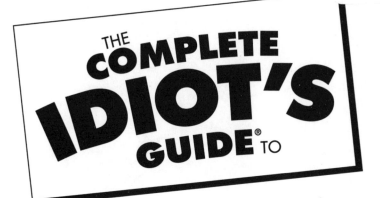

THE
COMPLETE
IDIOT'S
GUIDE® TO

Modern China

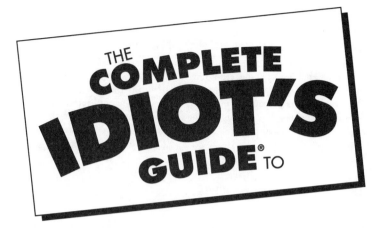

THE **COMPLETE IDIOT'S GUIDE**® TO

Modern China

by Vanessa Lide Whitcomb and Michael Benson

ALPHA

A member of Penguin Group (USA) Inc.

International Standard Book Number: 0-02-864386-0
Library of Congress Catalog Card Number: 2002110195

06   05   04   8   7   6   5   4   3   2

Interpretation of the printing code: The rightmost number of the first series of numbers is the year of the book's printing; the rightmost number of the second series of numbers is the number of the book's printing. For example, a printing code of 02-1 shows that the first printing occurred in 2002.

Printed in the United States of America

Publisher: *Marie Butler-Knight*
Product Manager: *Phil Kitchel*
Managing Editor: *Jennifer Chisholm*
Acquisitions Editor: *Eric Heagy*
Development Editor: *Doris Cross*
Production Editor: *Katherin Bidwell*
Copy Editor: *Cari Luna*
Illustrator: *Jody Schaeffer*
Graphics: *Steve Adams*
Cover/Book Designer: *Trina Wurst*
Indexer: *Brad Herriman*
Layout/Proofreading: *Becky Harmon, Mary Hunt*

Contents at a Glance

Part 1:   **From Empire to Republic**   1

  1   The Lay of the Land   3
China's land, culture, and people, from China's origins to the present day.

  2   The Dynasties   21
The rise and fall of the dynasties, from before the Qin Empire to its fall in 1912.

  3   The Empire Fades   37
The Opium War, the Taiping Rebellion, war with Japan, and the Boxer Rebellion presage the slow disintegration of the Qin Empire.

  4   The Revolution of 1911   47
Dr. Sun Yatsen brings the Republic of China into being, China's emperor abdicates, and Sun founds the Nationalist Party.

  5   From Chaos to Communism   59
Warlords run amok and are checked by Chiang Kaishek's forces. A burst of nationalism fuels the Chinese communist movement, and Mao Zedong emerges from the Long March as the leader of the Chinese Communist Party.

Part 2:   **China's Enduring Past**   71

  6   Cultural Legacies   73
Many traditional cultural legacies remain in contemporary China while others have faded. Daoism and Buddhism have taken a backseat to Marxist thought though they are on the rise again. The Chinese language is standardized and simplified, and Han nationalism remains strong.

  7   State and Society   85
The Confucian principles that underpin the governmental and social structure are reshaped by communism. This chapter looks at aspects of imperial society, today's party-state, China's education system, and the social order of China today.

8 China's Triumphs 103
*China's "four great inventions"—paper, printing, gun-
powder, and the mariner's compass—are not all that China
has contributed to the world.*

Part 3:   From Mao to the Millenium   **117**

9 Mao's Dream 119
*Civil war between the communists and the nationalists
ends with the flight of Chiang Kaishek to Taiwan and the
establishment of the People's Republic of China with Mao
Zedong as its social engineer and absolute ruler.*

10 Mao's Disaster 137
*The dream becomes a nightmare when Mao's programs
and plans take a back seat to thought reform and purges,
and the Red Guards and Gang of Four terrorize the whole
country.*

11 Deng's Doers 153
*Deng Xiaoping succeeds Mao as leader, and a new era of
opening and reform begins, marred by the 1989 Tiananmen Square crackdown.*

12 Jiang's Gang 165
*Jiang Zemin is named to succeed Deng. Jiang and his
team of nonideological technocrats continue Deng's reforms
and make major headway in creating a new economy.*

13 The View from Tiananmen Square 175
*In 1989, Deng Xiaoping, whose open reformist govern-
ment showed so much promise, shocked the world when
he ordered a military assault on pro-democracy demonstrators in Tiananmen Square. This chapter draws on
opinions from many sources on what the reasons for the
crackdown may have been, and whether a time will come
when the government will tolerate criticism.*

Part 4:   Inside Today's China   **187**

14 The New Generation 189
*Exactly what is "new" about China's new generation of
leaders and new middle class, and what hasn't changed
at all—and has even gotten worse.*

15 Pressure Points   203
*A traditional bureaucracy conflicts with an open economy,
and that's just the beginning. China has major problems it
is trying to address, such as a growing inequity between
rural and urban income, unemployment, government
corruption, and crises in every area of the environment.*

16 Strained Relations   219
*Most of Beijing's relations with China's regions, minorities,
and communities of faith are untroubled, but there are trouble
spots: Taiwan, Tibet, Muslim extremists in Xinjiang,
unregistered religious groups, and the banned Falun Gong.*

Part 5:   The Outside World   233

17 Asian Neighbors   235
*China is the major power of East Asia, and has friendly
relations and economic ties with all the region's countries.
Beijing does, however, keep an eye on Japan's proposed
military buildup, and is in disputes with several neighbors
who also claim sovereignty of the South China Sea's strategic and potentially oil-rich Spratly Islands.*

18 From Local to Global   247
*China is moving from a local to a global society, with joint
media ventures, a complete range of television programming, more books from more countries, and lifestyles that
reflect the influence of global mass culture.*

19 China and the United States   263
*China-U.S. relations include 22 years of ruptured relations
and U.S. pressure on China to clean up its human rights
record. Still, U.S. investments in China are growing, and
the trade balance is in China's favor.*

Part 6: China's Future: Place Your Bets   279

20 Running the Store   281
*Jiang Zemin, Li Peng, and Zhu Ronghi are top party-
state leaders who are reportedly scheduled to step down
in 2003. This chapter is a fill-in on who their likely
replacements will be and what challenges they'll be facing.*

21 The Globalization Game   295
    China's entry into the World Trade Organization requires
    major changes that will diminish Beijing's control and have
    far-reaching effects—some positive and some not—on the
    entire society.

Appendixes

    A Glossary   307
    B Further Reading   311
    C Chronology   315
       Index   321

Contents

Part I: From Empire to Republic   **1**

1 The Lay of the Land   **3**

The Land That Became China 3

China Shapes Its Land 6

Mapping Modern China 8

China's Diverse Regions 9

The East 10

    The Yellow River Valley 11

    The Yangzi River Valley 12

The South 13

Offshore China 14

    Taiwan 14

    Hainan 14

The West 15

    Xinjiang Uygur Autonomous Region 15

    Qinghai Province 16

    The Tibet Autonomous Region 16

    The Ningxia Hui Autonomous Region 17

The North 17

    The Northeast 18

    The Inner Mongolia Autonomous Region 18

2 The Dynasties   **21**

China Past 22

The Zhou Dynasty (1027–256 B.C.E.) 22

The Qin Empire (221 B.C.E.–1912 C.E.) 24

    The Han Dynasty (206 B.C.E.–220 C.E.) 25

    "Three Kingdoms" and "Six Dynasties" (221–618 C.E.) 26

    The Tang Dynasty (618–906 C.E.) 26

    The Song Dynasty (960–1279 C.E.) 27

Genghis Khan 28

    Ruler of Rulers 30

    Genghis's End 30

The Yuan (Mongol) Dynasty (1279–1368 C.E.) 31

Marco Polo 32

The Ming Dynasty (1368–1644 C.E.) 33
   Europe Arrives *34*
   Rise of the Manchus *34*

3 The Empire Fades   **37**
The Opium War 38
The Treaty of Nanjing 39
The Taiping Rebellion, 1850–64 39
The West Goes East 40
Restoration and Reform 41
War with Japan 42
The Hundred Days of Reform 42
The Boxer Rebellion 43
   The Open Door Policy *44*
The Beginning of the End 45
   The Empress Acts *45*
   Death and Succession *45*
   The Last Emperor, Pu Yi *46*

4 The Revolution of 1911   **47**
Dr. Sun Yatsen 48
Power Struggle 48
   Yuan Shikai *49*
   The Qing Court *49*
The Revolution 50
The Return of Yuan 51
The Republic of China 52
   The Empire's Final Weeks *52*
   President Yuan *53*
   Politics by Assassination *54*
Yuan Versus Sun 54
   The Second Revolution *54*
   Another Autocracy *55*
   The Death of Yuan *56*

5 From Chaos to Communism   **59**
Warlords in Command 60
The Intellectual Reformers 60
   The New Culture Movement *60*
   The New Tide Society *61*
   Chen Duxiu *61*
The May Fourth Movement 61

The Birth of Chinese Communism 62
Sun Yatsen 62
  The Three Principles of the People (San Min Zhu Yi) 62
  Dealing with the Soviets 63
  Sun and the Warlords 64
Exit Sun, Enter Chiang 64
  The Defeat of the Warlords 65
  The Purge of the Communists 66
Enter Mao Zedong 67
The Long March 68

Part 2: China's Enduring Past   71

6 Cultural Legacies   73
The Han Idea 73
  Philosophical Influences 74
Daoism 74
Buddhism 76
A Look at the Chinese Language 77
  One Chinese Versus Many 78
  You Say Peking, I Say Beijing … 79
  Chinese, a Language with Character(s)! 81
  A Word on Simplified Characters 83

7 State and Society   85
The Confucian Code 86
The Old Social Order 89
  The Gentry and the Commoners 89
  The Family 90
  Women's Place in the Family 91
Family and Society After Communism 92
Education 94
  Imperial Education 94
  Education Today 95
  Compulsory Education 95
  Higher Education 96
  Literacy 97
Today's Party-State 97
  The Central Government 98
  Local Governments 99
Modern China Revisits Confucius 100

8 China's Triumphs   **103**

Continuity in Change 104
The Four Great Inventions 104
   Paper 104
   Printing 105
   Gunpowder 106
   The Mariner's Compass 106
Keeping Records 107
Traditional Chinese Medicine 108
Arts and Letters 110
   The Bronze Age 110
   The Buddhist Era 111
From the Tang to the Qing 112
   The Tang Dynasty 112
   The Song Dynasties 113
   The Yuan (Mongol) Dynasty 114
   The Ming Dynasty 114
   The Qing (Manchu) Dynasty 114
Other Triumphs 115

Part 3:   From Mao to the Millenium   **117**

9 Mao's Dream   **119**

The Japanese Threat 120
   The Party vs. the Guomindang 120
   The Not-So-United Front 121
The Japanese Invasion 122
   Atrocities 122
   Japanese Occupation 122
Mao Zedong: Social Engineer 123
   Mao's Six Major Campaigns 123
   The Three Three Three System 123
The CCP's Leaders 124
   Deng Xiaoping 124
   Lin Biao 125
   Liu Shaoqi 125
   Zhou Enlai the Mediator 125
World War II 125

Civil War in China 128
Chiang Flees to Taiwan 128
Mao's New Government 129
Mao's Programs and Plans 132
    Land Reform *132*
    Agricultural Collectivization *133*
    Industrial Development *133*
New Foreign Policy 134

10 Mao's Disaster   137

Mass Campaigns 138
Thought Reform 139
The Hundred Flowers Debacle 141
The Great Leap Forward 142
    Mobilizing the Peasants *143*
    China Falls Back *144*
    Readjustment and Recovery *145*
The Great Proletarian Cultural Revolution 146
    Mao's Last Stand *147*
    The Red Guards *148*
The Gang of Four 149
Death and Succession 150

11 Deng's Doers   153

The End of the Gang of Four 154
Deng Xiaoping Leads 155
    Reversals of Policy *155*
    Paradigm Shift *156*
A Market Economy 156
    Reform on the Farm *157*
    Privatization *158*
The New Government 158
New Issues 159
Tiananmen Square, 1989 159
    A New Reform Plan *160*
    The Death of Hu Yaobang *161*
    The Massacre *162*
    China Moves On *163*

12 Jiang's Gang   **165**

After Tiananmen Square 166
The New Beijing Team 166
   Jiang Zemin *167*
   Zhu Rongji *168*
   Hu Jintao *169*
The New Economy 169
The Wild Card—the PLA 170
The State of Jiang's Party-State 172

13 The View from Tiananmen Square   **175**

The Square 176
April 15–June 4, 1989 177
   The Media *179*
   The World Reacts *179*
The View 180
   The '89 Dissidents *181*
   On the March *182*
   The Falun Gong *184*
The Legacy of Tiananmen 185

Part 4: Inside Today's China   **187**

14 The New Generation   **189**

What's New? 190
Jiang's "Cultural Revitalization" 190
The "Workers with High Incomes" 191
The Rural Picture 193
The Status of Women 194
China's Youth 197
Intellectuals 198
Social Responsibility: NGOs 200

15 Pressure Points   **203**

Recipe for Conflict 204
   Old Government, New Economy *204*
   Legal Reforms *205*
Growing Economy, Growing Inequities ...207
   Migrant Workers *207*
   Rural Poverty *208*

Corruption 210
  Corruption in Shenyang *210*
  Yu Baozhong's Case *212*
Environmental Crises 213
  Air Pollution *214*
  Water Pollution *215*
  The Three Gorges Dam *216*
The Rule of Law 217

16 Strained Relations   219
Taiwan: The "Other China" 220
Hong Kong 223
Tibet 225
Xinjiang and Islam 227
Religious Organizations 229
  Falun Gong *229*
  Christians *231*

Part 5: The Outside World   233

17 Asian Neighbors   235
Russia 236
The Koreas 237
Keeping an Eye on Japan 239
Vietnam 240
The South China Sea 240
Singapore, Malaysia, Indonesia, and the Philippines 241
  Singapore *241*
  Malaysia *242*
  Indonesia *242*
  The Philippines *243*
India and Pakistan 243
Regional Trade 244

18 From Local to Global   247
Media Roundup 248
  Newspapers and Magazines *248*
  Radio and Television *249*
  The Internet *251*
  Books *252*
Art in China 253

Music 254
    Foreign Film Distribution 255
Fashion 256
Food 258
Lifestyles 259
    "Generation Yellow" 259
    The Gay Lifestyle 260
    AIDS 261

19 China and the United States   **263**
Looking Back 264
    World War II 265
    After the War 265
    Korea 266
U.S.-China Detente 267
Taiwan Troubles 268
Nuclear Weapons Proliferation 269
Human Rights 269
U.S.-China Relations After 1989 270
    Most-Favored-Nation Status 270
    Permanent Normal Trade Relations 271
    Is U.S. Policy Effective? 272
    China Questions U.S. Human Rights 272
Trade and Investment Relations 273
    U.S. Investment in China 274
    Three Ways to Invest in China 276
Mixing Business and Politics 277

Part 6: China's Future: Place Your Bets   **279**

20 Running the Store   **281**
The State of the Party-State 281
The New Leadership 282
    Hu Jintao 283
    Wen Jiabao 284
    Li Ruihuan 285
    The Shanghai Clique 285
    Other Prominent Leaders 286
    Behind the Scenes 288
    The Role of the PLA 289

New and Continuing Challenges 290
   Growing Unemployment 290
   Government Corruption 291
   Pressure Points Outside of China 292
   Relations with the United States 293

21   The Globalization Game   295

Ready or Not 296
The Global Economic Picture 297
The WTO: Who Wins, Who Loses? 298
   Chinese Enterprises 299
   The Workforce 299
   Down on the Farm 300
   Foreign Investors 301
Playing by the Rules 302
Is China a Military Threat? 303
China-U.S. Relations 304
China's Future 304

Appendixes

  A   Glossary   307

  B   Further Reading   311

  C   Chronology   315

     Index   321

Foreword

Vanessa Lide Whitcomb needs no certification from peers or fellow China watchers for presenting this important book to the reading public. In several roles, as editor, analyst, and writer, she brings an admirable set of credentials—enlightened experience in and about China and skill in exposition. While no book speaks for itself, this one arrives in readers' hands ready for and deserving of careful scrutiny.

This book was written primarily for a Western readership, specifically American. It could not appear at a more suitable time, for Americans have "a China problem." That problem lies at the disjunction between two widely shared assumptions: that China more than any other part of the world will engage the United States in the new century and the reality that Americans largely are uninformed about China.

Reducing, if not closing, this knowledge gap surely ranks as an important responsibility of scholars, journalists, and well-informed lay leaders of all backgrounds. Modern China merits notice among those who would replace fiction with fact, distance with perspective, and bias with understanding.

Like other *Complete Idiot's Guides*, this one aims for an audience of attentive readers who have a great deal of curiosity about a topic but have limited prior exposure to that topic. For them, the step-by-step introduction in this volume will be convenient and comforting. This book is also comprehensive in that it still imparts a good deal of detailed information to other, more knowledgeable readers on all the basic social sectors of China—politics, economics, human rights, interpersonal respect, religion, health, family, and education. It also is a volume that is long on modern Chinese history and trends, and clearly describes basic factors underlying China as a developing society in a period of globalization and democratization.

The gap in Americans' knowledge of China will not be filled with this or any other single volume. However, the first solid steps in such a journey of inquiry and discovery are found here. An informational "long march" of modern China begins on page one.

—James A. Robinson, a policy scientist, is a former president of Macalester College in St. Paul, Minnesota, and president emeritus of the University of West Florida in Pensacola, Florida. During the last 15 years, he engaged in fieldwork on democratic innovations in Hong Kong, Japan, Singapore, Taiwan, and the People's Republic of China. He also is the author of the classic *Congress and Foreign Policy-Making: A Study in Legislative Influence and Initiative*, published in 1962 and still in print.

Introduction

China is both a land of tradition and one of rapid change, and it is keeping tabs on both the new and the old—as well as how they interact in a uniquely Chinese fashion—which makes any study of China so fascinating.

In this book we look at the vastly different regions that make up China; and we not only look at how China is, but how it got that way. Many lengthier books than this have been written on just a single dynastic period in Chinese history, or the birth of the Republic of China, or the Maoist regime, or China's new economy. We don't pretend to rival their ability to provide detailed background and analysis of these specific periods and events. What we do offer is a grounding in the history and culture of China, an understanding of modern China—after the empire fell in 1912—and some insight into contemporary China's economy, society, and government, as well as where they may be headed.

We hope you find reading this book as gratifying as it was for us to write it.

A Note on Chinese Spelling

There's still a lot of variation in the West in how Chinese words are spelled with an alphabet, or *romanized*. It's the age old problem of taking the Chinese writing system—which is based traditionally on characters that represent whole sounds and words—and finding a way to break them down into distinct phonetic letters. For instance the number "ten" is represented in Chinese by a character that looks much like a cross or plus sign. Its pronunciation is something like the sound made by running an English "sh" sound with an "r" to get the approximate sound "shr." Needless to say, it's an approximation. As such, many insightful scholars have come up with useful romanization systems to spell Chinese words. In this book we will use the same system that the Chinese government has adopted. It's known as the *pinyin* system.

We do not expect the reader to learn this system in order to read the authentic Chinese words provided in this book. In all cases, an English definition is provided within the text where it is used. However, we know readers will appreciate seeing some words spelled as they would approximately sound in Chinese. If a reader is so inclined to learn more about a word or words in this book they should consult a Chinese-English dictionary—most are based on pinyin today—for further insight into pronunciation, meaning, and usage.

How to Use this Book

Here's what's in the six sections of this book:

Part 1, "From Empire to Republic," is where you'll find an overview of the land and people of China and the dynasties that ruled the empire until it fell, and the founding of the Republic of China.

Part 2, "China's Enduring Past," takes you to the roots of Chinese culture, and looks at how many cultural legacies endure to this day, and even those that don't.

Part 3, "From Mao to the Millenium," begins with the Long March of Mao Zedong and the other future leaders of the People's Republic of China, and follows China's modern history through the leadership of Jiang Zemin.

Part 4, "Inside Today's China," briefs you on what's new in contemporary China, and which issues and problems of the past remain unresolved.

Part 5, "The Outside World," looks at China's relations with its Asian neighbors and with the United States, and gives you a feel for how Chinese society and culture are being influenced by the ideas and values of the outside world.

Part 6, "China's Future: Place Your Bets," is the place to go if you're looking for the latest on China's government, international investment and trade, social change, and future prospects.

Extras

As you read the text, you'll see lots of boxes that give you a little extra in the way of help, definitions, quotations, and opinions.

Han Help

Here you'll find extra background that will give you a better understanding of the text.

Hu Nu?

This is a fun box where you can enjoy tidbits of interesting, and sometimes bizarre, background to the goings-on in the text.

Language Lesson

Just what it sounds like, this box is for lessons in language, sometimes the translation of a Chinese term, and sometimes the connotation of an English term used in the text.

Wise One Says

Here you'll find quotations from a range of sources—ancient Chinese tomes, to scholarly works, to the latest news reports—that offer insight on the text and China itself.

Acknowledgments

The authors would like to thank the wide range of editorial staff at Alpha who made the publication of this book a reality. Special thanks goes out to Doris Cross, development editor, for her wonderful ability to synthesize a great deal of material on China and offer insight on how the book could be best presented. Great appreciation should also be extended to Kathy Bidwell, production editor, who showed enough wisdom and patience—editorially speaking—to match the likes of Confucius! She and her team of copy editors and proofreaders have certainly helped in making this book more readable than we ever thought possible.

Trademarks

All terms mentioned in this book that are known to be or are suspected of being trademarks or service marks have been appropriately capitalized. Alpha Books and Penguin Group (USA) Inc. cannot attest to the accuracy of this information. Use of a term in this book should not be regarded as affecting the validity of any trademark or service mark.

Part 1

From Empire to Republic

Chinese civilization has existed continuously for longer than any other civilization on earth, but that doesn't mean that China hasn't experienced change. Its land, people, and rulers have been changing since Chinese culture began 4,000 years ago in the fertile valley of the Yellow River. These chapters take you from China's ancient beginnings, through the rise and fall of the Qin Empire, to the birth of the Republic of China and the first stirrings of Chinese communism.

Confucius

Mao Zedong

Chapter 1

The Lay of the Land

In This Chapter

- How China got started
- Imperial China's diverse peoples
- China's landscape changes
- Modern China's regions and populations
- China's problems and prospects

China is not the world's most ancient civilization, but Chinese civilization has existed continuously for longer than any other—3,500 years. Perhaps that's why it's easy to get the impression that—even though dynasties came and went—the land and the people were changeless. That is not the case: While there were some dynasties that ruled for centuries, and there were equally long periods of time when China's borders remained the same, invasions, migrations, and natural disasters changed the lay of the land many times. This chapter starts with a sketch of where China began and who its people were, then looks at the people and land of China today.

The Land That Became China

Early China was a very different place from the People's Republic we know. There was a land of China more than a thousand years before there

Hu Nu?

Today, China is a land of largely Sino-Tibetan speakers, a language family that includes all the various dialects of Chinese, Tibetan, and some other "small" or minority languages (see Chapter 6).

Language Lesson

Many Chinese still call their country by its ancient name, **Zhong guo**. This term can be translated as "central land," or "middle kingdom," based on the ancient (and sometimes not-so-ancient) belief of the Chinese that China is the geographical center of the earth—and earth's only true civilization.

was a Chinese Empire, but it didn't look very "Chinese." It was populated by diverse peoples, some of whom bore no resemblance to the Chinese in language or race. In fact, China began with Chinese-speaking people living on a relatively small portion of land in the north.

It was the rulers of the small northern Zhou kingdom (1027–221 B.C.E.) who began to conquer the non-Chinese-speaking people to their south, who would greatly influence the geography of China today—a country in which varying dialects of Chinese are now spoken by nearly a fifth of the world's population in a land roughly the size of the United States, and where only small pockets of non-Chinese-speaking people still exist.

Much of the land to the south that was consolidated by the early Chinese would later become a major part of China's "breadbasket." The dynasties that followed the Zhou dynasty were able to grow enough grain (primarily rice) to sustain a large population, feed a trained army, draw taxes, and later trade goods through accessible southern ports—all key to China's ability to maintain its position for many centuries as the most powerful country in East Asia.

China, however, did not begin to take shape in earnest as a centralized state until the rise of the Qin dynasty (221–207 B.C.E.). Even at that time what was China covered only a portion of what became its central land, the region between the Yellow and the Yangzi Rivers, south to the China Sea.

It's important to keep in mind that China was not always the size it is today; it grew slowly, through its history of nearly 4,000 years. China's first significant territorial expansion came under the Han dynasty, an empire that ruled for 400 years. Under the Han dynasty, China's borders were pushed far to the west, nearly to the current western reaches of contemporary communist China. The Han period is seen as a time when a unified Chinese national identity solidly took shape. Today, the majority of Chinese citizens consider themselves to be ethnically *Han*, tracing the term's origin to the famed Han dynasty. Later in this chapter we also show that China's non-Han population is an integral part of the Chinese landscape.

Invasions by nomadic tribes from the north had been a continuous problem since before China was a unified empire, and had driven the population southward. During the Han dynasty, just before the beginning of the Common Era, massive flooding and a change in the course of the Yellow River created a major migration to south China. Han civilization displaced the indigenous people and took root there.

China's relative isolation from early outside influences—geographically imposed by vast arid lands to the north and west—turned it into a unique and inward-looking nation. It was not until the time of the Tang dynasty (618–907 C.E.)—often considered to be the high point of imperial China because of its spectacular achievements in the arts, religion, and government—that China's borders reached so far that its people could no longer remain isolated from foreign influences and ideas. Notably, traders began to connect China with the lands of Central Asia, the Middle East, and even Europe, via the *Silk Road*. Perhaps the most nourishing outside influence on the land of China during this period was Buddhism's religious ideas (see Chapter 6), which had found their way there from India.

Language Lesson

Today, 91 percent of China's people are considered **Han**. Though they are usually racially Chinese, to be Han is often loosely defined, and increasingly refers to Chinese people who speak the official dialect of Mandarin—or some other Chinese dialect—as their mother tongue, and share certain cultural characteristics that are traditionally thought of as Chinese.

Language Lesson

The **Silk Road** was a 7,000-mile route that linked China's Yellow River valley with the Mediterranean Sea. China's silk trade was never a major factor in its economy, but during the empire's many centuries of isolation, the few outside influences that trickled in did so via the Silk Road.

As China's land was opened, whether by or against its will, China would continue to absorb ideas, practices, and peoples into its vast empire and, in turn, make them its own. This is no better demonstrated than under the rule of the Manchus. A non-Chinese nomadic people from North Asia, the Manchus were the founders of the geographically largest and the last Chinese dynasty, the Qing dynasty (see Chapter 2). Yet, by the end of the Qing dynasty, Manchu rulers had practically forgotten their language and nomadic customs—royal court decorum was an exception—and had adopted the governing techniques of their Han subjects.

Since Qing leaders were outnumbered, they put into effect laws aimed at stopping the absorption of the Manchus into the dominant Han Chinese population. For instance, the Han Chinese were not allowed to move to the Manchu homeland, and it was illegal

Wise One Says

The population growth of Imperial China remained relatively modest until the end of the nineteenth century. By that time, writes John Bryan Starr in *Understanding China*, the country's population had tripled, and stood at roughly 450 million people.

for Manchus to engage in trade or manual labor. Intermarriage between the two groups was also illegal. Most of these efforts did very little to make the Qing Empire any less Chinese.

By the time the Qing dynasty came to an end—at the turn of the twentieth century—the land of China had reached a size of present-day proportions (in fact, it was larger). It was no longer a small kingdom of unified tribes all speaking the same tongue and living a similar pattern of life. Instead, it was a land that encompassed many different peoples, speaking various languages, following various religions, and living in widely different environments—but, no doubt, with a strong sense of belonging to a Chinese civilization. That powerful idea continues today; in fact, China would push hard for the renewed unity of land and people as it stepped into the modern age.

China Shapes Its Land

With mountain ranges to the north and west, and the Pacific Ocean to the east, China was a prisoner of its geography—isolated from the civilizations of western Asia, Europe, and Africa until the tenth century. The highly organized government used the time well: In the seventh century they created the Grand Canal to transport grain and other products from the Yangzi River delta to the Yellow River, where it could be off-loaded at various points, and from there to the seaport of Hangzhou. The ports and market centers that sprung up marked the first wave of China's urban growth.

By the tenth century, Arab traders began to reach China's seaports, and caravans were carrying goods—and news—back and forth along the Silk Road.

Han Help

Only 11 percent of China's land is arable, compared with 40 percent of the land in the United States. The U.S. population is about 300 million; China's is 3.4 billion.

The increase in trade began to produce cities of great splendor and gargantuan size. Hangzhou, the coastal end of the Grand Canal, had become China's capital in 1126. By the thirteenth century it was a candidate for the greatest city in the world—certainly in size. When Italian explorer Marco Polo visited the court of Kublai Khan toward the end of the century, he was stunned by Hangzhou. It had a population of at least one million; Venice, his native city, had around 50,000 inhabitants.

The Great Wall and the Grand Canal are the stars of Chinese engineering, but it was the sophisticated terracing and irrigation systems developed centuries ago that have kept China's ever-growing population from starvation. China's three great river systems—the Yangzi River (Changjiang), Yellow River (He Huang), and West River (Xi Jiang)—carry the grains, rice, and other crops from their fertile deltas to the rocky hillsides and barren deserts that dominate much of the Chinese landscape. Today, nearly half of the farmland is irrigated—more than in any other country—and nearly all of it is under cultivation.

By the late sixteenth century, Portuguese traders had arrived at Chinese seaports. It wasn't long before international maritime trade was underway, ending China's long isolation from the world (see Chapters 2 and 3), and catapulting coastal China into the limelight. The cities where the great inland waterways met the sea—Hong Kong, Shanghai, and Ghangzhou (Canton)—grew into sprawling cosmopolitan centers, leaving most of the rest of China behind.

 **Han Help**

During his rule, Kublai Khan created a new and improved version of the Grand Canal that had made his capital a world-class metropolis. It was renovated again in the 1960s, and now goes from Beijing to Hangzhou. It is the world's longest canal, and a primary means of transportation.

Hu Nu?

Cotton that was grown in the north was transported through the inland waterways to southern mills. Textiles made their way back through the river system to every corner of China. Today, there are 67,900 miles of navigable inland waterways, and China's textile industry is the largest in the world.

Hu Nu?

The early rulers of China built all kinds of fortifications to keep out foreign invaders. Construction of the Great Wall started in the seventh century B.C.E. The vassal states under the Zhou dynasty in the northern parts of the country each built their own walls for defense purposes. After the state of Qing unified China, it joined the walls to hold off the invasions of tribes to its north. This is the origin of the name, Great Wall. It was far later, during the Ming dynasty (1368–1644), that much of what survives today as the Great Wall of China was built. It is 4,160 miles long—without counting its branches or secondary sections.

Mapping Modern China

Sometimes called "Mainland China" or "Red China," the People's Republic of China (PRC) is the third largest country in the world by land area (3,695,000 square miles), and it is the largest by population—1.3 billion. More than one out of every five of the world's people lives in China—more people than were living in the entire world prior to the twentieth century.

China is bounded by 19 countries: To the north is the Republic of Mongolia and Russia; to the northeast, Russia and North Korea; on the east China is bounded by the Yellow Sea and the East China Sea; on the south by the South China Sea, Vietnam, Laos, Myanmar (better known as Burma), India, Bhutan, and Nepal; to the west lie Pakistan, Afghanistan, and Tajikistan; and to the northwest, Kyrgyzstan and Kazakhstan.

China also includes 1,300 islands off its east coast.

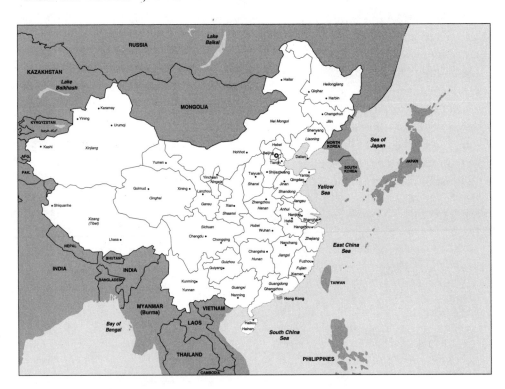

Some of the world's highest mountain ranges—the Tien Shan, Kunlun Mountains, Qin Ling, and the Himalayas—are in western China. Forty-three percent of China's land is mountainous. The North China plain is the largest area of flat lowland in the country. North central China's Mongolian Steppe is a gravelly desert in the west, a forested range in the east, and a fertile plateau in between. In the Northwest, the Junggar Pendi Basin supports irrigated agriculture; to its south is the Takla Makan, the driest desert in Asia. The mountains, deserts, and plateaus of the west are subarctic; the weather in the southeast is subtropical.

Han Help

Even though China is still an agricultural country, the industrial sector now contributes 42 percent of the gross domestic product.

Despite the growth of the new economy's urban commercial centers, China is still an agricultural country: 79 percent of the population lives on 15 percent of the land, most of it in the fertile river basins of the east. In the 1980s, industry increased dramatically in the rural areas. The government became concerned when it began to encroach on the short supply of arable land, and passed a strict land-use law that makes it very difficult to take farmland out of cultivation. Heavy industry complexes as well as light industry are now widespread.

China has abundant natural resources:

◆ The world's largest coal reserves are in China.

◆ China is the world's fourth largest oil producer.

◆ It has the world's largest reserves of antimony, manganese, natural graphite, tin, and tungsten.

Fishing along the eastern shore is another strong area of the economy. The total annual catch of fish, shellfish, and mollusks in China is estimated at about 13.1 million metric tons—greater than any other country's.

China's Diverse Regions

The people who live in the 19 eastern provinces where the population is concentrated are almost exclusively Han. The Han account for 92 percent of China's population. The remaining 8 percent, or 100 million people, are of 56 distinct minority nationalities: They inhabit 50 to 60 percent of China, most of it in the largest three of five autonomous regions—Xinjiang, Inner Mongolia (Nei Mogol), and Tibet (Zizang). (See Chapter 7 for more about autonomous regions and the PRC's government structure.) Minorities are distinguished from Han not by race, but by religion or ethnicity.

The United States is often thought of as an assemblage of geographical regions (Midwest, Northeast, Southwest, and so on). There is no such convention for the regions of China. Scholars have used systems as simple as dividing the country into eastern and western regions, to the thoughtful scheme of G. William Skinner, who divided it into macroregions based on the major river drainage basins. To give you a concise overview of China's diverse geography, culture, and economy, we will divide the country into the east, the north, and the west.

> ### Han Help
>
> China is divided into 22 provinces, 5 autonomous regions, 4 municipalities, and 2 special administrative regions (SARs). The autonomous regions are Guangxi, Inner Mongolia, Ningxia, Xinjiang, and Zizang. The four municipalities that are governed directly by Beijing's central government are Beijing, Shanghai, Tianjin, and Chongqing. Hong Kong, a British Crown colony until 1997, and Macao, a Portuguese colony until 1999, are the two SARs.

The East

The east includes the 19 provinces that are primarily inhabited by Han people. This is the heartland of imperial China's Han culture. The northern part of east China begins just south of the Great Wall in Hebei Province where Beijing, the capital, was settled more than 3,000 years ago. To the southeast is Tianjin, a city of 10 million, which has a warm, semi-humid climate. Tianjin is where the Grand Canal that links China's two greatest river systems—the Yellow and Yangzi Rivers—begins. It is a major agricultural and industrial center that ranks sixth in population and is fifth on the list of China's richest regions. Chinese industry was born in Tianjin during the days of the Republic of China (1911–1949), and today it is home to 12,000 industrial enterprises.

Hu Nu?
Beijing, which means "northern capital," was the capital for the Chinese dynasties, and for the Mongol horde that breached the Great Wall and founded the Yuan (Mongol) dynasty (1279–1368). They chose it because it was the major Chinese city closest to their home. It was China's capital for most of the twentieth century (81 percent); for the remainder of the century the capital was Nanjing, and for a short period, Chongqing. Beijing is not just the PRC's capital, it is also one of China's major cultural and business centers.

South of Tianjin on the coast of the Yellow Sea is the Shandong Plateau on the hilly Shandong Peninsula. In the interior, south of Beijing and Tianjin, is the arid North

China Plain, known for its Siberian weather and its dust storms. The soil is fertile because it is *loess*, but the North China Plain's lack of rain makes it difficult to farm.

Language Lesson

The Yellow River got its name for a reason. **Loess** is a mixture of sand and clay that has a yellowish color. Along the route of the Yellow River's Great Bend, the river picks up great quantities of loess, and deposits it on the North China Plain. Still, its load of 40 percent sediment in the summer (3 percent is considered heavy) slows it down considerably, and raises its bed, increasing the danger of floods in the low-lying farmland. The Yellow River has brought floods—and the inevitable famines that follow them—of disastrous proportions to the North China Plain throughout history.

The Yellow River Valley

The great northern agricultural region begins where the Yellow River crosses the Great Wall in Shaanxi Province, and extends eastward to the coast. It stretches south as far as Xian, west into Gansu Province, and through Hebei and Henan Provinces (excluding the Luliang Mountains) to the coast. Most of China's wheat, corn, millet, beans, and tubers are grown in this region.

Gansu, the eastern province that is farthest west, shares some of the characteristics of both regions: Like the west, it is rich in minerals, has oil fields, and mines nickel, zinc, and platinum. Like the northern area of the east, it has roughly a 90 percent Han population, and a much higher population density than that of the west. The Yellow River runs through it, but at Gansu's high elevation, it does not support a great agricultural yield. In fact, because of Gansu's elevation (3,300 to almost 10,000 feet), as much as half the silt the Yellow River carries every year is soil picked up in Gansu and sped down to the river's lower reaches. Gansu's soil depletion is a critical problem. Gansu does, though, still have abundant exotic wildlife such as giant pandas, snow leopards, and bactrian (two-humped) camels. Such creatures have virtually disappeared from the overpopulated eastern provinces.

Far from Gansu, on the Yellow Sea coast, is the province of Jiangsu, where Shanghai, China's wealthiest, second most populous, and most culturally sophisticated city is situated. The climate along the coast is temperate but humid. Monsoon rains make their appearance every year, and offshore earthquakes are not unusual. Down the coast from Shanghai is Hangzhou, where the Grand Canal ends and the Yangzi River meets the Yellow Sea.

Han Help _____

The sources of the Yellow River and the Yangzi River are high in the Tibetan Plateau. As they flow to lower elevations (the Yangzi flows at 40 times the Yellow River's rate because of the Yellow River's loess suspension), they produce a major source of hydroelectric power. China is one of the world's leading producers of hydropower, but it only meets 20 percent of the country's need for electricity. Coal-burning supplies almost all the rest, and is the major source of China's critical air pollution problem.

The Yangzi River Valley

The Huai River in Anhui Province marks the agricultural dividing line between the northern and the southern regions of the east. From the fertile Yangzi delta's Jiangsu, Anhui, and Zhejiang Provinces, across south central China as far as Sichuan and Yunnan Provinces in the west, the climate is warmer, and wetter, due to the regular summer monsoon rains. South of the Huai is where the ancient method of "wet rice" agriculture begins. It is a highly labor-intensive type of farming that is, for the most part, still carried out without mechanization.

Wuhan is the capital of Hubei Province, and the great central city of central China. It has two new airports, two international harbors, several railways, and many highways. It's a leader in scientific research and technology, with more than 500 research institutes, and it's also an industrial center with iron and steel mills and a major shipbuilding industry.

The climate and terrain are variable in south central China, and Sichuan Province is one of the regions with the best conditions for growing rice. The Sichuan Basin has an 11-month growing season, and sometimes produces three crops a year. For that reason, Sichuan has the highest population in China, and Chongqing, a separately administered municipality in Sichuan, is China's largest city.

Hu Nu?
Chongqing has a population of almost 31 million. The combined population of Chongqing and Sichuan Provinces is 107,000,000—greater than the population of any country in Europe except Russia.

The Three Gorges, as in the highly controversial Three Gorges Dam project, is on the Yangzi River between Chongqing and Wuhan. The dam would control flooding, generate hydropower, and deepen a section of the river's channel that would allow bigger ships to get to Chongqing. The plan was on the table for years before work got underway in 1993, but very little progress has been made because of a range of issues—local, national, and global.

The main points of contention are that it will displace more than a million people and place many species of fish in danger of extinction; it is plagued with infighting, corruption, technical problems, and environmental issues; it will cost an estimated $30 billion; and the site of some of China's most important ancient artifacts will be lost

Han Help

The Yangzi is China's longest river and has 3,000 tributaries. Many major cities such as Shanghai, Nanjing, Wuhan, and Chongqing are Yangzi ports.

forever before archeologists can recover them. (For more on the Three Gorges Dam and China's environmental problems, see Chapter 15.)

The South

In the south, the climate ranges from subtropical in the basins and high plateaus of the southwest, where higher elevations make for cooler summers and milder winters, to tropical on the southeast coast.

In Guangdong Province, the Yangzi River, the West River (Xi Jiang), and the Pearl River (Zhu Jiang) come together with the climate (steamy in summer, mild in winter) to form one of China's most fertile agricultural regions. Crops grow year around in Guangdong, and its capital Ghangzhou (Canton) is a thriving seaport that always makes the top of the list for the quantity of goods it produces and exports. Ghangzhou has 3,200 factories that make everything from canned goods to cars. The special administrative regions of Hong Kong and Macao that abut Ghangzhou's harbor also do well: Hong Kong is one of the world's major financial centers, and Macao is a favored vacation spot.

Hu Nu?

South China has many pockets of minority nationalities scattered through the provinces. In Sichuan and Yunnan there are Yi, and there are Miao people, an ancient Chinese group, throughout the south.

China also has many linguistically diverse regions. In the south around Guangdong, Hong Kong, and Macao, Cantonese is the spoken dialect. The Guangxi Zhuang Autonomous Region, in the southwest, is populated by Zhuang people who have their own language. The Zhuang, who are related to the Thai people (of Thailand), are China's largest minority. Hakka speakers are widespread in China, as well, but are found primarily in the region between Guangxi and Fujian in the east (see Chapter 6).

Offshore China

China does include 1,300 islands, but the only 2 we look at here are Taiwan and Hainan.

Taiwan

Taiwan is an island in the East China Sea, 90 miles off the coast of China's Fujian Province. It is about 240 miles long by 90 miles wide. Taiwan has a unique history, and a relationship with the People's Republic of China that is still evolving.

Following the establishment of the Communist People's Republic of China, China's Nationalist Party, led by Chiang Kaishek, fled the mainland and established the independent Republic of China, widely known as "Nationalist China," on the island of Taiwan (then called Formosa). (See Chapter 16 for more about Taiwan.) The Republic of China claimed to be the legitimate government of China, and was recognized by the United Nations as such until 1971, when the People's Republic of China assumed China's UN seat. Taiwan has only recently backed away from its claim to be China's legitimate government, and is cautiously negotiating a "one country, two systems" compromise with Beijing. It is officially a province of the PRC; in practice, however, it is in effect self-governing.

Han Help

The Chinese Matzu and Jinmen Islands off Taiwan's coast are under the jurisdiction of Fujian Province but are administered by the Taiwan government. China claims sovereignty over the strategically important and potentially oil-producing Spratly Islands. They are also claimed by Taiwan, Vietnam, and other governments in the region.

The heavy monsoon rains from October through March support rice-growing on Taiwan's arable land (25 percent of Taiwan's land), but industry and commerce are the basis of its economy. Its occupation for 50 years by Japan (1895–1945), which was the most industrialized country in Asia, has been a major factor in Taiwan's economic development. Its heavy industry (steel, military hardware, automobiles) in particular has made it one of the world's largest and fastest-growing economies. It has also helped create severe air pollution in Taiwan's cities.

Hainan

A tropical island in the South China Sea, Hainan was under the jurisdiction of Guangdong Province until 1988. It is now the Hainan Province, and also China's largest "special economic zone," a designation that marks it for the development of foreign investment, trade, and tourism (see Chapter 11). With its location (just across the Qionghou Strait from the mainland) and one hundred miles of coastline, fine beaches, and scenic seaside resorts, the hope is that it will compete with Hawaii as an international tourist destination.

The West

What we designate as the west includes the autonomous regions of Ningxia, Tibet, and Xinjiang, and the province of Qinghai. They share very high elevations, abundant mineral resources, pasture lands (limited in Tibet), and plenty of wild animals—many that are endangered species under the government's protection. Except for Ningxia, they have vast desert areas, arctic temperatures, and therefore minimal arable land. With the exception of Xinjiang, they all have large non-Han populations, but not many of China's major minority groups, which are …

◆ **Zhuang.** The largest minority, the Zhuangs live primarily in the southwest's Guangxi Zhuang Autonomous Region.

◆ **Man (Manchu).** Originally from historical Manchuria, Manchus are found throughout China, where they are quite assimilated.

◆ **Hui.** They differ from the Han primarily in their religion, which is Islam.

◆ **Miao.** Aboriginal people of southwest China, they live primarily in their own communities in the southwestern provinces.

◆ **Uygur.** A Turkic-Muslim people, they constitute most of the population of Xinjiang Uygur Autonomous Region.

The Huis and Manchus share the Han languages. The rest of the minority nationalities have their own spoken and written languages. (See Chapter 6 for more about China's languages and dialects.)

Han Help

Xinjiang not only has a large non-Han population, the ratio is the opposite of China's national average. Xinjiang's Uygurs and 46 other ethnic nationalities, most of them of Turkic-Muslim origin, constitute 94 percent of its population, the rest being Han. China's average Han population is 91 percent.

Xinjiang Uygur Autonomous Region

Xinjiang is the most sparsely populated region in China, at about 26 people per square mile (compared with 2,000 in the rich agricultural regions of the east). In the east are two deserts, the Gobi and the Ordos. The west is dominated by the Tian Shan mountain range, which has peaks over 20,000 feet above sea level. At its southern edge is the Turpan Depression, an oasis that is 505 feet below sea level—the lowest point in China. The Tarim Basin to the southwest holds some of China's greatest oil reserves. Farther south is the dry Takla Makan Desert, bounded by the Altun Shan mountain range that meets Tibet's northern border.

Xinjiang is rich in minerals, and has 40 percent of China's coal reserves and 25 percent of its natural gas. In addition to oil, the region produces textiles, petrochemicals, and some grain, and is known for its carved jade and porcelain.

Qinghai Province

Qinghai occupies the northeastern side of the Qinghai-Tibet Plateau, with elevations from 10,000 to 16,500 feet. Between the Qilian Mountains to the north and the Qinghai Plateau, which is rich in minerals, lies the Qaidam Basin, with natural gas and oil, and salt lakes with proved reserves of 70 billion tons of salt. Fifty percent of the province is taken up by pasture land. As in many areas of China, Qinghai has the serious problems of soil erosion, water deficits, and deforestation.

Qinghai Province has a Han population of 56 percent; 44 different ethnic groups make up the remaining 44 percent.

The Tibet Autonomous Region

The major land mass of Tibet is the Qinghai-Tibet Plateau. It is bordered by the Pamir Mountains on the west, the Kunlun range to the north and, at its southern border with Nepal and Bhutan, the Himalayas, known as the "roof of the world." The major Himalayan peak is Mount Everest—at 29,035 feet above sea level, the highest mountain in the world.

Hu Nu?

In the fifteenth century, Tibet developed its own version of Buddhism, in which the spiritual leader, the Dalai Lama, was also the head of state. In the centuries that followed, there were intermittent skirmishes over Tibet between the Qing dynasty's rulers, the Nepalese, the Russians, and the British. After the revolution that established the Republic of China in 1911, the new government recognized Tibet's independence. It lasted until the new communist government of the People's Republic of China invaded in 1950, and killed great numbers of Tibetans in 1959, including many monks, and destroyed monasteries and holy places. (There is more about Tibet in Chapter 16.)

Tibet is cold and dry; there is very little land where crops can grow or animals can graze. There are substantial reserves of several industrial minerals, and Tibet produces 30 percent of China's hydro-energy, but it is a poor country that is the focus of long-term government programs to build Tibet's agricultural infrastructure. The land is home to a dizzying array of wild animals; many of them, such as the Tibetan antelope, wild yak, and wild donkey, are under state protection.

As of 1998, the population was 96.4 percent Tibetan, 2.8 percent Han, and under 1 percent of other ethnic groups. For some time, Han technicians, teachers, and other professionals have been moving to Tibet, while many of Tibet's people continue to hope for independence.

The Ningxia Hui Autonomous Region

Ningxia, bordered by Inner Mongolia in the north, Shaanxi Province in the east, and Gansu in the south, has rich irrigated farmland and is 1 of the 10 major pasture lands in China. With modern agricultural techniques it now produces melons, apples, and grapes in addition to grains, and more paddy rice than is grown anywhere else in western China. It also has abundant mineral resources and reserves of coal. Desertification (the changing of arable land into a desert), which is widespread, has been addressed with some success in Ningxia, which has also made strides in preventing industrial pollution—also a problem throughout China.

The population is 34.1 percent Hui, which equals one fifth of China's total Hui population.

The North

The north, for our purposes, includes the autonomous region of Inner Mongolia (Nei Mongol), and the three provinces east of it that were created out of historical Manchuria: Heilongjiang, Jilin, and Liaoning.

> **Han Help** _____
>
> Manchuria was the country of the Manchus, a semi-nomadic people who conquered China and established the Qing (Manchu) dynasty in 1644. It was the last dynasty to rule China before the Qin Empire fell in 1911. Japan invaded Manchuria in 1895, and held it until the end of World War II. In the chaos of the post-war period, because of Manchuria's location between China and Russia, both countries struggled to gain sovereignty over it. The Chinese Communist Party succeeded in conquering it, and in 1949, Manchuria became three provinces of the People's Republic of China.

The Northeast

This region, generically called the northeast, has a rich agricultural region called the Manchurian Plain where most of the population lives. It is surrounded by mountain forests that make northeast China a prime source of timber, but deforestation poses a problem for the future, in the northeast as well as in other forested areas of China.

When the communists took control of China in 1949, Changchun, the capital of Jilin Province, became the choice location for state-run industry. Harbin, a very busy river port, and Heilongjiang's capital, is a communications hub and an industrial center. It produces airplanes, automobiles, and machinery. Shenyang, the capital of Liaoning, is also a major industrial center that makes steel products such as tools, machinery, and electrical equipment. The region also has oil refineries and coal mines, and huge iron and steel mills at Anshan, a stone's throw (in China) from the major Beijing-Tianjin industrial belt, and from Shanghai down the coast—both major producers of iron and steel products. Products are shipped through the inland waterways (Harbin, Dalian, and Shenyang are river ports) to Dalian, at the tip of the Liaoning Peninsula. It is northeast China's principal seaport.

The northeast is China's most industrial region, but its outdated and inefficient plants have turned much of it into a rust-belt. As state-owned companies have continued to shed workers who are left without the state social benefits they were accustomed to, the region has become unsettled. In March 2002, tens of thousands of workers who felt cheated of benefits by corrupt officials demonstrated in the oil-drilling center of Daquing and the iron-working center of Liaoning. Daquing's oilfields are the most productive in China.

Hu Nu?

The Mongolians formed a close bond with the Tibetans early in their history, and practice the Tibetan form of Buddhism.

A group of 6,000 to 7,000 Mongolians, descendents of the horsemen who remained after Kublai Khan's conquest of Yunnan, still live in a close-knit community in Yunnan Province.

The Inner Mongolia Autonomous Region

The Mongol people are descendants of Genghis Khan, who first broke through the Great Wall in 1209, and his grandson Kublai Khan, who established the Yuan dynasty that ruled China from 1271 to 1368. Both Outer and Inner Mongolia were part of the Qin Empire when it fell in 1911, and competition ensued between Russia, Japan, and the succeeding government of China for domination of the region. Outer Mongolia declared itself the Mongolian People's Republic in 1924, and in 1949, Inner Mongolia became the Inner Mongolian autonomous region of the People's Republic of China.

The new PRC government, wary of the Russian influence in the region, lifted a prior ban on the emigration of Han Chinese to Inner Mongolia, with the result that, as of 2002, the population was only about 10 percent ethnically Mongolian.

> ### Han Help
>
> In 1904, when the Russians finished laying the tracks for the Trans-Siberian Railroad, it ran 5,000 miles, from the Ural Mountains in Siberia, across China, to Vladivostok on the Sea of Japan. The PRC built new railway lines that now extend the two major north-south routes into the northeast, Mongolia, Russia, and the southeast. China's major east-west line runs from Lianyungang on the East China Sea coast, across China to Urumqi, the capital of the Xinjiang Autonomous Region.

The land of the Mongolian Steppe ranges from gravelly deserts in the west to high grass-lands in the east, where some Mongolians raise horses and camels, or live a semi-nomadic existence following their flocks of sheep and goats in the summer months. There are resources such as coal and iron, but the region's major exports are timber and wool.

The forested Da Xing'an Mountains border the three provinces that make up the northeast, and the Gobi Desert overlaps Inner Mongolia's border with Outer Mongolia (the People's Republic). Another desert, the Ordos, lies south of the Yellow River, and Inner Mongolia's southern border parallels (and in some places is marked by) the Great Wall, from its western end to where it meets the Yellow Sea.

The Chinese lived on the land of the Yellow River basin in the north long before there was a China. At the same time, other peoples such as the Miaos and the Uygurs were living on their land in the northwest and the southeast. They did not emigrate to China; they stayed on their land and became part of China, as Chinese culture became part of them.

The Least You Need to Know

- China is the world's oldest continuously existing civilization.
- Chinese civilization came together during the Han dynasty (206 B.C.E.–220 C.E.), so it is called the Han culture.
- From China's beginning, non-Han peoples of the region became integrated into Chinese culture.
- Seventy-five percent of China's people live on 15 percent of the land, in or near the river basins where the food is grown.
- Despite 50 years of industrialization, China's economy remains farm based.

2

The Dynasties

In This Chapter

- ◆ The Zhou dynasty establishes a feudal aristocracy in 1027 B.C.E. and produces three great poets.

- ◆ Confucius teaches moral principles that guide Chinese thought until modern times.

- ◆ The despot Qin Shihuang establishes a Chinese empire that will last for 2,000 years.

- ◆ The Han dynasty creates the earliest definition of "Chinese."

- ◆ Genghis Khan and his Mongol hordes invade and conquer China.

- ◆ European traders bring new ideas—and problems—to China's shores.

Modern China began in 1911 with a revolt that ended the rule of the Qing (also known as Manchu) dynasty, and with it, the 2,000-year-old Chinese Empire. The patchwork of disparate provinces, called China, had survived foreign conquerors, rebellions, corrupt dynasties, and wars with its neighbors keeping its ancient ideals and traditions relatively intact. The mid-nineteenth century's Industrial Revolution and developments in transportation made China vulnerable to incursions of a new kind.

China had been at a great distance by sail from the trading centers of Europe. New ships powered by steam engines brought China into much closer range. Steamships, mostly British, crowded Chinese ports to take on raw materials for manufacturing, and offload—along with Protestant missionaries—opium from colonial India. When opium addiction reached alarming proportions the Qing government banned it, and then confiscated it when the ban went unheeded. What followed was the Opium War, a series of sea battles that Britain won hands down. (The Opium War is covered in more detail in Chapter 3.)

To put an end to the decimation of its fleet, China signed treaties with foreign governments that legalized opium and opened more ports to bargain-rate foreign trade. Hong Kong was ceded to Britain, and concessions of various kinds were made to other European powers. The people rebelled. When China suffered a crushing defeat by Japan in the Sino-Japanese War of 1895, nothing could save the Qing dynasty from the revolutionaries. Their leader, Sun Yatsen, became the father of modern China.

China Past

The next three chapters summarize the end of the Qing dynasty, and the period between the revolution of 1911 led by Sun Yatsen, and the emergence of Mao Zedong as leader of the Chinese Communist Party.

The rest of the book follows the evolution of modern China into the twenty-first century; its wars and alliances, restrictions and reforms, successes and shortcomings. We also look at China's relations with the West, its military potential, and its prospects for economic growth through participation in the global economic community. But Chinese civilization has existed far longer than any other, and to understand modern China and what its future may hold, we first have to look at its past.

As we race through China's long history at a frightful pace, you will notice that ancient China was not, as is commonly believed, under the control of a single power structure. On the contrary, China was ruled by a series of dynasties (regimes), each with its own achievements and failures.

The Zhou Dynasty (1027–256 B.C.E.)

China's first known civilization, the Shang dynasty (which began in approximately 1600 B.C.E.), had a calendar based on the movements of the stars that was accurate enough to be used to plan ahead for the planting season. Examples of written Chinese characters dating back to the Shang dynasty have been found, though it is possible the writing system dates back even further. Not all of the land that we know as China today was ruled by the Shang; some of it was part of other kingdoms, some of whose histories have been erased by time. The Shang dynasty lasted until 1027 B.C.E. when there was a successful invasion from the west. The invaders were known as the Zhous.

The 800 years of the Zhou dynasty encompassed the dawn of China's Iron Age. It was a time of great advances in Chinese culture. For the first time, the Yangzi Valley was colonized, a currency system was introduced, and iron was used to make tools and weapons. And there was plenty of need for weapons. The Zhous were just as prone to warfare as the Shangs before them, and the last 200 years of the dynasty saw many more periods of war than of peace.

It was also during this time that the first segments of wall were built along the southern border of Mongolia to prevent an invasion of nomads from the north. In later dynasties these sections of wall would be joined to form the Great Wall of China.

This dynasty ran on a system known as feudal aristocracy. The nobles owned large areas of land. Everyone who lived there paid rent to the noble and in times of war the men fought in the army of their landlord. Though the king was technically in charge of the kingdom, as the years went along, the king's power diminished while that of the feudal lords increased. By the end of the Zhou dynasty the king had lost power completely and China had split up into seven separate states, each ruled by its own feudal lord.

The Zhou dynasty produced three great philosophers: Confucius, Mencius, and Laozi.

Kong Fuzi lived from 551 until 479 B.C.E. His name has been translated into English as Confucius. He lived in the feudal state of Lu, located in what is now known as Shandong Province.

Confucius's philosophy, which he believed applied to men of all classes (including feudal lords) was very similar to what we in the West call the Golden Rule. Confucius said, "Repay kindness with kindness. Repay evil with justice." He did not believe that the feudal system itself was unjust, just that it was being run by unjust men.

Wise One Says

Confucius says: "Do not worry about people not knowing you, but strive so that you may be worth knowing."

We have much more to say about the unique influence of Confucius on Chinese culture when we explore the religions and philosophies of China in Chapter 7.

The great Chinese philosopher to follow Confucius was Mengzi, whose name is often written Mencius in Western books. He lived from 372 until 289 B.C.E.

Han Help

During Mencius's lifetime Alexander the Great conquered most of the known world and established Alexandria, Egypt, as the center of Hellenistic culture.

Language Lesson _____

Confucian ethical teachings include the following values:

Li   includes ritual, propriety, and etiquette

Xiao   love within the family: love of parents for their children and of children for their parents

Yi   righteousness

Xin   honesty and trustworthiness

Ren   benevolence, humaneness toward others—the highest Confucian virtue

Chong   loyalty to the state

Mencius believed that man was born good and he remained essentially good. Evil came, he believed, when man strayed from the natural path. One of Mencius's most famous sayings is: "A great man is one who has not lost the child's heart."

Mencius, like Confucius, believed that the problems of the world were caused by the misdeeds of the feudal lords rather than by any injustice within the system itself. He believed that the lords ought to be compassionate, and that it was their moral duty to relieve the suffering of the lower classes.

Laozi was the third great philosopher of the Zhou period. He lived at approximately the same time as Confucius and believed the key to a happy and successful life was to remain harmonious with nature. He called this style of living Dao, or "The Way."

Wise One Says _____

Laozi says "Soldiers are instruments of evil. He who delights in slaughter will not succeed in his ambition to rule the world."

His philosophical writings have been preserved in *Tao Teh Ching*, or *The Book of Tao* (also known as the *Daodejing*, in pinyin romanization), and are still extensively studied today. The philosophy in *Tao Teh Ching* has evolved into a full-fledged religion, with priests, multiple gods, and intricate ceremonies. It is discussed in greater detail in Chapter 6.

The Qin Empire (221 B.C.E.–1912 C.E.)

The crumbling pieces of the Zhou dynasty were united in 221 B.C.E. when the feudal ruler of the Qin state conquered the lands of his fellow lords and declared himself "First Exalted Emperor."

Qin Shihuang proved to be a cruel leader who treated the people as his own personal slaves. It was under his leadership that the 2,000-mile Great Wall of China was built to prevent invasions from what was then China's northern border. But he is perhaps best known today for the thousands of life-sized terra cotta warriors buried to protect his tomb near Xian.

In a move typical of tyrants, Qin Shihuang ordered that all books be burned so that there would be no knowledge of what had come before he took power. Priests who tried to hide books were executed. Luckily, attempts to preserve history were occasionally successful, or the memory of Confucius, Laozi, and other philosophers would have been forever lost.

Qin Shihuang, as one might imagine, was not a popular leader, and he was forced to sequester himself in a fortlike palace where only a trusted few were allowed access to him. Immediately after he died, a successful rebellion ensured that his descendents would not have an opportunity to rule.

The Qin family was out of power, but the imperial system set up by Qin Shihuang lasted longer than two millennia, from 221 B.C.E. until the last day of the Chinese Empire in 1912.

The Han Dynasty (206 B.C.E.–220 C.E.)

After Qin Shihuang's descendents were ousted, the Han family seized power. The first Han ruler was a commoner. While the Roman Empire to the west reigned supreme, the region of Asia ruled by Han leaders was transformed into a united state with characteristics that we would recognize today as "Chinese." Appropriately, Confucianism, which embodied the moral principles on which China's social and legal systems were based, was declared by the Han leaders to be the official religion of China.

During the course of the Han dynasty there were attempts made to restore the feudal system—the same system that had led to the end of the Zhou dynasty—but they were always subdued before they could take root. From the point of view of Chinese heritage, there was no dynasty more important than the Han. A great majority of Chinese people today consider themselves to be Han—that is, directly descended from the leaders of this dynasty. The Han dynasty came to an end in 220 C.E. and was followed by 350 years of disunity.

> **Hu Nu?**
>
> It was during the Han dynasty that written examinations were first required for those wishing to qualify for civil service positions.

"Three Kingdoms" and "Six Dynasties" (221–618 C.E.)

The three-and-a-half centuries of disorder that followed the end of the Han dynasty saw constant fighting among several dynasties, including the Wei, Shu, and Wu. During this time China split into three separate kingdoms and was frequently invaded from the north by nomads. Reunification came briefly during the Chin dynasty (265–317), but invaders from the north quickly took advantage of the feuding states and moved in. For the first time, non-Chinese controlled at least part of China.

Hu Nu?

Hua Mu-Lan is the heroine of a famous Chinese poem written during the Northern dynasties (420–589 C.E.). In the story, Mulan disguises herself as a man to serve in the army in her father's place. While serving, she is recognized as a courageous soldier and offered a government post. She turns down the position in favor of going home and living a peaceful life with her family. After she returns home, she puts on her lady's clothes again—and shocks her fellow soldiers who didn't know she was a woman when they were on the battlefield. The story was expanded into a novel during the late Ming dynasty (1368–1644 C.E.). Nobody knows for sure if there really was a Hua Mu-Lan, but of course her character was popularized in America by the Disney film *Mulan*.

Although this period was not a time of stability, several noteworthy events occurred: Buddhist missionaries from India first arrived and Buddhism began to be practiced in China; coal was first burned for heat; and a period of innovation in Chinese sculpture took place.

The period of disorder officially ended with the commencement of the Tang dynasty.

The Tang Dynasty (618–906 C.E.)

In the West the great Roman Empire was coming to its end, and in Arabia the Prophet Muhammad had founded a new religion, Islam, that in time would have a profound impact on the whole world.

China was again united in 618 when it was conquered by Tai Zong, the first Tang emperor. The Tang conquered land in what we know today as India, Korea, and even Afghanistan, making the Chinese Empire larger than it had ever been. Learning also flourished, as astronomy and mapmaking became finely honed sciences at this time. The Tang dynasty was another fruitful time for Chinese arts. Great strides were made in painting, glazed porcelain, printing, and lyric poetry. Tang painters worked both in color and in black ink, and used long scrolls of paper or panels of silk as their canvases. Chinese artists were somewhat ahead of their Western counterparts when it came to techniques such as gradations of light, perspective, and shadow. Chinese pot makers borrowed shapes and techniques from the Greeks, Persians, and Indians, but added a new dimension: color. The new Chinese pots were made in beautiful bright colors, including oxblood red and ultramarine blue.

> ### Hu Nu?
>
> It was during the Tang dynasty that the Chinese came up with one of their most famous inventions: fireworks. Gunpowder, as it came to be known, was invented by the Chinese, but it was not used in conjunction with weapons until it became known to Europeans.

Poetry was not unknown before the Tang dynasty; Confucius's poems, for example, had been extremely popular. But in this era lyric poetry flourished as an art form. The two most famous poets of the Tang dynasty were Li Po and Tu Fu who lived at the same time and were friends. Li Po wrote poems that were filled with colorful images of nature.

One of Li Po's most famous poems is the following, called "Song of Pure Happiness" (as translated in 1929 by Witter Bynner):

> Her robe is a cloud, her face is a flower;
> Her balcony, glimmering with the bright spring dew,
> Is either the tip of earth's Jade Mountain,
> Or a moon-edged roof of paradise.

To administer the expanded empire the Tang maintained capitals in the cities of Luoyang and Changan, but the empire proved too vast to manage effectively. In time the peoples of what are now Thailand and Tibet revolted against Chinese rule. But it was eventually that old nemesis, invaders from the north—Mongols—that brought an end to the Tang dynasty in 906. It took 54 years for the Chinese to regain control of most of China.

The Song Dynasty (960–1279 C.E.)

When the Song dynasty gained power in 960 they returned much of China to Chinese rule, but not all of it. The northernmost sections of China remained under Mongol control. Throughout its more than 300 years in power the Song dynasty was intermittently at war with the Mongols. Nevertheless, for the first time, large public buildings were built in China as architecture made great strides—and was becoming increasingly ornate. Up until this time wood had been by far the predominant building material; now it gave way to stone.

Masons were now able to build tall pagodas composed of many square, and sometimes octagonal, platforms arranged in a tapering design. Other new design elements in Chinese structures included colorful decorative tiles. Waterways were now crossed with humped bridges. Marble and bronze statues grew in size and variety, now depicting dragons, animals, and gods and goddesses.

By the eleventh century, the emperors of the Song dynasty were remarkably modern in their thinking. The empire was run efficiently and with compassion for the welfare of the people—the poor as well as the rich.

Much of this enlightenment was brought about by a man named Wang Anshi who, despite strong opposition, carried out radical reform programs. Wang traveled around the country and made a list of things the people needed; he then saw to it that the necessary changes were made in the Chinese economy, government, and education systems.

Whereas poetry evolved during the Tang dynasty, prose writing developed dramatically during the Song period. It was during this time that the first great histories of China were written. Two major encyclopedias were developed. Mathematicians made progress as well. Algebra was developed, though it's unclear whether it was independently developed in China or borrowed in rudimentary form from the Arabs. It was also a good time for Chinese medicine; Chinese doctors inoculated people against smallpox seven centuries before the smallpox vaccine was developed by the English physician Edward Jenner.

The center of innovative Chinese thinking was Luoyang, which had become a Chinese capital during the Tang dynasty. It was in the province of Henan not far from the Yellow River, and those who lived there at the time considered it the greatest city in the world.

Genghis Khan

The early thirteenth century in China was an especially violent period, the only time that the protective barrier from the north, the Great Wall of China, had buckled under the relentless pressure of the Mongol hordes—an army of warriors commanded by a supreme warrior—Genghis Khan.

The man who came to be known as Genghis Khan was born in 1162. His father was Yesugei the Brave. Nothing is known about him. Originally known as Temujin, Genghis was nine years old when his father was murdered, poisoned by warriors of a rival tribe, the Merkits.

When Temujin turned 13, he became engaged to a young woman named Bortei. In 1177, Temujin had his first opportunity to demonstrate ruthlessness when he and his brother killed their half-brother after catching him spying on them for a rival tribe, this time the Tanguts. After the killing, the Tanguts kidnapped Temujin and he was put in prison to await his execution. He managed to escape two days before his scheduled death and returned to his tribe and married his fiancée.

When Temujin was 18, his tribe was attacked by the Merkits. The warriors lost control of their village and Temujin was forced to abandon his wife to the mercy of the Merkits. Two months later he led a successful raid of his old village and freed his wife. In the three years after that successful raid, Temujin performed many feats of legendary bravery. He organized large armies, fought in many battles, and was always victorious. He was given the name Genghis (originally pronounced Chingus, by the way) Khan, which translates as Invincible Ruler.

> **Wise One Says**
> Genghis Khan, as a young man unaware of what the future held, once said "Violence never settles anything."

> **Han Help**
> When Genghis Khan was born the Crusades were going on in the Holy Land. They were still in progress after his death, when the crusaders formed an alliance with the Mongols in the hope of defeating the Muslims.

Genghis Khan's military victories were not a matter of luck. He won because he was a military innovator. He invented a system of warfare based on a self-sufficient cavalry, one that could live off the land. He defeated his enemies by being more mobile than they were. He surrounded and destroyed opposing armies.

He was a good leader and was adored by his men, who fought hard for him. He, in turn, was intensely loyal to them. On the other hand, he was ruthless to his enemies; he did not take prisoners except temporarily, when he could elicit information from them. When he conquered a village, the buildings were burned and the inhabitants were slaughtered.

While Genghis Khan was being (mythologically) brave, his forces moved steadily westward. He conquered, and thus united, the three major empires that made up China at that time: the Xi Xia, Qin, and Na Zhong. During the first six years of the thirteenth century C.E. Genghis Khan built up an impressive combat record. His armies defeated Jamuga's army in 1203, which wasn't the grandest of his feats as Jamuga's army consisted of only about 50 men, but the victory gave him control of half of Xi Xia.

In 1203, Genghis Khan defeated the other half of Xi Xia's army—the half led by a warrior named Togrul. In 1204, Khan headed for the Qin Empire, an empire defended by a small tribe of mercenaries known as the Naimans. The mercenaries were easily vanquished. However, conquering the Qin Empire would have to wait for the time being. Before he could move his conquering forces any farther he was going to have to figure out a way to get past the Great Wall.

Ruler of Rulers

In 1206, Genghis was given the new, even bigger title of Khan of Khans—a ruler amongst rulers! His title meant that he was in supreme command of all of China, though this was not yet the case. There were still some problems. A portion of the Xi Xia Empire reemerged in 1209 so that Genghis had to conquer it again. Luckily, it was easily done.

In 1215, Genghis concentrated his efforts on busting a hole through the Great Wall of China. Although it took two solid months of battering, his hordes finally made it through and the war against the Qin Empire was on. Before the year was out, Genghis's army had conquered the Qin capital, Beijing, and destroyed the capitol building.

Genghis's End

Guchluk, the ruler of the Qin Empire, managed to hang on to power for another two years after the fall of Beijing, but he was finally captured by Genghis's men and beheaded.

Despite his title as ruler of rulers, Genghis Khan still had one empire left to conquer before he would truly be the ruler of all China. In the year 1218, Genghis and his hordes rode to the empire of Na Zhong for a war that lasted four years. The Mongols were again victorious. Several years later, while Genghis was returning from a successful mission to prevent his enemies from uniting against him, he fell off his horse. He was severely injured and, on August 21, 1227, he died of his injuries.

Although the Song dynasty officially ended in the year 1279 when its last ruler died, this was actually a full 19 years into the reign of Genghis Khan's grandson, and his heir as ruler, Kublai Khan.

The Mongols remained in power after Genghis's death, with the leadership of the country passing down from father to son, as is true of royalty. The thinking is that the leadership is in the blood. But if Genghis Khan thought a continuation of his policies would be automatic as long as leadership remained in the hands of his descendants, he couldn't have been more wrong. Only two generations down the line a completely different type of Mongol leader emerged.

The Yuan (Mongol) Dynasty (1279–1368 c.e.)

Kublai Khan, the grandson of Genghis Khan, inherited his position as ruler of the Yuan dynasty and had a great influence on China—but his type of influence couldn't have been more different from his grandfather's.

Whereas Genghis was a military champion and innovator who is best known as a conqueror, Kublai forever changed China by showing the people what effective leadership was.

There had been compassionate rulers in China's past, but none of them had been Mongolian. The Chinese, for good reason, expected Kublai Khan to be a barbarian; he was anything but. He had given up the nomadic ways of his people and become in every way—including his personal style—effectively Chinese.

Perhaps it was because he was the Mongol with a heart that his powerful influence did not last after his death. Things may have gone differently for the Chinese who regained control of the country that had been lost ever since Genghis Khan had burst through the Great Wall.

Kublai was the second oldest of the brothers, and when his oldest brother Mongke took the throne, Kublai was put in charge of the military. When Mongke was killed in a battle between Buddhists and Daoists, Kublai assumed the throne.

His leadership did not go unchallenged, however. In fact it was challenged by his own brother, Arigh Beki, who was younger than Kublai and running southern portions of China. Kublai squelched the challenge by cutting off supplies to his brother's territory.

In 1260, Kublai was named Great Khan, leader of the Yuan dynasty, although it would be 19 years before the Song dynasty would officially come to a close with the death of its final emperor.

To administer the vast area under his rule, Kublai followed the example of China's previous rulers and established a bureaucracy. He also ensured the support of the diverse population he ruled by enlisting a committee of strong religious leaders of different faiths to advise him. Religious tolerance was not the only innovation to come to China during Kublai Khan's reign. He did not hesitate to appoint foreign officials who had skills useful to him; he created government aid agencies to care for people who

---

Hu Nu?

Kublai Khan was born to Toluia and Sorghaghtani Beki. Kublai's father died when he was young and he was raised, along with his three brothers, by his mother. His mother was a strong woman. When Toluia's brother tried to take control of the throne, she fought him and won.

desperately needed help; he brought the Chinese mail system out of the stone age; and he reorganized and greatly improved the transportation systems—the waterways as well as the roads. He also increased trade and diplomatic contact with the West. Scholarship and art flourished.

Not everything Kublai Khan did, however, met with the approval of all the competing groups he ruled. The Han resented the Mongolians, the Mongolians resented the Han, and everyone resented the foreigners.

He proclaimed that China's two capitals were to be Dadu for the winter and Shangdu for the summer. (The summer capital, Shangdu, became known as Xanadu.) The winter capital had previously been in Mongolia, but the new winter capital was in China, and is present-day Beijing. Kublai's decision to move China's winter capital out of Mongolian territory incensed the Mongolians, who saw it as a betrayal of his heritage.

Late in life Kublai tried to appease his Mongol critics by conquering new lands as his grandfather had done, but it was not what he was built to do. It was clear that even the gods were not on Kublai Khan's side when it came to expansionism. When he tried to conquer Japan a typhoon wiped out his entire expedition. The attempts of his army to conquer Java and Japan eventually failed, but not until they had drained the treasury.

Things went from bad to worse. The system of paper currency Kublai had devised ended up causing drastic inflation. His policy of religious freedom could not stop the battles going on between the various religions.

In 1281, after the death of one of his favorite wives, he became very depressed, and in his later years he grew hideously fat and became an alcoholic. Even so, despite his self-indulgent ways, he lived to be 79.

Kublai Khan had the wisdom to realize that he could not bring peace and stability to the domain he ruled by following the barbaric ways of the Mongols. After his death, predictably enough, there was a return to brutal and corrupt leadership, and eventually a civil war that brought the Ming dynasty to power.

Marco Polo

Marco Polo was born in Venice, Italy, in 1254. He was educated in accounting, foreign languages, and matters of the Christian church. His father, Nicolo, and uncle, Maffeo, were merchants who became explorers. They began their first journey to the Far East in 1260, first visiting Constantinople (today's Istanbul) and then making their way to the domain of Kublai Khan, ruler of China.

Kublai Khan sent the Polos back to the Pope in Rome as his ambassadors with messages of peace and interest in converting areas of China to Christianity. They then went home to Venice for two years before they returned to China, as they had promised Kublai Khan they would, and to the large profits they would make from trade with distant lands.

On this journey, they took the 17-year-old Marco Polo with them. After three-and-a-half years of travel, the ambassadors humbly appeared before the emperor.

The Europeans were amazed at the things, still unheard of in Europe, that were available in China, such as paper, sophisticated art, and mechanical devices.

Wise One Says

Marco Polo wrote a book about his travels, called, appropriately enough, *The Travels of Marco Polo*, that is still read today. When he was near death, a priest entered his room and asked him if he wanted to confess that his stories about China were false. "I did not tell half of what I saw because no one would have believed me," he replied.

Young Marco Polo, with his father and uncle, lived for many years—until the 1290s—in China. Upon his return to Italy as a 40-year-old man, he told of the jade, porcelain, silk, ivory, and other riches of Asia. He described the festival of the emperor's birthday in which everything from clothing to ornaments was laced in gold. He also related that he'd seen people using "black stones" (actually coal) for fuel. Trouble was, people in Italy did not believe his wild stories. He was called the "man of a million lies."

It was through Marco Polo that most Europeans learned of China. Although he never wrote about the Great Wall or foot-binding, he taught the Western world about Chinese trade and the many wonders that the Eastern world had to offer.

The Ming Dynasty (1368–1644 c.e.)

After civil wars drove out the Mongols who had destroyed the Yuan dynasty, the Mings, a family that rose from humble beginnings, picked up the pieces that remained. They restored traditional Chinese culture. Chinese scientists and doctors once again advanced humankind's knowledge. Artists again became innovative. Porcelain was again an art form. During the sixteenth century most of the Great Wall of China was greatly expanded and reinforced.

Especially busy during the Ming dynasty were the historians. They launched the largest historical undertaking of all time—an encyclopedia that would contain all of the knowledge of humankind. It is said that at one point the encyclopedia comprised 11,095 volumes. Sadly, only a few volumes survive.

Europe Arrives

It was also during the Ming dynasty that European explorers began to explore the world by ship. The New World was discovered. The Portuguese reached China by sea in 1514 and in 1557 established their first colony in China at Macao. Ships soon arrived from England, Spain, and Holland. European culture had begun to penetrate the unique, pristine culture of China.

Rise of the Manchus

The leaders of the Ming dynasty had the usual problem: They needed to defend themselves against the constant threat of invasion from the war-minded Mongols to the north. To bolster their efforts the Ming leaders enlisted the aid of a people from the northeast known as the Manchus. In exchange for their protection services the Manchus were granted a certain amount of regional authority. To the horror of the Mings, the formerly competitive tribes that comprised the Manchus organized under a powerful leader into a cohesive force that eventually took control of China. When the Manchus captured Beijing in 1644 they founded what came to be known as the Qing dynasty, the last in China's long history of dynastic rule.

> **Hu Nu?**
>
> It was during the Qing dynasty that Taiwan first came under strict Chinese rule. It had been a remote and irrelevant hinterland until it became a haven for the last remnants of the Ming dynasty. (Three hundred years later Chiang Kaishek would flee to the same island.) The Qings then dispatched a force to Taiwan that rooted out the Ming loyalists and took control of the island in the process.

The Qing dynasty was very strong during its early years, and by the middle of the eighteenth century China had expanded its empire to encompass Tibet, Mongolia, and much of southeast Asia. The empire was prosperous and relatively war free, by Chinese standards, and the increasing trade with the West was proving very profitable. By the early 1800s, however, the Qing leaders had become corrupt and complacent. It did not bode well for the future of China.

The Least You Need to Know

◆ China's history is the oldest on Earth.

◆ Confucian philosophy was a major influence on Chinese culture until the advent of modern China.

◆ Genghis Khan, whose Mongol hordes breached the Great Wall and conquered China, fell off a horse and died of his injuries.

◆ Genghis's grandson, Kublai Khan, rejected Mongol ways and became a product—and advocate—of Chinese culture.

◆ Marco Polo introduced Chinese culture to the West.

◆ European traders descended on China's ports and brought wealth, ideas—and trouble—to the fractured empire.

Chapter 3

The Empire Fades

In This Chapter

- ◆ A foreign dynasty and a deluge of foreign interlopers bring unrest to Chinese society.
- ◆ Great Britain assaults China with opium and gunships.
- ◆ The Treaty of Nanjing cripples China's sovereignty.
- ◆ A disaffected would-be savior leads the Taiping Rebellion.
- ◆ China suffers a humiliating defeat by Japan.
- ◆ The Boxer Rebellion breaks the Qing dynasty's spirit.

As the eighteenth century came to an end the Qing dynasty controlled the largest land area in China's history, and the empire was at peace. But peace, along with the importation of high-yield crops such as sweet potatoes and peanuts, led to a sudden leap in population that brought new miseries to the peasants. The foreign Manchu rulers, widely accepted by the gentry and the civil servant class who had benefited from their administration, were not looked upon favorably by the peasants. The increasing number of other foreigners trading at the port of Ghangzhou added to the mounting tension in the countryside.

From 1842 until well into the twentieth century the Europeans nibbled away at the Chinese Empire. Southeast Asia went to France, Manchuria to

Russia and Japan, and Burma to Great Britain. Foreign wars, famine, and rebellions plagued the country while its leaders struggled, and ultimately failed, to hold on to its traditions in a world that had moved on.

The Opium War

The British, who had established a brisk trade in opium, a highly addictive drug, were, in effect, planting the seeds of a Chinese drug problem that has never gone away. But worse things would happen during the last days of the Chinese Empire.

Opium got its hooks into China quickly. In 1800, an estimated 4,000 chests of opium were being imported into China per year. In his book *The Search for Modern China*, Jonathan Spence estimates that 40 years later that number was closer to 40,000 chests per year. Absolutely none of this was legal, but so much money was being made that there was no problem bribing the officials who would have been responsible for stopping the opium inflows.

In 1839, the Chinese decided to crack down on the opium trade. Twenty thousand chests of opium were seized. The British lost a fortune. The seizure sparked a series of clashes between the Chinese and the British that is technically known as "The Anglo–Chinese War" but is more commonly known as the Opium War. The British were highly outnumbered of course, but this was more than compensated for by their superior military power. Small groups of British ships sat off Chinese ports and caused great damage with their bombardments. The continuous threat of attack added to the building tensions. The Industrial Revolution, which had spawned a flurry of inventions in the Western world, had not reached China, and the Chinese had no defense against the British cannons.

Hu Nu?

When opium was first introduced in China by the British in the seventeenth century, it was smoked as an additive to tobacco. Around 1760, the Chinese discovered how to prepare the drug so that it could be smoked on its own. During that century, opium was smoked mostly by the rich. Those in the employ of the wealthy had taken up the habit by the nineteenth century, and by the early twentieth century even peasants were smoking opium. To give you a strong idea of how entrenched opium usage was in Chinese culture, it is estimated that during the early years of the twentieth century, half of China's adult population smoked opium daily.

The Treaty of Nanjing

The Opium War came to an end in 1842 when a humiliated China was forced to sign the Treaty of Nanjing. The treaty gave Hong Kong, an island off China's southeast coast, to the British. Great Britain also picked up $21 million in cash in the deal, and five Chinese ports were opened up to British traders, who were now allowed to set up residences there. This was the first of several treaties the Chinese signed with the European powers, and they later became known by the Chinese as the "Unequal Treaties." The European powers began to treat China as a colony—and the Chinese were letting them do it.

The Taiping Rebellion, 1850–64

While China was fighting to maintain control of its land and economic power, a population explosion was taking place that would have devastating consequences. A country that had been able to feed 150 million people was now struggling to feed 400 million. An already restive peasantry, deeply resentful of the Manchus who controlled the government and the Christian missionaries and traders who were flooding in from the West, now had to contend with starvation and abject poverty.

Onto this scene stepped Hong Xiuguan, a young man from a poor *Hakka* family in south China. He'd repeatedly failed the civil service exam, thereby closing the only door to self-improvement open to him, and was consumed with hatred of the Manchus who dominated the government. After he'd come across some commentaries on the Christian Bible written by a Chinese convert to Christianity, Hong believed himself to be the younger brother of Jesus. He committed himself to leading a holy rebellion against the Manchu rulers. Even though Hong's rebellion lacked a clear purpose, it stirred an already dissatisfied peasantry enough to take up arms and fight with him.

Hong and his ever-growing band of peasant revolutionaries fought from south China to the

Han Help

Christian missionaries earned the right to go into China in 1844, and at their peak, there were about 1,400 Protestant missionaries in the country. By the end of World War II, it is estimated that there were four million Chinese who had converted to Christianity, both Protestant and Catholic.

Language Lesson

The **Hakka** people are an ethnic group who originated in central China and migrated to the south centuries ago. Many Hakka now live in Gaungdong, Fujian, and Taiwan and maintain their distinct dialect and customs.

Yangzi River and conquered much of it. This, Hong said, was the start of the Taiping (Great Peace) dynasty, and he was its ruler. Hong might have been a military match for his Chinese opponents, but he could not fight the British and French. When he and his men got to Beijing he found the city at war with the British and French over treaties and trade disputes. It was up to the Europeans in 1860 to put down the Taiping Rebellion and it took them until 1864 to finish the job. All in all, Hong's own version of Christianity fused with revolutionary zeal had kept the Manchus and the Europeans busy for 14 years.

The help of the Europeans cost China dearly: Ten new ports were opened to them and they were allowed for the first time to sail their ships up Chinese rivers into the heart of the country. An undeveloped piece of land outside Shanghai was given to the Americans. This and other foreign trade would mark a beginning for Shanghai as a leading center of commerce. Other foreign investment—especially British and Japanese—would figure greatly into Shanghai's nineteenth-century economic growth.

The West Goes East

The world was modernizing fast, a fact that most Manchus did not seem to realize. China was being left behind. It wasn't that there were no attempts to modernize; it was just that compared to the rest of the world's leaders, the Manchus were not terribly successful at it.

An influx of Western ideas entered China during the first half of the nineteenth century when Protestant missionaries published a Chinese translation of the Bible. For a time almost all Chinese knowledge of Western thought had to do with Christianity, but during the mid-nineteenth century, Western works were available in translation on a variety of subjects.

Yan Fu was a Chinese scholar from Fujian Province who lived from 1854 to 1921. As a young man he studied in England and became familiar with Western philosophy, including the works of Charles Darwin. Upon his return to China, he became a pioneer in understanding Western thought and helped other Chinese understand it as well with his translations of heady Western works such as T. H. Huxley's *Evolution and Ethics* and J. S. Mills's *On Liberty*.

> **Hu Nu?**
>
> During the latter half of the nineteenth century, approximately 85 percent of the foreign works translated into Chinese were American. The remainder were Japanese. By the end of the nineteenth century, almost all translated works were about science and technology.

Yan Fu's writings taught that the Western way of life was healthier because it encouraged humans to be energetic and assertive, whereas Chinese life forces tended to be stifled by the teachings of their sages.

But the very cultures that those who sought to modernize China were seeking to understand were also becoming, in several ways, China's oppressors. More and more the Chinese land and people were being exploited by men from the other side of the world. The Qing dynasty's economy was generally strong, making more money than it spent during the first half of the nineteenth century. But as time went on, the black ink changed to red. The reason was that the Chinese economy was being dominated by influences that did not have the best interests of China in mind. Economic ventures in banking, shipping, and railroads were increasingly controlled by foreigners. As a result, most of the profits from foreign investment in China were sent back to foreign lands and were not used to sustain China in any way.

Restoration and Reform

British and French troops had stopped the Taiping rebels from taking Beijing because the Qing forces couldn't. During the rebellion the inept imperial forces had also had, with great reluctance, to rely on the regional militias of the Chinese gentry. It was their most prominent member, Zeng Guofan, a military leader and Confucian scholar, who had suppressed the Taiping movement in the provinces. Afterward, Zeng and his fellow scholar-military commanders developed a plan for China's recovery and its defense against foreign aggression (known as "Self-Strengthening"). They took their proposals to Cixi, the Empress Dowager, the regent who had been China's de facto ruler for many years.

Han Help

Cixi (also spelled Tzu Shi), the Empress Dowager, first ruled in place of her ineffectual son, Tongzhi, and later her nephew, Guangxu, who was sickly but intelligent and assertive. Cixi was born in 1835, and though no one is sure, it has been said that her father was a guard at the emperor's home, the Forbidden City. She was a member of the Manchu family, and as a child, she had little contact with Chinese people. The Empress Dowager was known for her extravagance. One story relates that she would only use golden chopsticks to eat! Furthermore, her fear of foreigners and resistance to change did not make her an effective leader for such a dynamic period.

Cixi and her cohorts were mounting their own effort, called the Restoration, to restore the now-endangered dynastic traditions. The world had changed, and Cixi was too self-centered and obtuse to know it; Self-Strengthening was never even considered.

In yet another quarter another scholar, Kang Yuwei, had conceived of an imaginative new approach to reforming China's policies: using a different version of Confucian text that would allow for some creative solutions to China's resistance to change.

For the rest of the nineteenth century, bureaucrats and scholars alike tried to bring about the reforms and modernization that could give China a fighting chance in a world that had changed. Western methodologies and technologies were known of and appreciated, but in China's traditional culture, they just wouldn't take.

War with Japan

China had stuck fast to its old traditions, arrogantly believing in the superiority of its culture and disdaining contact with foreigners. The United States opened trade with Japan in 1854—with a bang. It took "gunboat diplomacy" to get Japan to open its doors, but the result was that, under the Meiji period that followed, Japan's industrialization took off.

Japan saw that the Industrial Revolution was changing the world, and wanted to become part of that change. The country set about to modernize itself as fast as it could, and by the end of the nineteenth century it had emerged as a world power.

The Japanese began a period of military expansionism that would continue until it was ended by Japan's defeat in World War II. Tokyo's first choice for a test of strength was with China.

The Sino-Japanese War began in 1894, sparked by a conflict involving Korea. In a replay of the Opium War when China found itself defenseless against Britain's battleships, the Chinese army and navy alike were decimated by Japan's modern weapons. China sued for peace in 1895 and ended up ceding Taiwan (then known as Formosa), the Liaodong area in southern Manchuria, and the Pescadores Islands.

The power gap between China and the modern world steadily grew. Other countries took what they wanted. Russia built railroads through Manchuria and opened a naval base on the Chinese coast. Great Britain, France, and Germany also continued to move right in like they owned the place. It started to look like, if the trend continued, China would soon be divvied up between the world's powers and cease to exist altogether.

The Hundred Days of Reform

China had been defeated by foreign powers again and again in the past, but its humiliation by Japan in 1895 was intolerable. Japan not only had military superiority, it had evolved into a modern society. For many of China's people, Japan's supremacy brought into question the very idea that had made China the oldest civilization on Earth, the idea that Chinese culture was superior, and superior cultures prevail. The reform-minded took it another way: They were in awe of what Japan had achieved and sought the advice and help of Japanese mentors.

Meanwhile, Kang Yuwei had not given up his quest for ways to infuse progressive reforms into China's traditional mind-set. By 1898, the country was on the verge of collapse. Kang had some promising ideas but he knew it would be useless to take them to Cixi, the Empress Dowager. Instead he approached Guangxu, the nominal emperor, who was deeply impressed with Kang's advice. On his own initiative Guangxu ordered what was called the Hundred Days of Reform: modernization of China's railroads, military, legal system, education, and economy. Manchu officials who opposed the changes were fired. The Empress Dowager, still the power behind the dynasty, banished Guangxu to a palace where he was kept under house arrest with four guards along with his wife, who was Cixi's spy. Kang fled, and his reforms disappeared with him.

The Boxer Rebellion

At the turn of the twentieth century, a secret society called the Boxers—their name in Chinese translates more literally into "The Righteous Fists"—quickly became an anti-foreigner movement that spread throughout China. Combining martial arts with mystical rituals, they went into trances and then attacked foreign targets, believing that their powers could make them bulletproof.

With the collusion of the Empress Dowager, who shared their xenophobia, this unorganized rabble began their violent revolt in 1900, roaming the northeastern section of China, killing and destroying any evidence of a European presence. Also on the Boxers' list of enemies were Chinese people who had converted to Christianity. Church-burning became a favorite Boxer activity and many thousands of Chinese Christians were killed. An international force of British, American, German, French, Russian, and Japanese troops arrived to rescue their nationals and the besieged Chinese Christians from the Boxers. Declaring war on all of them, the Empress Dowager and her cohorts fled the Forbidden City for Xian, where they set up a temporary capital.

Han Help

During the eighteenth and nineteenth centuries, revolutions had been toppling imperial powers all over the world: the American Revolution in 1776, the French Revolution in 1789, and the formation of independent states in Latin America in the 1800s. Karl Marx had published *The Common Man* in 1848, three years before the beginning of the Taiping Rebellion.

Wise One Says

When the international force arrived in China to quell the Boxer Rebellion, Cixi was incensed and declared that her desire was to "eat the flesh and sleep on the skins" of the foreigners. Even as a mature woman, Cixi had never actually met a white person. She had been told, and firmly believed, that Europeans were not quite human, and that their knees didn't bend.

The international force sent 19,000 more troops to China, but not to fight a war; they went on a looting spree in Beijing, and killed and tortured great numbers of Chinese people.

Rather than fight a war, the international powers and the Chinese provincial governors came to an agreement: The Chinese would keep the peace in China if the foreign forces moved out. But once again China was forced to sign a humiliating treaty, this one called the Treaty of Beijing. All of the trade agreements already in place were amended to the benefit of the Europeans, and China was compelled to make huge payments in gold for the next 39 years as compensation for the loss of some 200 foreign lives and damage to foreign property.

The Chinese people grew more frustrated and more hostile than ever toward the Manchu rulers, including their Empress Dowager.

The Open Door Policy

If the international force that had crushed the Boxer Rebellion had wanted to, they could have divided China among them, and China as we know it would have ceased to exist. The only thing that prevented China's demise was the inability of the parties to agree on how to carve it up. What they did finally agree on was called the "Open Door" policy. It stated that none of the powers with trading privileges inside China would use their privileges against those of another power. Each nation would have equal trade rights and China would be left intact.

Wise One Says

The Anglo-American Open Door Doctrine marks the first clear phase of transition to a Far East out of control, and from rivalry between similar competitors to rivalry between competitors dissimilar from each other and hostile to each other in ideology, social and political structure, and economic operation.

—Owen Lattimore, *The Situation in Asia* (Little, Brown, 1949)

The Beginning of the End

In 1901, when Cixi returned to her palace in Beijing, she was a changed woman. With her dynasty in jeopardy of extinction she had finally accepted the fact that modernization was the only road to take.

The Empress Acts

The Empress Dowager created a comprehensive 10-year plan for reforms in every area of Chinese life:

- Opium was outlawed.

- The military was strengthened.

- The civil service exams were abolished and the educational system was modernized—a break with a millennium of Confucian tradition in government and education.

- The people were promised a constitution and a representative government.

- Provincial self-government would be established and funded by Beijing.

The Manchus drew on their best leaders, including Zhang Zhidong and Yuan Shikai, to put the plans in motion. But by this point, as far as most of the Chinese people were concerned, the Manchus couldn't do anything right, and the people were taking things into their own hands.

In 1905, students and workers in Ghangzhou mounted a protest against the discriminatory practices of American manufacturers toward Chinese labor. It was followed by a boycott of U.S. goods that spread to other cities and lasted for months. The local governments set up in major cities such as Shanghai and Tianjin couldn't get off the ground because the Qing dynasty had a hopelessly inept fiscal, financial, and administrative structure. In addition, the punishing treaties and wars of the recent past had drained its treasury.

Beijing's reform plan had merit, but in the maelstrom that China found itself in, it was too late for reforms.

Death and Succession

In 1906, a son, Pu Yi, had been born to Prince Chung, Emperor Guangxu's brother. Two years after his birth, Cixi suffered a stroke and, further weakened by dysentery, realized that she did not have long to live. She chose Pu Yi to be the next emperor. The next day, oddly enough, Emperor Guangxu, 37 years old, died, and Pu Yi, a toddler, succeeded him.

Soon thereafter the Empress Dowager passed away at the age of 73. Though she was never officially the leader of China, she had been in power for half a century. Her extravagance followed her into the grave; she was buried with gems adorning her body from head to toe. In 1928, revolutionaries looted her tomb and made off with all her fabulous jewels.

The Last Emperor, Pu Yi

During the four years between Cixi's death and the death of the dynasty, the last emperor was Pu Yi, who was still a boy. Chaos, not the boy emperor, reigned in China as the Chinese people's wrath toward their government boiled over. The revolt that was to come would end the dynasty system in China.

The Least You Need to Know

- ◆ Great Britain's opium trade made addicts of half the adult Chinese population.
- ◆ Punishing "unequal treaties" with foreign powers weakened the Qing dynasty's hold on the people.
- ◆ Hatred of the foreign Manchu rulers and the encroaching foreign powers fueled the Taiping Rebellion.
- ◆ Japan's crushing victory over China shook the Qing dynasty to its foundations.
- ◆ The Boxer Rebellion brought dynastic China to its knees.

Chapter 4

The Revolution of 1911

In This Chapter

- Hatred of the Manchus leads to a revolutionary movement.
- Dr. Sun Yatsen becomes the founder of modern China.
- The Republic of China is born and the Qing dynasty dies a slow death.
- President Yuan Shikai and the foreigners fight to retain dynastic rule.
- Sun Yatsen founds the Nationalist Party (Guomindang) and the Revolutionary Party of China.

By 1909, all that remained of the Qing dynasty was a three-year-old emperor and a stillborn modernization program. The Western world was being wired for electricity. Railroads made cross-continental travel not only feasible but quick and easy. The first automobiles were being built. Telephones had been invented. But China, even though pushed this way and that by an array of foreign influences, had continued along its own peculiar course. The need for modernization was evident but the means of adapting China's traditional culture to meet the demands of modern life had yet to be found.

The world had changed in other ways, too. In Europe, Karl Marx and Friedrich Engels had published their blueprints for socialist revolution. Socialist movements had taken hold in Germany and Great Britain and had been part of the failed Russian Revolution of 1905 against the Czarist regime. In China, anti-Manchu sentiment had reached critical mass. The concepts of representative government and individual rights had begun to resonate. The scattered uprisings that had been taking place since the Boxer Rebellion were about to coalesce into a movement, and it already had a leader.

Dr. Sun Yatsen

Sun Yatsen was a Christian who had studied in Hawaii and Hong Kong, where he earned a medical degree, and was thoroughly familiar with the political philosophies and economic concepts of the West. He was the most prominent of a group of revolutionaries who, late in the nineteenth century, demonstrated their contempt for the Manchus by cutting off their own *queues*.

Language Lesson

A **queue** is a long braid of hair that had to be worn by Chinese men during the Qing dynasty. In China, the queue was known as a *bianzi*. The penalty for cutting off one's queue was death, but some men risked it anyway and wore hats in public to hide the evidence of their crime.

In 1905, Sun had joined forces with other anti-Manchu groups in Japan to form the Tongmeng hui, or Revolutionary Alliance. Many of these students returned to China and set up revolutionary "cells." Between 1906 and 1908 they mounted seven uprisings to overthrow the Qing government. Then Sun took three years off to do some planning, and continue his extensive recruitment and fundraising efforts overseas.

Power Struggle

With no one in charge of the central government things were at a standstill, except for the competition that had begun for the leadership of China. In the provinces where regional self-government had been established, the landlords were happily reinventing feudalism and arming to the teeth. The reformers could be found in the provincial assemblies. The revolutionaries were organizing and waiting for an opening.

Yuan Shikai

In Beijing, Zhang Zhidong and Yuan Shikai, who had been key players in the Empress Dowager's reform movement, now hoped to achieve control of the leaderless Qing government.

Yuan had been a star in the Qing dynasty for a long, long time. He had first distinguished himself as a young officer sent to Korea in 1883. Japan and the United States were threatening China's suzerainty over Korea, and he had seized the Korean king and sequestered him from the Japanese, thereby saving the country from Japanese annexation—for the time being, anyway. He was well rewarded; at the age of 21 he was appointed Chinese resident in Seoul.

After Emperor Guangxu's death in 1908 Yuan had fully expected to come into power, but he had been snubbed by the Empress Dowager who chose the two-year-old Pu Yi instead. In 1908 Yuan had been forced to retire from public life.

> **Han Help**
>
> From 1903 on, Yuan led the movement for military modernization of the Qing army. He built up six divisions in North China and, borrowing a trick he had learned from the Japanese, hired German instructors to establish discipline.

The Qing Court

In the Forbidden City the struggle for power continued. Pu Yi's Qing title was Emperor Xuan Tong, but his father, Zi Feng, wielded the real power because Pu Yi was a child.

Even though the Empress Dowager's reform plan was a shambles, the Manchus just couldn't give up. In 1910, Zi Feng supervised the establishment of provincial consultative councils and a National Consultative Assembly in Beijing. Had they been formed 25 years earlier they may have preserved the Qing dynasty and begun the orderly transition to democratic government. But they were too late. There was no one strong enough to root out the corrupt *eunuchs* and government functionaries who were busy amassing their own fortunes at the expense of the Qing dynasty—and the Chinese people.

Language Lesson

A **eunuch** *(huan quan)* was a castrated male. Known in China as making excellent, passive servants, eunuchs were also cherished for their high-pitched singing voices. Their positions of trust, however, made them privy to the inner workings of the court, and many of them engaged in intrigues that benefited them at the expense of their masters. Many, in fact, robbed their masters blind.

It was a situation where the more things changed, the more they stayed the same. In the spring of 1911 a cabinet was appointed, but 9 of the 13 ministers were Manchu noblemen and 5 of them were members of the imperial family clan. Power tended to stay in the same hands.

The Revolution

In 1911, in its hopeless pursuit of the reform program instituted a decade earlier, the government addressed the poor shape of China's railroads. The only railroads in China had been built by the Japanese, and in Manchuria, by the Russians. The Chinese themselves had only 250 miles of railroad under their control, and the government announced its decision to "nationalize" the rail lines under foreign control.

The truth of the matter was that the Chinese, without a clue as to how to run a railroad, intended to turn the seized railroads over to foreigners to operate. The move adversely affected transportation and commerce in the provinces of Sichuan, Hunan, Hubei, and Guangdong. In Sichuan, the move caused an immediate, violent uprising.

Finally, in the autumn of 1911 tensions were at fever pitch. Uprisings grew larger and more frequent. On October 10, a revolt in Wuchang organized by several of the secret revolutionary societies had monumental consequences: Most of the provinces declared their independence from the Qing dynasty. Sun Yatsen was in the United States at the time.

Hu Nu?

Today the occasion of the first shots fired at Wuchang, one of the three cities clumped together today as Wuhan, is celebrated as "Double-Ten Day" because it took place on the tenth day of the tenth month.

Throughout the Wuhan tri-city area, revolutionary groups seized the momentum. More and more troops mutinied, and provincial assemblies sided with the rebellion. By early December, a group of rebels who refused to tolerate the continuation of the old guard's power overthrew the provincial government in Nanjing. On December 29, the provisional assembly in Nanjing elected Sun Yatsen, who had just returned to China, provisional president of the Chinese Republic. He took office on January 1, 1912. Li Yuanhong was elected vice president. A republican regime was established, and Sun Yatsen became the founder of modern China.

The Return of Yuan

But the Qing dynasty didn't go altogether quietly. On November 11, the Beijing Provisional Assembly elected Yuan Shikai premier, a move the Qing court quickly approved. Yuan was also put in charge of what was left of the Qing troops. And Pu Yi's mother made a last-ditch effort to keep some role for the emperor, while recognizing Yuan Shikai as premier. For a brief time, China had a child emperor, a premier, and a new president. Whoever was in charge, it certainly wasn't the Manchus.

Wise One Says

By 1911, not only was it impossible to salvage the dynasty; even the nomination of Yuan Shikai as a "strong man" to maintain the security of loans and investments was far from successful. The Western formula for a strong man called for a man strong enough to carry out policies urgently demanded by foreign diplomats, but not quite strong enough to defy foreign control.

—Owen Lattimore, *The Situation in Asia*

Foreign governments, though claiming neutrality, were watching these developments closely. The worry, of course, was that a new, non-Qing regime would be bad news to foreign interests in China.

The revolution had finally succeeded, but not everything went smoothly. The rebels were indebted to the old reformers for their support and intellectual leadership in bringing about the revolution, and to the provincial military establishment's troops, a third of whom had fought with the rebels.

Han Help

Even after October 10, 1911, the old Qing officials continued to retain most of the power in China. In Jiangsu Province the governor of the Qings, Cheng Dequan, simply changed his signboard from "civil government" to "military government."

The Republic of China

The new government sought to modernize China in its own way and at its own pace. The major problem of land reform was not addressed, but the new government did take on political, social, and economic issues:

- Opium traffic was prohibited.

- Trade in indentured labor was banned.

- Laws to protect Chinese investment were passed.

- Laws were passed removing many of the privileges foreigners had enjoyed.

The reforms reflected the deep respect the lawmakers had for democratic principles but they also indicated a failure to understand the source of power in China—which was and always had been the land and its people.

Understandably, foreigners who'd taken their privileges for granted were not impressed with the new government. In fact, there was nothing about the new government that boded well for their interests. Shortly after Sun had proclaimed the founding of the Republic of China, they joined forces with what was left of the Qing regime to try to end the revolt. They had, after all, succeeded in ending the Taiping Rebellion in 1864.

A dozen British, American, Japanese, German, and French warships assembled on the Yangzi River opposite Wuhan in a show of strength against the revolutionaries. The foreigners also hoped to bankrupt the new government by continuing to collect taxes and customs duties to send to the Qing treasury in Beijing.

Russia incited several Mongol princes to declare "independence," hoping in this way to persuade Outer Mongolia and part of the Heilongjiang Province in the northeast to secede from the Chinese Republic.

The Empire's Final Weeks

Yuan marched troops down to Wuhan and captured the city of Hanyang, one of the three in the Wuhan complex. The foreign powers supported him completely, and they persuaded the Sun government to hold talks at Shanghai.

Sun saw how the wind was blowing and he was smart enough to know what to do. Yuan's troops outnumbered those under revolutionary control. The foreigners would support Yuan, so he would make a deal with him: Sun would resign as president, letting Yuan take his place if Yuan could get Pu Yi, the boy emperor, to abdicate.

Yuan, who was itching for more power, naturally agreed, and on February 12, 1912, Pu Yi was packed off to a nice palace and the Qing dynasty—as well as the Chinese Empire—came to an end.

Sun resigned as president of the Republic of China. Yuan was elected president at Nanjing and inaugurated as provisional president at Beijing. Thus, in a whirlwind of events and before the astonished eyes of the foreigners, China's government turned around. The Qing dynasty had become so weak by this time that it gave way to the republic.

President Yuan

The day after Yuan took office, Sun Yatsen proclaimed a provisional constitution that had been drawn up overnight in Nanjing by the provisional senate to stop Yuan from seizing power outright. According to the constitution, a full parliament would be convened within 10 months, and Yuan would step down and let new presidential elections be held.

On February 25, a delegation went up from Nanjing to Beijing to escort President Yuan south. The party was received with all the pomp of the Qing days. All seemed serene, but on the night of February 29 a revolt broke out among the troops and Yuan used it as an excuse to avoid leaving North China, where he was in full command of his troops.

On March 10, he assumed the presidency, but he remained in Beijing rather than go south and into the hands of the revolutionaries. So the legislature moved up to Beijing and held their sessions there.

Yuan's idea of a republic was not even close to what had been envisioned by the revolutionaries. Yuan liked the style of the Japanese, whose government had the outward signs of democratic rule but was essentially a dictatorship.

Sun Yatsen was not about to go quietly, either. He ordered his Tongmeng hui to become a centralized political party, with the goal of running candidates for the December 1912 elections. Sun's new National People's Party, or *Guomindang,* wanted to limit the president's powers so that the new parliament would have ample authority to enact true democratic reforms.

Language Lesson

Guomindang, often written as "Kuomintang" in earlier references, still exists today as a political party in Taiwan. *Guo (Kuo)* means country, *min* means national people, and *dang (tang)* means party or group. To the non-Chinese world, this party is now generally referred to as the "KMT."

Politics by Assassination

One of the leaders of the Guomindang Party was Song Jiaoren, who became known as "China's first parliamentarian." After the party won a majority of seats in the national parliamentary elections held in 1912 and 1913, Sun knew that he now had the power to rid China of Yuan.

Yuan wasn't going to take it lying down, however, so he formed his own party, the Republican Party, which attracted old Manchu supporters. Yuan also did something that Sun had not expected; he fought dirty. Whereas Sun was practicing revolution by election, Yuan practiced politics by assassination.

On March 20, 1913, Song Jiaoren was shot to death at the Shanghai railroad station. The assassin was arrested a few days later and identified as a soldier who said he had been hired by a local gangster to kill Song. The gangster wouldn't talk but it was assumed he was doing a favor for Yuan. Before there could be a trial, the alleged assassin was killed in his prison cell. The case was dropped. The gangster died shortly thereafter as well, shot to death on a train.

Yuan vs. Sun

Yuan continued in power, but not without stirring up trouble. He negotiated with a consortium of five foreign powers for a loan of 25 million pounds sterling for China without telling the legislative body he was going to do it. Sun and his followers were furious. Sun wanted to rebel against the government right then and there, but he was persuaded to hold back and to try to keep his framework for parliamentary democracy cohesive. Yuan Shikai was equally determined to destroy that framework.

The Second Revolution

The sinews of Guomindang (KMT) power lay in south China, that fertile field of rebellion for over 200 years. The military commanders of the Chinese republic in the south were southern men with southern ties.

In June 1913, Yuan Shikai set about replacing those southerners with northern generals. To reinforce his decisions, he sent units of the northern army, which was loyal to him, to the south. The influx of northern troops angered the southerners, and in July, the seven provinces of Jiangxi, Anhui, Jiangsu, Guangdong, Sichuan, Fujian, and Henan announced their secession from the Chinese Republic and declared war against the Yuan government. This was called the Second Revolution.

It came to nothing, ending in two months because there was no popular support for it. As far as the common people were concerned, it was just a quarrel among politicians. Sun Yatsen did very little during this period. Seeing that his own safety was in jeopardy, he escaped to Japan.

In September 1913, Yuan's forces, led by General Zhang Xun, finally captured Nanjing. It was a bloodbath. For three days soldiers ran wild in the streets, raping, murdering, and looting. (It is sad that the city of Nanjing, less than 30 years later, would be once again the scene of a violent terror campaign, this time by the Japanese.) By the end of 1913, Yuan Shikai's northern army controlled all of the provinces south of the Yangzi River except Guizhou, Yunnan, and Sichuan.

Yuan then set out to legitimize his version of government. He pushed the parliament into electing him president once again. On the second anniversary of the Double-Ten incident, on October 10, 1913, Yuan was installed in office for another five-year term. He held a military review at the gate of the Heavenly Peace in Beijing, and almost immediately, virtually all of the European nations recognized the new Chinese government as legitimate.

Another Autocracy

By November 1913, Yuan had sufficient power to dissolve any threats to his power, including the Guomindang. Early in 1914, he removed another threat to his power by dissolving the parliament. The Republic of China, for which so many had such high hopes, had become, in effect, another autocracy. Yuan was the undisputed dictator of China. He had the unrestricted power to declare war, sign treaties, appoint officials, and issue emergency decrees.

In December 1914, Yuan came as close as it was possible to declaring himself emperor. He went to the Temple of Heaven where, in a formal ceremony, he made sacrificial offerings to the gods. That was precisely what emperors used to do, and no one could miss the implication that he was casting himself in that role.

Then Yuan called a convention of "citizens' representatives" that, though it was presented as a random sampling of officials, actually was entirely composed of citizens' representatives who supported Yuan. The group heaped laudatory hyperbole on top of laudatory hyperbole on Yuan, calling for him to declare himself emperor. The people, they said, were not ready for republicanism. It's highly unlikely that this was a true representative sample of the Chinese populace, as there was not a single vote against the cry that Yuan should be named emperor.

This was a miscalculation on Yuan's part, as mass protests quickly followed, and many of his military allies abandoned him.

Sun Yatsen, in the meantime, had been planning for a more democratic regime. In 1914, he founded the more radical Gemindang, or Revolutionary Party of China. Then he made contact with all the secret societies of the past and renewed all his old relationships with many Chinese that were living abroad, especially in the United States. He would need support from outside China's borders if he was going to organize another rebellion and see his vision of democracy in China become a reality.

> **Hu Nu?**
>
> Yuan tried to hide the fact that he was the only one in power by appointing a political council consisting of 69 members from the provinces, but they were really 69 yes men, as they all represented Yuan's followers.

> **Wise One Says**
>
> In describing why Yuan should not be ruler of China, Yan Fu said, "His obstinacy and his wrong choice of subordinates cause much dissatisfaction. To expect him to change society and lay the foundation of a stable regime is out of the question."

By the beginning of 1915, Yuan had appointed himself president for another 10 years with the proviso that if he decided for any reason that he did not want to continue in office he had the exclusive right to choose who would replace him.

Within China, many of those who had supported Yuan were now becoming disillusioned with his course. One of them was Yan Fu. For a time he had been Yuan's adviser on foreign affairs, casting his lot, irrevocably it had seemed, with the last of the Qings. But in 1914, he remarked that although Yuan was an outstanding man, he did not have the knowledge and experience necessary to cope with the leaders of the foreign powers. Yan Fu had once believed that China was not ready for democracy. He now thought that China was not ready for a return to imperialism.

Yuan then sealed his fate in 1915, when Japan presented Yuan with a list of demands for extensive economic privileges in China (called the 21 Demands). Yuan granted them.

The Death of Yuan

In the winter of 1915, the provincial governor of Yunnan sent a message to Yuan telling him to abandon the idea of empire. He did not respond, so Yunnan seceded from the Beijing government. Guizhou followed. Suddenly, Yuan discovered that all of his maneuvering had cost him the loyalty of his generals, who were now setting themselves up as independent warlords of the areas they controlled.

Guangxi Province also joined the rebellion. Yuan's generals there announced that he must give up the idea of empire and resign from public office. One by one the other provinces seceded from Yuan's government: Guangdong, Zhejiang, Sichuan, and Henan.

By June 1916, Yuan had lost the support of most of China. On June 6 he died, bitter in the knowledge that he had failed to realize his ambitions.

The Least You Need to Know

- ◆ Democratic ideas and anti-Manchu sentiment combined to create a revolutionary movement.

- ◆ Sun Yatsen led the movement for change and competed with Yuan Shikai, a reactionary and opportunist, for control of China.

- ◆ The Republic of China was founded in 1911.

- ◆ Traditionalists, foreign powers, and President Yuan fought hard to retain dynastic rule.

- ◆ Sun Yatsen founded the Revolutionary Alliance, the Nationalist Party (Guomindang), and the Revolutionary Party of China.

- ◆ Yuan's attempt to return China to the way it had been was unsuccessful, and he died a bitter man.

Chapter 5

From Chaos to Communism

In This Chapter

- ◆ Chaos prevails throughout China.

- ◆ The May Fourth Movement revitalizes Chinese nationalism.

- ◆ Dr. Sun Yatsen tries to create unity and reform with his Three Principles of the People *(San Min Zhu Yi)*.

- ◆ Chiang Kaishek leads a militant new nationalist government that decimates the communist movement and overthrows the warlords.

- ◆ Mao Zedong leads the Long March and emerges as the leader of the Chinese Communist Party.

The period following the death of Yuan was utterly chaotic. China's honeymoon with Japan was over, and Western ideas were being extolled by Chinese intellectuals. Regional military leaders fought each other, while warlords sought to carve out their territory. The Nationalist Party and a new force, the communists, were setting the stage for a power struggle.

For once, the Western powers were too busy with their own crisis—World War I—to intervene much in China's affairs.

Warlords in Command

With no central government in China, all power had passed into the hands of the generals who commanded the armies. Throughout the country, warlords, many of them once loyal to Yuan Shikai, competed with each other for control of the land, which they plundered. Trade—so vital to China's economy—almost ceased to exist. This anarchic period lasted for more than 10 years. A "warlord" might be stereotyped as unprogressive. Some were ruthless and violent; others worked hard to revive the lucrative opium market. Many warlords, though, sought to modernize the regions they controlled.

The Intellectual Reformers

The revolution of 1911 and Yuan Shikai's tumultuous regime left many of China's intellectuals wondering just what sort of regime would best serve the country's interests. Many of China's intellectuals had returned from their studies abroad with new ideas about government. And Bertrand Russell, Henrik Ibsen, Albert Einstein, and other great Western thinkers found receptive audiences when they visited China during this time.

As often happens when a central government is in default, individuals and groups begin to take more responsibility for themselves and for their society. A similar reaction took place in China at this time and spawned a major movement:

Language Lesson

The **compradors** were the *nouveau riche* (new wealthy class) Chinese go-betweens for big-market foreign investors.

Han Help

Hu, and a number of other Chinese intellectuals in the 1920s, were educated in the United States. They took advantage of special scholarships the U.S. government set up with some of its share of the Boxer Rebellion indemnities.

- ◆ Social service organizations and advocacy groups sprang up.

- ◆ In Shanghai the *compradors* severed ties with the government and began to form a new, independent bourgeoisie.

- ◆ Great advances were made in higher education.

- ◆ Intellectuals developed alternative ideologies.

The New Culture Movement

Hu Shi, a Phi Beta Kappa graduate of Cornell University, led the movement to increase literacy by using vernacular speech, or *baihua* as the written language rather than classical Chinese, which had previously been used for all written communication. A professor of philosophy at Beijing University, Hu was very much a pragmatist, and sought to find a rational middle ground in the search for solutions to China's biggest problems.

The New Tide Society

In 1918, a politically active librarian named Li Dazhao was publishing a journal called *New Tide* that rejected family-centered Confucian values and advocated the primacy of the individual. Born into a peasant family in Hebei Province, Li welcomed the Russian Revolution and urged China to "adapt itself to the new tide of the world." Li and a group of student activists formed the New Tide Society to take their ideas about cultural and social values to the people through lectures and discussions. (Significantly, Li had an assistant named Mao Zedong, from whom we will hear more very soon.)

His society, along with its sister organization, the Marxist Research Society, was very popular with students.

> **Han Help**
>
> In 1917, the Bolshevik Revolution toppled the Russian Empire.

Chen Duxiu

The most important of the new political activists was Chen Duxiu, who organized demonstrations and served time in jail for his protests. As dean at Beijing University, Chen was editor of *New Youth*, and worked with Li Dazhao to explain Marxism to the Chinese people. In 1920, Chen founded the Marxist Study Society and the Socialist Youth Corps, organizations that would later evolve into the Chinese Communist Party.

The May Fourth Movement

The European war had not been without its influences on China's trade and economy, but on May 4, 1919, it precipitated a turning point in Chinese history.

World War I was over. The Germans had surrendered to the Allies, and the Treaty of Versailles had been signed by all parties. One of its stipulations was that Germany's rights in the Shandong peninsula would now be transferred to Japan. Three thousand of Beijing's university students took their rage—against imperialism, against Japan, and against Chinese people who had been cozy with the Japanese—into Tiananmen Square. They assaulted high-level government officials and clashed with police. Most of them were jailed. Similar protests took place in other major cities.

In an unprecedented show of cohesiveness for China's fragmented society, attacks on Japanese people, strikes, and boycotts of Japanese products went on in Chinese cities for a year. The events of May 4, however, would have far greater implications for China's political evolution (covered in Chapter 13). In the short term, hundreds of new publications sprang up, advocating the rejection of Confucian traditions, and urging various directions to be taken by Chinese culture and politics.

The Birth of Chinese Communism

Many Chinese intellectuals had been heartened by the Russian Revolution of 1905 and the work of Karl Marx, which had been translated into Chinese in the same year. Now the Bolshevik Revolution found resonance in China because of its utopian ideals and its moral superiority over capitalism. Communism also gained favor in China because the communist Russians treated China with far greater respect than the previous Russian regime under the Czar.

Hu Nu?
The Chinese Communist Party, in its first years, went along with Chen's philosophy, though Li Dazhao's thinking would have its day when Mao, his former assistant, rose to power. Li was executed by the warlord Zhang Zuolin in 1927.

The Chinese Communist Party was not officially formed until 1921. Chen Duxiu and Li Dazhao became its co-leaders, but did not agree on the details of how communism should be implemented in China. Chen believed that the urban workers would lead the way to revolution and a new form of government. Li believed that it was the farmer who had the moral right to found the utopian state.

It is fascinating that intellectuals—who took their ideas to the common people—drove the May Fourth Movement and formed the Chinese Communist Party.

Sun Yatsen

Sun Yatsen had not been idle during this time. He had a plan for China's recovery and unification, and he was doing everything he could to promote it.

The Three Principles of the People (*San Min Zhu Yi*)

Sun proposed that China unite under his *San Min Zhu Yi*, Three Principles of the People. They were …

- **Nationalism.** It was the uniting part. China had to stick together as a single nation and be willing to defend itself against interlopers or it would be subject to foreign imperialism.

- **Democracy.** Sun believed that this goal could not be achieved all at once.

  The first step was to gain military control over all of China, so that the democratic government would be able to represent all of China.

  Then, there would be an education program. The people would have to be taught the intricacies of self-government before they could be expected to handle the responsibility of the vote.

  Local government would start first. Then there would be provincial government. Only after the people were represented in their village and in their province would national elections be feasible. (In other words, if his principles were applied, Sun wouldn't have to worry about being defeated in a national election anytime soon.)

- **The People's Livelihood.** The principle referred to Sun's vision of the China of the future, a modern China in which industry and agriculture flourished. The roads and railroads would be greatly improved.

Until the nation was "ready" for democracy, Sun believed, it was essential that China be united under a single political party. Of course he believed that the party should be his, the newly resurrected Nationalist Party (Guomindang). The Guomindang had begun as a group of Sun supporters but had grown beyond that and now included students, soldiers, shopkeepers, and bankers.

Sun appealed to the United States for support but received no encouragement. His attempts to win the aid of various European governments were equally unsuccessful. He had failed to acquire foreign support and he had failed in his efforts to organize the regional alliances he needed to spread his vision.

Dealing with the Soviets

There was one country that was willing to help the Guomindang (nationalists): the Soviet Union. Ah, but there was a hitch. In 1922, the Soviets, seeking to increase their influence in Asia, agreed to help Sun's cause if he agreed to let members of the newly formed Chinese Communist Party (CCP) into his government. Though Sun did not believe that communism would work in China, he acceded to their wishes;

Han Help _____

Why didn't the Soviet Union leap at the chance to help the fledgling CCP directly? They were pragmatic and knew they had a better chance working with a big-name political leader like Sun Yatsen, rather than with a handful of unknowns leading a paltry group of 300 Chinese communists.

there were only about 300 members of the CCP at the time anyway, so it seemed to be a small concession. To make sure that Sun kept his word, the Soviets sent an advisor to be at his side, Mikhail Borodin.

Sun set up a regime in the south of China, in Ghangzhou in 1923, which was the area where he had been most popular all along. He sent Chiang Kaishek to Russia to study military organization. Chiang returned and established a military academy at Whampoa for the training of the Nationalist Party's forces.

In January 1924, the Guomindang was reorganized with help from Borodin, its Soviet advisor. Now, regional representatives would be elected to the Party Congress, which would elect the Central Committee. As Sun had agreed, CCP members would be eligible to run for office.

Sun and the Warlords

Shortly after the party reorganization, a new wave of anti-imperialist sentiment sent people into the streets again. The Guomindang, the CCP (which maintained its separate party organization), and Chinese business owners mounted demonstrations against the treatment of Chinese workers in foreign-owned factories in Ghangzhou and other cities. They struck foreign businesses and carried on a boycott of British goods that lasted for a year.

The nationalist uprisings had further secured the Guomindang base in Ghangzhou and, in 1925, Dr. Sun decided that he was going to try to sell his Three Principles to the warlords in power in North China. As he started out on his mission, he was already a very ill man.

Warlord after warlord told him that they had no plans to unite anytime soon, under his or anybody else's principles. Sun got as far as Beijing and became bedridden. He died of cancer on March 12, 1925.

Exit Sun, Enter Chiang

With the death of Sun Yatsen, there emerged a new leader, a forceful figure who was a general of one of the nationalist armies and commander of the Guomindang military academy at Whampoa—Chiang Kaishek. He would become one of the twentieth century's most influential Chinese leaders.

Born near Shanghai in Zhejiang Province in 1887, Chiang had trained to become a philosopher of Confucianism as a youngster, but during his teenage years decided that the military offered the life he wanted.

He had learned his military skills at various schools, including the Tokyo Military Staff College in Japan. Chiang had become a major player in the Guomindang during the 1911 revolution. By 1923, he was one of Sun's most trusted men. When Sun died, Chiang was one of two Guomindang leaders who the party began to consider as his replacement.

Chiang represented the right wing of the party and had the support of the domestic and foreign capitalists and the landlords. He had an army of 100,000 under his command, and he knew how to use it to quell anti-imperialist strikes and peasant rebellions.

Wang Jingwei, the other possible heir to Sun Yatsen, was supported by those whose major issue was the presence of foreign interests in China's economy and the threat of Japanese aggression.

Han Help

Chiang's wife was Meiling Soong, who had graduated from Wellesley College in the United States. She was a member of the Soong family, who became very influential in the Nationalist Party. The Soongs were later one of the "Big Four" families that owned tremendous chunks of China—and having a daughter who was married to Chiang didn't hurt their chances in finance one iota. Charles Soong had three beautiful daughters and they all married into power. One married Sun Yatsen, another married Chiang Kaishek, and the third married into the powerful Kong family, who were wealthy industrialists.

The Defeat of the Warlords

Chiang picked up where Sun had left off. He continued to try to put China back together again. For a time, nationalist and communist soldiers worked well side by side—a necessity if the Chinese army was going to overthrow the warlords in the north and once again unify China.

The Chinese army marched north in 1926 for what Chiang called his "Northern Expedition." Thanks to advance teams who distributed propaganda, the warlords, as it turned out, had no support from the people and not much more from their own soldiers. Dozens of warlords were quickly overthrown with remarkably little bloodshed. Others formed agreements to cooperate with the government.

> ### Hu Nu?
> How much cooperation the nationalist government actually received from the warlords was always questionable. Even after the warlords were "defeated" by Chiang, many remained in control, keeping their own large armies for "self-protection." Chiang's unified China was not nearly as unified as he would have liked.

Emboldened by his success, Chiang courted conservatives in every quarter to ensure his leadership of the Guomindang.

The Purge of the Communists

With the north of China once again under control of a centralized government, Chiang could see that his next problem was coming from within. He had agreed to allow the communists into his military and now they were trying to take over.

After months of planning, in April 1927, Chiang launched an all-out attack against the communists, Chinese and Russians alike: He split with the Guomindang's left wing, which had no troops to oppose him with; he crushed Shanghai's labor unions; and many communists were arrested and promptly executed. Few were able to escape the terror campaign, which took place in the cities; those who did went into hiding in the countryside.

With his only competitor being Wang Jingwei, who was now out of the picture because he lacked the military support Chiang enjoyed, Chiang established his new capital in Nanjing in 1927. It soon was given diplomatic recognition. His offensive against the communists had interrupted the Northern Expedition, which now continued north, overthrowing warlords on its route. In June 1928, Chiang's Guomindang forces captured Beijing, and achieved the submission of the warlords to the new Nanjing government under Chiang. Nevertheless, the northern warlords would continue to prove troublesome for years to come.

Language Lesson

A Russian word, **soviet** means a small independent government. The word was first coined by Russian communists to describe a governing council.

The communists, because their movement was so popular, quickly regrouped and established pockets of power. In the province of Jiangxi and in other southern provinces, the communists assumed control and set up *soviets*.

Enter Mao Zedong

After the terror campaign that had all but destroyed the CCP, some of the communists who had managed to escape to the rural areas joined forces with warlords unfriendly to the Nanjing government. It was in Jiangxi Province that Mao Zedong and the warlord Zhu De established a communist base. When the Guomindang attacks on the CCP in the cities made it impossible for the Central Committee members to remain in their headquarters in Shanghai, they moved the Central Committee of the CCP to Mao's Jiangxi base. That was when Mao first emerged as a figure of power within the Chinese Communist Party.

Mao Zedong was born in 1893, the son of a peasant farmer in Hunan Province. He was rebellious and revolutionary in nature even in his youth. Though both of his parents were unschooled (his mother was illiterate), Mao was well schooled in the Confucian classics. His favorite stories when he was young were about peasant rebellion. He also enjoyed the translated works of Rousseau, Voltaire, Napoleon, and even Thomas Jefferson. When the Manchus were overthrown, Mao was among those who chopped off his queue in protest.

When he was a young man he saw an event that changed his life, a peasant rebellion in Hunan in which the peasant leaders were executed and their heads placed on poles.

Mao worked as a library assistant at Beijing University and as a headmaster in Changsha, in his native Hunan Province. He was the chief of propaganda under Sun Yatsen but was fired after Chiang took over the Nationalist Party. Mao was 28 years old and among the founders of the Chinese Communist Party when it formed in 1921.

In Jiangxi, Mao, knowing that his military forces would be no match for the Guomindang army, taught his troops guerilla warfare techniques. The enemy may have been more powerful, but he and his armies were infinitely more cunning.

On four separate occasions Chiang used his army to try to destroy Mao's soviet in Jiangxi, and every time, Mao's forces had been able to fight off the attack. On his fifth try, Chiang tried a different tactic. He completely blockaded the region in an attempt to starve out the communists.

> **Wise One Says**
>
> Mao described his military tactics against Chiang's forces: "When the enemy advances, we retreat; when he halts and camps, we harass him; when he seeks to avoid battle, we attack; when he retreats, we pursue."

The Long March

Trapped and facing disaster, the communists at Jiangxi—80,000 strong—broke out of Chiang's blockade and made a hasty escape that took them 6,000 miles across China on foot. They left behind some 20,000 of their colleagues, most of them wounded and unable to make the trek. "The Long March," as it was called—though it was actually a retreat—began in mid-October of 1934. For more than a year the communists zigzagged through much of western and southern China, some of them carrying all their worldly belongings on their backs. They fought, on average, a battle a day; some were only skirmishes but others were heated firefights. Exhaustion, frostbite, and disease took a heavy toll on the communist troops.

Early in 1935, Mao became the head of the Chinese Communist Party.

> **Hu Nu?**
>
> In addition to marching and battling, Mao's troops also effected land reforms, staged allegorical plays about the advantages of the communist way, and held huge recruitment drives.

The Long March ended when Mao and the less than 10,000 soldiers who remained with him reached the safety of China's northwest, where they set up the new CCP capital in Yan'an. For a time, until office space could be built, the Chinese Communist Party was operating out of a cave. Mao's forces had walked through 12 provinces, seized 62 cities, and crossed 18 mountain ranges and 24 rivers.

> **Han Help**
>
> The world first learned about the Long March through the book *Red Star Over China* by reporter Edgar Snow (1905–1972). This book, published in 1937, is considered one of the great pieces of journalism of the twentieth century and remains one of the best sources on the subject. Snow spent four months in communist-controlled northwest China in 1936, where he found Mao and his comrades uncharacteristically willing to discuss their experiences with a foreigner. Interestingly, not only did the Western world learn of the Long March through Snow's book, so did the people of China. Government censorship precluded legal distribution of *Red Star Over China* in China, but illegal translations made it readily available. Snow's reputation took a bit of a hit in the 1960s when he wrote that it was impossible to have a famine in a communist nation. History proved him very wrong on that one.

Being a bona fide Long March survivor would have important implications on the Chinese political scene for much of the twentieth century. The handful of men who survived the 6,000-mile trek became the leaders of the revolution that created the

People's Republic of China in 1949, and reigned supreme as the elite of the Chinese Communist Party for many years. The story of the birth of modern China continues in Chapter 10.

The Least You Need to Know

- ◆ A decade of chaos followed the death of Yuan Shikai.

- ◆ Sun's Three Principles of the People were Nationalism, Democracy, and the People's Livelihood.

- ◆ Intellectuals led the reform and revolutionary groups that drove the nationalistic May Fourth Movement.

- ◆ Sun's protege, Chiang Kaishek, took over after Sun's death and formed a militant new government.

- ◆ Chiang's forces slaughtered most of China's communists.

- ◆ Mao Zedong emerged as a leader of the Chinese Communist Party.

Part 2

China's Enduring Past

Today's People's Republic of China is a rapidly modernizing country with a world-class economy that seems to bear little resemblance to the China Marco Polo visited in the thirteenth century. But the continuity of Chinese culture has never been broken. The idea of what it is to be Chinese has prevailed through periods of foreign rule, the influx of non-Han peoples, and the powerful influences of Buddhism and Western ideas. These chapters look at the legacies of the past that have endured and are echoed in modern China: the power of Han culture; the role of language, philosophy, and innovation in Chinese culture; the Confucian underpinnings of governance and social behavior; the unwillingness of the government to tolerate dissent; and the ongoing commitment of China's leaders to improve the land, economy, government, and lives of its people.

Chapter 6

Cultural Legacies

In This Chapter

- ◆ The power of the Han identity lives on in Chinese culture.

- ◆ Daoism greatly impacted Chinese thought and has had a lasting influence on Chinese concepts of health and medicine.

- ◆ Buddhism stands as one of the most powerful outside religious ideas to sweep early China but has a mixed status in current Chinese society.

- ◆ The Chinese language is more diverse than many may think.

- ◆ Chinese written characters have a deep history and continue to help define Chinese cultural identity.

Before modern China began in 1912, China's borders, dynasties, ruling families, and population groups were always in motion. Chinese culture itself, however, never strayed far from its roots, and aspects of many of China's cultural legacies are visible even today.

The Han Idea

As we noted in Chapter 1, Chinese culture is called "Han" because it was during the Han dynasty (206 B.C.E.–220 C.E.) that the strands of the culture meshed into the distinct entity called China. Its hallmarks were a centralized government whose authority was undisputed, a highly sophisticated bureaucratic system, an examination program that afforded upward mobility, an elaborate and precise structure of family and community relationships, a written language of stunning complexity, and—the factor that unified it all—China's powerful sense of its unique identity and cultural superiority.

Philosophical Influences

The earliest and most profound influence on Chinese culture was Confucianism and its later neo-Confucianist admixtures. Because imperial China's state and society were, in effect, inseparable, and for much of its history, were built on Confucian principles, we take a close look at Confucianism in the chapter on the Chinese state and society (see Chapter 7).

A countless number of philosophical schools flourished during and after the time of Confucius. Mencius added his perspective on Confucian thought (see Chapter 2), and the Legalists and Naturalists had varying degrees of influence on its evolution. But Confucianism wasn't the only doctrine in China; Buddhism and Daoism emerged to challenge, and eventually influence it—even bringing about revivals of Confucian thought.

Daoism

Daoism started as a blend of psychology and philosophy. It evolved, however, into a religious faith, and for a time Laozi, who is believed to be its founder, was popularly worshipped as a god. *Daoism*, with Buddhism and Confucianism, was one of the three great religions of China.

Daoism, unlike Confucianism, does not concern itself with the role of the individual in society. It's a sophisticated philosophical system built on the idea of Dao as the primary, unifying principle in a world of dualities.

Because Dao could not be understood intellectually, Daoists pursued a mystical state that they attempted to reach through controlled breathing and other exercises. Laozi said, "Be still like a mountain and flow like a great river."

Daoism's practices and beliefs include the following:

Language Lesson

Daoism translates into English as "the Way."

- ◆ Dao is the first-cause of the universe. It is a force that flows through all life.

- ◆ Each believer's goal is to become one with the Dao.

- Priests do not pray to a god; there is no god to hear the prayers or to act upon them. They seek answers to life's problems through inner meditation and outer observation.

- Time is cyclical.

- Yin (the dark side) is the breath that formed the earth.

- Yang (light side) is the breath that formed the heavens. They symbolize pairs of opposites that are seen throughout the universe, such as good and evil, light and dark, and male and female.

- Health and vitality are to be promoted.

- The five main organs and orifices of the body correspond to the five parts of the sky: water, fire, wood, metal, and earth.

- Each person must nurture the Qi (air, breath) that has been given to them.

- Development of virtue is one's chief task.

- The Three Jewels to be sought are compassion, moderation, and humility.

- Daoists follow the art of *wu wei*.

Wise One Says

According to *Our Beliefs*, the book of Western Reform Daoism, "[Dao] (pronounced "Dow") refers to a power which envelops, surrounds and flows through all things, living and nonliving. The Dao regulates natural processes and nourishes balance in the Universe. It embodies the harmony of opposites (that is, there would be no love without hate, no light without dark, no male without female)."

Language Lesson

Wu wei means to let nature take its course. For example, one should allow a river to flow toward the sea unimpeded; do not erect a dam, which would interfere with its natural flow.

Aspects of Daoism were absorbed into Neo-Confucianism (read more about neo-Confucianism in Chapter 7), and Daoism was supported by the state until the end of the Qing dynasty in 1911. After the fall of the Qing, and the period of warlordism (regions under separate military rulers) that followed, much of the Daoist heritage was destroyed. Then, when the communists came to power, they restricted freedom of worship. The practice of Daoism was halted and Daoist monks were forced into manual labor. There were several million practitioners just prior to that time, but by 1960, slightly more than a decade later, that number had been reduced to 50,000.

What remained of Daoist culture was then obliterated by the Cultural Revolution (1966–1976). Since Deng Xiaoping restored a degree of religious freedom in 1982, there has been a slight resurgence of Daoism in China.

Because of Daoism's focus on the cultivation of the body, alchemy was a significant part of early Daoist practice. Many early Daoist thinkers preoccupied themselves with finding the "elixir of life" or mixing rare elements to gain immortality. Needless to say, Daoists made more lasting contributions to traditional Chinese medicine (often abbreviated TCM) and its concepts of illness and medical treatment than to alchemy. The Daoist idea of physical transformation lives on today in TCM (see Chapter 8). TCM, which is now integrated with Western medical practices in China, has also had a significant impact on the West, and particularly North American health and fitness approaches in areas of acupuncture, acupressure, herbalism, holistic medicine, meditation, and martial arts.

> **Hu Nu?**
>
> It's interesting to note that even some early Western scientists were obsessed with finding the secret to immortality, much like early Daoists. We now know, for instance, that Isaac Newton—father of scientific method and thought—was simultaneously performing alchemy with precious metals as he worked out some of his most influential scientific discoveries!

It is believed that there are about 20 million Daoist practitioners today in East Asia, Most of them are in Taiwan where they do not have to contend with the restrictions of the Chinese Communist Party. About 30,000 Daoists live in North America.

Buddhism

Like Daoism, Buddhism has a long, established history in China. But unlike Daoism, Buddhism originated from outside of China. This makes Buddhism's role in China all the more special since it marks one of the most successful foreign influences on Chinese society predating the modern era.

> **Han Help**
>
> There are two branches of Buddhism that became popularized throughout Asia. The earliest is called Theraveda or Hinayana ("Lesser Vehicle") which spread throughout portions of South and Southeast Asia. The other branch, called Mahayana ("Greater Vehicle"), became widely adopted throughout East Asia, finding wide appeal in China.

Buddhism found its way to China from India in the first century C.E. by means of the Silk Road (see Chapter 1). During the chaotic centuries that followed the fall of the Han dynasty in 220 C.E., Confucianism was on the wane, and Mahayana Buddhism slowly began to take hold. Mahayana's appeal for the Chinese was that it was not necessary to be a monastic to achieve salvation; the monastic life was out of bounds for the family-oriented Chinese society. Mahayana offered universal salvation for any who could achieve it through their individual efforts. Mahayana also had an array of Buddha-type and bodhisattva-type (enlightened beings) deities that were easily merged with local figures of worship.

They later figured prominently in the transformation of Chinese art, architecture, and literature that took place during the fifth through the ninth centuries (see Chapter 8).

By the sixth century, four Chinese branches of Buddhism had evolved: Pure Land, Tiantai, Huayan, and Chan.

Hu Nu?

In the sixth century, Chan Buddhism found its way from China to Korea, and then to Japan, where it became "Zen" Buddhism and was established as the state religion. Chan or Zen are translated as "meditation" or "sitting." Zen can be thought of as a kind of Buddhist Daoism in which enlightenment can be attained through harmony and spontaneity. During the nineteenth and early twentieth centuries, China's intellectual revolutionary leaders were greatly influenced by Japan's Zen Buddhists.

Pure Land Buddhism was distinguished by its elements of reincarnation and cyclical cosmic cycles. During the centuries of disorder after the Han dynasty, it held the most appeal—for obvious reasons. It is the most popular school of Buddhism in Japan today. Chan Buddhism, with its Daoist aspects, also gained a great following in China.

Tibetan Buddhism took its own course, and in the seventeenth century became one with the government of Tibet. The Tibetan theocracy was ruled by successive reincarnations of a bodhisattva called the Dalai Llama until 1959, when the People's Liberation Army reasserted Beijing's rule over Tibet and the present Dalai Llama fled to India.

Currently, Buddhism is thriving in Taiwan. Contrasted to China, where Buddhism—though recognized by the Chinese government as a religion—is closely linked to a bureaucratic office known as the Buddhist Association of China, Taiwan's Buddhists are free to worship in any temple they like. (It's interesting to note that even Taiwan initially installed a government-led association to legislate Buddhism. It ultimately failed.)

The number of Buddhist devotees in Taiwan has skyrocketed since the 1980s and '90s, with nearly 3.7 million Taiwanese identifying themselves as Buddhist. It is estimated there are over 4,000 Buddhist temples (of various sects) now founded in Taiwan (these figures are from Taiwan's Government Information Office website).

A Look at the Chinese Language

The Chinese language and writing system continue to influence what it means to be Chinese, perhaps even more profoundly than the great religious philosophies of Daoism and Buddhism do today.

There have been many forms of Chinese over the long history of its development. Its written form is probably more than 3,000 years old. The spoken form of Chinese (or as discussed in the following section, the many spoken variations of Chinese) likely has even more ancient origins. Even now, an incredible number of Chinese still spend most of their youth memorizing the complex Chinese characters and learning not only their grammatical use but also their significance in ancient poetry, classical prose, and art.

One Chinese Versus Many

Non-Chinese speakers are often confused about what Chinese really is and isn't. For a clear definition ... well, there isn't one. The reason is not because of some inadequacy with Chinese, but instead because of the way Westerners have traditionally defined China and the wide variety of languages spoken by its people.

What English speakers usually call Chinese is actually Mandarin—a *dialect* of Chinese that almost every member of Chinese society today can speak. You can hear it in Beijing, Hong Kong, Taiwan, and even San Francisco if you know where to look. It's the official language in both China and Taiwan today, and nearly every Chinese child receives an education in the dialect of Mandarin. But this was not always the case. A broader view of Chinese will show us that it's more accurately made up of a continuum of language dialects.

> **Language Lesson**
>
> A **dialect** is a variety of a language that is distinctive because of the grammar and vocabulary used by its speakers. Dialects are usually found in distinct regions where a continuous population has lived for a long period of time. There are a number of Chinese dialects, some of which may be very close and only differ in certain vocabulary and grammar while others are mutually unintelligible and are nearly separate languages altogether.

For many thousands of years, language in China was not uniform. Dialects were varied and widespread, since regional communities were often isolated and quite resistant to outside influence. Even today, Chinese people often speak Mandarin in official situations or academic settings, but then will fall back into speaking the dialect of their native community when in a casual setting, simply because it is more comfortable (with younger speakers Mandarin is becoming a mainstay, however). The variety of dialects is astounding and represents the inherent richness in the broader use of the term "Chinese language." The following is a description of some of the main Chinese dialects still widely spoken:

◆ **Mandarin**   The most widely spoken Chinese dialect. It has been adopted as the standard language throughout China and in Taiwan, used in schools and most major media. It's what the West recognizes as Chinese. Also known as *putonghua* in China and *guo yu* in Taiwan, Mandarin is itself a broader term for many northern Chinese subdialects found from Sichuan to Heilongjiang.

◆ **Shiang**   Spoken in the south-central region of China, primarily in Hunan.

◆ **Cantonese**   A distinctly different dialect from Mandarin, Cantonese is still widely spoken in south China around the areas of Guangdong, Guanxi, Macao, and Hong Kong. Interestingly, many of the dishes found on a Chinese menu in the United States will most likely reflect the Cantonese pronunciation rather than Mandarin. This is because some of the first Chinese restaurants were established by Cantonese speakers!

◆ **Kan**   A dialect spoken mainly throughout Shaanxi and southwest Hebei.

◆ **Min**   Spoken in large areas of Zhejiang, Fujian, and Hainan Island. The local dialect of Taiwan—known as Taiwanese—is actually Min. The predominance of Min speakers in Taiwan attests to the massive wave of displaced Fujianese that settled the island during the Qing dynasty.

◆ **Wu**   Spoken in parts of Anhui, Zhejiang, and Jiangsu. Wu is widely used in Shanghai, and therefore is often called Shanghaiese.

◆ **Hakka**   A unique dialect spoken by what many scholars consider to be a distinct ethnic group. The Hakka dialect is widespread throughout southern China—most especially Fujian and Guangxi. The original Hakka homeland is not clearly known since they were forced to move and resettle many times over China's history. In fact, the name "Hakka" is a term meaning guest people.

You Say Peking, I Say Beijing ...

By the Qing dynasty, the common Chinese vernacular (words used in common speech) had boiled down to about 1,300 syllables (which could be single words or combined to form other words), meaning that the Chinese language has a huge number of *homonyms*. Thus, the syllable "*wu*," depending on the exact character used, can mean a crow, dirt, a witch, a house, tungsten, a parasol, and the number five! Each meaning has a different character, and is also pronounced in Mandarin with one of four tones (level, rising, down-and-up or dipping, or falling pitch). Thus, if you don't pay attention to the correct tones, you could find yourself calling for a horse or some morphine (a semantic piece of a word) instead of your mother (*ma*)! Other dialects, like Cantonese, use the same characters, but the corresponding syllables and tones can be quite different.

> ### Language Lesson
>
> A **homonym** is one of two words or more that are written and pronounced the same way but have different meanings. English has many homonyms: an "ear" can mean an anatomical part attached to our heads or can be a measure word for corn, for instance "I ate only one ear of corn." Chinese has an overabundance of such words, and they can only be distinguished by their use in a sentence or by their unique written character.

A typical Chinese dictionary contains around 40,000 words; the vast majority of them are combinations of characters. For example, *dian*, or "electricity," combined with *hua*, or "speech," becomes *dianhua*, a telephone. *Dianche*, or "trolleybus," would translate literally as "electric cart." *Dianying*, or "movie," translates as "electric shadow." There are sometimes phonetic clues guiding the pronunciation, but Chinese children, like foreigners, usually learn written Chinese by memorizing the characters.

Westerners have long tried to render the complexities of the Chinese language into the Latin-based alphabet. Beginning in the 1890s, the Wade-Giles romanization system, developed by two British scholars, was commonly used to spell out the Chinese syllables phonetically into words a Westerner could read more easily. This helped, to be sure, though place names and personal names were often transliterated loosely. During the 1950s, for a time, Mao Zedong reportedly gave serious thought to abandoning the use of pictographic characters altogether, with the goal of adopting China's own romanization system, *pinyin*, to boost literacy rates.

China stayed true to its characters, though the number of strokes needed to draw many of the most common characters has been pared down significantly on the mainland. (Taiwan and Hong Kong, for the most part, still use the traditional or more complex characters.)

Since 1979, though, the world has largely abandoned the Wade-Giles romanization system in favor of China's pinyin system. China had been using pinyin since 1958, mainly as a way to help children learn the proper Mandarin pronunciation. Once China opened its doors to renewed contact with the Western world in 1978, the official *Xinhua* news agency made it clear that the pinyin romanizations of Chinese names and places were the official versions. The rest of the world soon followed suit. Mao Tse-tung became known as Mao Zedong, virtually overnight.

The only problem with the switch is the large number of books in English and other languages that use the Wade-Giles versions of Chinese names and places. How can you tell the difference? Some of the syllables are exactly the same in Wade-Giles and pinyin, but others have an apostrophe to show an aspirated, or throaty, consonant sound. So if you see "k'ung" written out, you're looking at an old book that uses Wade-Giles. In pinyin, the same syllable would be written *kong*. And the transliteration of some Chinese words is just going to be confusing, no matter what. Historically, China had a capital in Beiping, which means northern peace. At least that's the Wade-Giles way of spelling it. Most of the world knew the capital as Peking, a spelling and pronunciation that was haphazard, like that of many Chinese place names. It took the official word of the Chinese government and the pinyin system to get everyone in agreement that China's capital should be romanized as Beijing.

Chinese, a Language with Character(s)!

The foundation of Chinese civilization is closely tied to the development of the Chinese character system—a nonalphabetic form of writing that originated during the Shang period between the sixteenth and eleventh centuries B.C.E.

A mountain of books have been dedicated to the topic of Chinese writing—and for good reason—it has remained one of the greatest hallmarks of Chinese culture to date. The overall influence that the character system has had even outside of China should be emphasized, contributing to the early writing traditions of Korea, Japan, and Vietnam particularly. It has also been the glue that holds the diversity of spoken dialects together in China. Even though so many dialects and subdialects have long been spoken throughout the land, people have always referred to a single written language—the Chinese character system—and still do today.

> **Hu Nu?**
>
> It's a telling example to watch two individuals speaking Putonghua (official Mandarin) clarify their pronunciation or word usage by tracing an outline of the word's character on their hand! It happens occasionally and illustrates nicely how useful Chinese characters are as mutual reference points for cross-language (dialect) communication.

The technique for writing Chinese characters is complex and requires a massive amount of rote memorization. Though the details about writing Chinese characters go well beyond the scope of this book, it is useful to note that character script has gone through a long evolution and was not originally used to convey the kind of direct communication that is does today.

The roots of the Chinese language, in fact, were more closely connected with fortune telling, or divination, in the ancient world. Oracle bones, also called dragon bones by those who dig them up and sell them to pharmacists for medicinal purposes, are examples of some of the earliest Chinese symbols. These bones were used to predict future events and, over time, the symbols that were written on the bones to account for a prediction developed into more stylized characters. Slowly, these stylized characters came to take on more complex and abstract meanings.

The oracle bone script was pictographic in nature (depicting a general, direct image of some object or event) and was undoubtedly the forerunner of modern Chinese script. That is not saying they bear much resemblance to today's characters, most don't. A few modern characters are still pictographic, like the word for *ren*, or people. Still, the vast majority of characters fall into one of three other categories:

♦ Characters depicting abstract concepts such as for the word "good" (*hao*), which originally depicted a woman with a child.

♦ Characters that have both a meaning symbol (sometimes called a radical) and a sound symbol combined to make a new word. The word "sing" (*chang*) combines the meaning symbol for "mouth" with a sound symbol (*chang*), hence the pronunciation of the word.

♦ Borrowed characters that have been given a new meaning but preserve their original pronunciation. These can almost be thought of as recycled characters in a way. The verb "to come" (*lai*) was originally a term for wheat. Its sound, however, matched that of the verb and the character was borrowed to approximate it in writing.

These types of characters are all represented in Chinese to varying degrees.

Chinese characters are unique in that each one is almost like a picture. Unlike our Latin alphabet in the West, there is no one element in a Chinese character that is repeated in exact form in all other characters. Chinese characters were not formed systematically, but there are recognizable patterns in the way they are constructed.

Chinese characters comprise several different styles, and each style is commonly used for different purposes:

♦ **Clerical and Seal Script** Two very early forms of character script that were developed in the early dynastic periods. They are still used today, but are reserved for stamps and chops used on official documents, much as they have been used in the past.

♦ **Grass Script (*Caoshu*)**   A free-flowing script form that is something like cursive in English. Chinese calligraphy (*shufa*) often favors this style because of its highly personalized and artistic form.

♦ **Standard Script (*Kaishu*)**   The script has been the standard writing for Chinese for over two thousand years. Its style is clean and very legible. This script is still used today in Taiwan and is widely used in most print media. It also served as a model for the simplified characters (see the following) that were developed only decades ago in China.

♦ **Modern Cursive Script (*Xingshu*)**   Used by most adult Chinese as an everyday cursive script. Its form is not as free-flowing as grass script but it's less restricted by formal rules of style than standard script, and therefore is much faster to write.

A Word on Simplified Characters

In 1956, the Chinese communist government under Mao undertook a massive project to change the way Chinese people wrote characters. Today, that policy has resulted in two separate character systems that are distinct in many ways. The traditional standard (*kaishu*), mentioned previously as the writing system currently used in Taiwan, has been replaced in China by a simplified character script that relies on fewer writing strokes to complete a word. The Mao government thought this would be a solution to the rampant illiteracy in China that had developed over the imperial period and continued into the modern age. To some extent it has made Chinese easier to learn, but in reality it has not entirely solved China's illiteracy problem. Those barriers are more socioeconomic and especially acute in the rural regions of the country where formal education is not as readily available. (See more about illiteracy in Chapter 7.)

The result of China adopting a simplified system of writing still causes disagreement, even within China. Some scholars of classical Chinese argue that the simplified style has killed off traditional elements of the language that are important to preserving Chinese culture as a whole. Others worry that the system makes too many characters indistinguishable (less writing strokes for distinction) and creates inherent confusion. Still others worry that two writing systems—one in China and the other in Taiwan—will only serve to confuse an international audience.

The reality is most likely somewhere in between. Some traditional standard characters are still used in China, and Taiwanese people will often adopt simplified characters for writing shorthand. The rest of the world seems content to wait and let things get sorted out. Currently, the majority of language primers and dictionaries sold abroad will provide both traditional standard and simplified standard scripts.

The Least You Need to Know

◆ Daoism is a native philosophy-religion of China founded by Laozi. It looks toward nature as an inspiration for its ideas, espousing that the free flow of energy—the Way—holds a key to understanding oneself and the world.

◆ Buddhism came to China through its Mahayana branch and influenced not only religious thought, but everything from art to government.

◆ The religious traditions of Daoism and Buddhism were intricately mixed with Confucian thought in China and are still practiced by large numbers of followers in Taiwan.

◆ China defines both Buddhism and Daoism as religions but keeps them under heavy state control.

◆ Chinese is actually an amalgam of several spoken dialects. The official dialect spoken throughout China, Taiwan, and many other Chinese communities is Mandarin.

◆ The Chinese character system is more than 3,000 years old and is responsible for uniting all the various Chinese dialects under one broad writing system.

◆ Today, two distinct character systems exist in Taiwan and China—the former is traditional while the latter is simplified.

Chapter 7

State and Society

In This Chapter

- ◆ Confucian concepts shape China's political and social principles for much of Chinese history.

- ◆ The Chinese family traditionally followed strict rules of social relations.

- ◆ Education, once only for the elite, reaches all of China's children.

- ◆ China trades Confucian ideals for the Marxist doctrine of the party-state.

During the course of Chinese history, the sway of Confucianism waxed and waned, but its ability to absorb aspects of other philosophies and schools kept it alive until the end of the Qin Empire. With the birth of the Republic of China in 1911, China's Confucian-based government and social system came to an end—nominally, anyway. But Confucian thinking did not disappear overnight, and even today, in China's rapidly globalizing economy and society, it echoes in several aspects of Chinese life. But to track where Confucian thought begins and where it leaves off in contemporary China, it is best to start at the roots of its thought.

The Confucian Code

Confucianism, which greatly influenced Chinese culture from the fourth century B.C.E. on, was not a religion by Western standards; it was a humanistic philosophy, but like a state religion, it established the values and moral principles of China's government and the codes of conduct for its society.

Like many great founding figures in a culture's history, Confucius—most Chinese still call him *Kongfuzi* or Kongzi—is a mixture of fact and fiction.

Scholars today believe that a man known as Kong Qiu lived in China between the sixth and fifth centuries B.C.E. and is a likely source for the legend of Confucius. But they are not sure if the philosophical tradition we call Confucianism can be traced to just one individual. Most likely the origins of this philosophy have many contributors that were inspired by Confucius's early teachings and elaborated on them as they wrote them down, preserving them for posterity. Confucius's followers were called *ru*, a term roughly translated as "scholar," and it was their job to teach the ruling class of China at that time the proper codes of ritual and conduct, or *li*, as instructed by their master (see more about *li* in the following section).

Language Lesson

Kongfuzi is translated into Latin as "Confucius." The Jesuit missionaries operating in China in the seventeenth century introduced his latinized name to the West.

Hu Nu?

The parallels between Confucius and Socrates, the great Greek thinker, are interesting to note, since both are said to have had a set of devoted followers that listened to their philosophical teachings and passed them on to others, and both are credited with founding the great traditions of thought defining the East and West, respectively. In the case of Confucius, however, we can say he enjoyed more popularity among leaders than poor Socrates, who was finally offered hemlock for his profound ideas!

Confucian ideas fit nicely into early Chinese thought about social order, harmony, and the worship of family ancestors. Before Confucius, China's rulers found it difficult to maintain their legitimacy through a Mandate of Heaven—the belief that heaven gave them the moral right—provided that they were morally upright—to rule the common people. Particularly during the Zhou period, there was great strife, conflict, and corruption, so the question followed: If heaven has a mandate to replace evil rulers with good rulers, and influence the overall pattern of human events, why does it allow humans to suffer so greatly? Something was wrong. Confucius provided an answer by introducing three key ideas:

- **Ren** This "cardinal rule" of Confucianism stresses that people practice love and kindness. Ren basically means humanity, and for Confucius, understanding this concept was essential to fulfilling the real potential of humanity. This love and kindness is shown in respect and loyalty to others: parents, friends, and leaders.

- **Li** Along with humanness, Confucius believed people should practice *li*, or ritual. This meant that everyone needed to show respect, kindness, and good faith, not only in official ceremony, but in everyday interaction with family and friends. In short, everyone was expected to make a habit of showing their humanness.

- **Junzi** This means "superior person," an individual who understands humanness and practices ritual. Moreover, a superior person was superior not by bloodline (a common assumption in earlier Chinese society), but by virtue of moral character and honest self-examination.

This was a revolution in thinking for the Chinese, and it preserved an ethical standard that is alive in portions of Chinese culture today. Through these principles, Confucius and his students forged a philosophy that outlined how social harmony could be achieved. The rules were to be followed by all members of Chinese society, and most of all by its leader, the emperor. By being the embodiment of these virtues, the emperor would set a good example that could be followed throughout the land.

The Confucian principles that had begun to have a strong influence during the Zhou dynasty were made official doctrine during the Han. The Confucian code, in its various reformulations along the way, continued to be of great influence during many later dynasties. In China's rural areas, it was the bedrock of family and community relations up until the communist revolution.

The basis of Confucianism lies with the five virtues:

- Uprightness

- Decorum

- Wisdom

- Faithfulness

- Reverence for parents and ancestors

Confucius also defined everyone's position in society and the ways that each position interacted with the others.

He saw five kinds of relationships:

♦ Husband and wife

♦ Parent and child

♦ Ruler and subject

♦ Sibling and sibling

♦ Friend and friend

Each role had its own responsibilities; for example, parents were responsible for their children until they were grown and could care for themselves. In turn, children were responsible for their parents; to honor them, care for them when they became unable to care for themselves, and see them through the end of their lives and the rituals attendant to their death and burial.

Status, in traditional Chinese society, both within the family and in public, was ensured by the roles mapped out by Confucian thought. Wealth, family position, and education were also contributing factors. There was a correct way to relate and communicate with others, and much of that depended on an individual's relative station in society. If a person's actions caused someone, or even themselves, to lose pride or self-dignity—and thus tarnish his or her status—it was seen as a loss of *face*.

Every Chinese person would have face to lose and face to gain, sometimes in the most seemingly mundane situations. A father with a child, a boss with a worker, and even an emperor with his country would stand to lose face if they committed an act that was unacceptable in their position (though who would have ever pointed it out!).

Language Lesson

Personal dignity tied to social status has always been very important in China as in all of East Asia. It is still called **face** and still plays an important role in modern society. Officials and wealthy people have much face; manual laborers, for example, have less. Others with much face include scholars, professionals, authors, artists, and entertainment stars, including athletes. Sometimes face can get in the way of criticizing a superior who has done something wrong, because it will ultimately challenge that individual's status, perhaps bringing negative repercussions.

Confucius believed that by being practiced in behaving correctly toward, and being loyal to, their family and their class in the hierarchy, people would be well prepared to serve the interests of the society. They would also be obedient to those above them in the system. That meant control from the capital. Government was to set the highest example for the citizens. According to Confucian principles a virtuous ruler ensured that the state would be in harmony with the people.

The Old Social Order

In the empire's early years, the literate gentry (nobility) and the commoners were distinct classes that did not intermarry, but neither was China a feudal society. Peasants owned their land, and after the examination system was in place, they were free to study their way into the civil service—the most honorable of professions. Of course they had to pass an examination to obtain a title (or "degree") in their field, then a civil service placement test, and then further tests if they wanted to rise in the bureaucracy.

Later, during the Tang dynasty, after centuries of disunity and incursions by Inner Asian tribes, the civil service was opened to non-Han candidates on a merit basis. The Song dynasty that followed doubled the number of officials recruited through exams rather than kinship, and imposed regional quotas.

Han Help

Commoners could rise in status through the examination system and civil service placement test, but candidates who were from land-owning civil service families could skip the scholarly degree and just take a placement test.

The Gentry and the Commoners

When the Song dynasty began, a strain of fast-growing rice was imported that greatly increased China's rice yield. The population shot up. There were more people to govern, but the bureaucracy was already stretched to its limits. At the same time, the country was full of gentlemen scholars who competed for fewer civil service jobs. Many of them turned their attention to their home regions. Acting on the Confucian message, they took charge of the management and administration of the land. Because they helped the local public officials collect taxes (and made personal contributions when asked), they became intermediaries between the farmers and the government—quelling rebellions or supplying troops for the government, and being community advocates and leaders in many ways.

Wise One Says _____

In the idealistic view that comes down to us through the gazetteers and other writings, the gentry-elite were moved by a sense of dutiful commitment to community leadership. So inspired, they raised funds for and supervised public works—the building and upkeep of irrigation and communication facilities such as canals, dikes, dams, roads, bridges, ferries ... They supported Confucian institutions and morals—establishing and maintaining academies, schools, shrines, and local temples of Confucius ... In time of peace, they set the tone of public life. In time of disorder, they organized and commanded militia defense forces. From day to day they arbitrated disputes informally ... The gentry also set up charities for their clan members and handled trust funds to help the community.

—Fairbank and Goldman, *China: A New History*

Han Help _____

The relationship between the commoner family and the gentry class was one of give and take. The family was responsible for providing for its own subsistence, and beyond that, it was relied on for a surplus of both labor and product that could be tapped by the gentry for its private purposes, and by the government for its public purposes.

The gentry did such a great job in the communities that, even though China's population continued to grow, the bureaucracy remained the same size for the next 500 years, into the seventeenth century.

During the Song dynasty, the gentry who were neither in official posts nor looking after their communities were not idle. They created many works of art and literature; they made advances in history, geography, cartography, astronomy, and philosophy; their mathematics may have been more advanced at the time than it was in any other country. It was also during the Song dynasty that everything that could be found or learned about China's historical past was collected and organized in comprehensive encyclopedic tomes.

The Family

In a preceding section, "The Confucian Code," we noted that in imperial China, relationships in the society were modeled on the relationships within the family. Confucius pointed to the father-son relationship of mutual responsibility—of the father to set an example of moral behavior and of the son to respect and obey the father—as the guide to the individual's relationship with the ruler. The family line passed from father to son, and the father reigned over the family as males dominated females, and the aged dominated the young. Children were expected to obey their parents, and wives were expected to be faithful to their husbands (but not husbands to their wives).

Relations among siblings and within the extended family were very strictly defined in terms of obligations and expectations. Daughters' marriages were usually arranged, and daughters moved into the household of their husband's father. One thing is certain: Everyone knew his or her place.

Filial piety—the act of honoring one's elders—was another important aspect of the Confucian brand of family life. The Chinese belief in worshiping one's ancestors made it easy to also require great respect toward any senior, particularly those within the immediate family. Seniority has played and continues to play a central role in Chinese families and in public authority, though there have been moments in the nation's modern history when concern for seniority has been pointedly disregarded.

Hu Nu?
The unusual system of inheritance in China had a major effect on the land and family, and also served to limit the power of individual landowners. Unlike European civilizations, in which primogeniture (inheritance by the eldest son) was the rule, in China, the eldest son did not inherit everything. Rather, the land was divided among the sons, none of whom could acquire enough property to dominate his region or threaten the central authority.

Language Lesson

One way members of a Chinese household are reminded of each other's position is in the formal kin terms used to address each other. The terms *ba ba* (father) and *ma ma* (mother) are used by all Chinese children. But rank between children—strictly defined by age—is distinguished within the family by kin terms. For instance, a younger sister would call her older sister by the term *jie jie*, while the older sister would call her little sister *mei mei*. These distinctions are so pronounced that each member of the family is assigned a distinct kin term. This closely follows Confucian thought, that family relations should be clearly defined. In fact, even in today's China it would be considered rude to not address a relative by his or her proper kin term.

Women's Place in the Family

Traditionally women were expected to be passive and obedient, even when abused by their husbands, and to refrain from demonstrating too much affection toward their sons. Infanticide, which was a documented practice in imperial China, most often was carried out on female children since male children were preferred. Girls were not sent to school, and remained illiterate. Women whose husbands died had little chance of remarrying, and those whose husbands had abandoned them were denied employment.

The dire position of women in earlier Chinese society was most evident in the practices of foot binding and concubinage. Both have been given a great deal of attention in Western literature and have become stereotypes of women's stature in imperial Chinese society.

The old Chinese custom of binding a young woman's feet to impede growth was perpetuated by Chinese men's insistence that it was a symbol of beauty. In reality it caused unrelenting pain for the rest of the woman's adult life due to resulting deformity and subsequent bouts of infection.

The practice of concubinage—that is the act of a married man taking a woman as an extra wife—could, in its own way, be as brutal as foot binding. If the female concubine, usually sold to a man by her family, could not give the man a son, or compensate in some other way, she would not be given full rank as a wife and therefore was susceptible to mistreatment by family members, including the man's other "successful" wives.

There is some evidence that concubinage was not as widespread as is often inferred in popular Western literature. In fact, usually only wealthier men were apt to take concubines because of the sheer cost of maintaining a larger household. Nevertheless, it is widely known to have existed throughout China prior to communism.

In both cases, the wholesale removal of these customs can be credited to the communists. Foot binding continued in China until 1949 when the communists outlawed it. During the First Five Year Plan (1952–1957), new marriage laws were put into place that outlawed polygamy (the taking of more than one wife), effectively halting the widespread practice of concubinage.

Family and Society After Communism

The Maoist-led revolt targeted China's old social system, and the gentry class in particular. As a result, the gentry were seen as an enemy of socialist progress. The accumulation of wealth and property by the gentry, particularly in the form of land ownership, was frowned upon by the communists, and land was eventually confiscated. Mao looked not to the gentry, but to the commoners to inspire his vision of a new Chinese society. After Deng Xiaoping's reforms, the old communist hard line distaste for wealth and material gain gave way to a new means of raising China's standard of living: today's free market economy. Once again, it is considered great to be rich. Yet, today's prosperity, unlike that of the gentry of the imperial age, is not strictly guided by a Confucian-style philosophy of social responsibility and decorum.

Some traditional Chinese family values have survived into the present: Parents, and other elders, are still treated with great respect; household kinship terms are still used as before; children are obligated to a large degree to follow their family's wishes when choosing a career, perhaps even a spouse. However, the impact of years of strong Marxist-Maoist ideology, China's drastic economic shifts, and the devastation brought on by the Cultural Revolution have reshaped other aspects of traditional family and community life.

The adoption by the early communists of the *danwei*, or labor unit, system had a profound effect on the traditional extended family unit (where families of more than one generation lived together). Under this system young adults were assigned to specific work units and often stayed with them for the rest of their lives. This made the traditional closeness of the Confucian family difficult, if not impossible, to maintain. In many cases, husbands and wives would work in different cities hundreds of miles apart, seeing each other only on rare occasions.

Han Help _____

It should be noted that the *danwei* system was never adopted in Taiwan or Hong Kong.

The Cultural Revolution had an even more adverse effect on the traditional Chinese family. By most accounts, the Cultural Revolution was a frenzied revolt against Confucian ideals, manipulated by a powerful few. The time-tested value of filial piety was shattered as young communists—many part of the Red Guard brigades—enthusiastically followed orders to turn in parents and respected elders of their community who had been branded bourgeoisie sympathizers, and therefore enemies of the communist state.

Now that the social upheaval of the Cultural Revolution is in the past—though it remains a painful memory—and the old *danwei* system fell by the wayside with the economic reforms of the mid to late '80s, Chinese families are falling back into a more familiar mode. The constraints on today's families are no longer due to ideology—but, paradoxically, for many families, they are a result of China's new economy. With more freedom to move about and hence be together and not with a work unit, Chinese families are still forced to make hard choices. The less affluent, particularly those from rural areas, routinely travel long distances to cities to find work. As a result, many families are still split apart for long periods of time.

Han Help _____

It's interesting to note that, in contrast to women's poor position in imperial China, today's young urban Chinese women are successfully navigating the new economy in unprecedented numbers—though they still earn less on average than their male counterparts.

In the cities, where larger numbers of couples have extensive education, family life is stable and children have more opportunities. For these families, the concern may be getting their children into top schools or deciding on which new car they should purchase.

For the most part, disparity in the standard of living between contemporary Chinese families is incredibly wide. And that disparity is determined more and more by the uneven economic growth of China's geographic regions (see more about this concern in Chapter 15).

Education

In imperial China, a very small number of common folk received an education; in China today, there is a nine-year compulsory education requirement for all children. Some things about education haven't changed, but when compared with the past, that is a major leap.

Imperial Education

When we look back into education in imperial China, we find Confucius taking center stage again. During his lifetime (551–479 B.C.E.) only the nobility were educated, and could therefore be considered for public service. Because one of his basic beliefs was that man was perfectible, it followed that anyone, gentleman or commoner, could be educated to become a good public servant. When he was 22 he started a school where, for a small fee, anyone could study for a government career. In Confucius's school, that meant studying culture and tradition, but the major emphasis was on the self cultivation of balance through emulating the examples of those who had achieved it and through the practice of rituals.

Language Lesson

Chung yung, translated as the "constant mean" or the "golden mean," requires that every impulse or course of action—no matter how virtuous—had to be brought into balance by another. The epigram "Discretion is the better part of valor" is a familiar example of the Confucian chung yung.

Confucius believed that in order to serve the society, one's own personal desires had to be in balance with the good of the people. That meant achieving chung yung, or the "constant mean."

Confucianism, and later neo-Confucianism, was the major influence on education during most of imperial Chinese history. The purpose of Confucian-based education was to engender moral responsibility and the "right conduct" that went with it. Officials who cultivated those characteristics could expect to receive the respect of the people and the serious attention of the ruler.

Even after obtaining a degree and passing a local and a central government exam, though, the hopeful job candidate would typically have to wait years for a post to open up. But it was worth it: There was no greater status in imperial China than to have a career in public service. Sadly, and ironically, Confucius himself was never awarded an official post.

Education Today

After 1911, the New Learning movement worked on reassessing Confucianism and deciding which aspects of it were relevant to China's new era.

During the 1950s and '60s, while the rest of the world was feeding its intellect with the fruits of modern communication systems, the Chinese consciousness had been shut down by the Cultural Revolution. Mao was distrustful of all innovation that didn't fit his personally micro-managed version of the universe. He distrusted scholarship, thinking it was tainted by foreign influences, as well as scholars—natural enemies of the peasant proletariat and tireless critics of Mao's way.

"Education for all" said Mao. It was interesting that he employed the Confucian concept of rectification through education as a basis for his indoctrination campaigns, thought-reform movement, and the "rectification" movements themselves.

In 1978, the government made education a priority. The progress made in the years since has been astounding; 91 percent of China's districts have compulsory education. In 1983, Deng Xiaoping said, "Education should be geared to the needs of modernization, of the world and of the future."

> **Hu Nu?**
>
> Vestiges of Confucian practice still remain in Taiwan, Hong Kong, and Singapore, where students and their family worship in Confucian temples, and teachers extol Confucian principles in their teaching practices.

> **Han Help**
>
> Though Mao worried about the infiltration of foreign ideas through education, Western ideas reached China through missionaries and Yen Fu's translations of Western classics long before Mao was on the scene. In fact, many of the party's founders were Western-educated or Westernized through being Christians (including Sun Yatsen and Chiang Kaishek).

Compulsory Education

Today, Children three through six years of age usually attend kindergarten near their homes, where they learn their native dialect. The primary school occupies the next six years, where they take Chinese language, fundamental mathematics, and moral education (shades of Confucius again). They may also study foreign languages; English has become very popular.

After they finish primary school, if they pass an entrance exam, children then attend junior middle school for three years, studying sciences, Chinese history, world history, geography, and English, which at this level is the official second language.

After two or three years of upper middle school, students can take an exam, based on which they may go on to an academic or vocational high school.

Higher Education

To go on to postsecondary educational institutions, after they finish high school, students must pass the national college entrance examinations. Universities, colleges, and institutes offer four- or five-year undergraduate programs, and some offer junior (two-year) college programs.

There are now more than 1,000 colleges and universities in China, and almost 3.5 million college students. There are 736 graduate schools and 200,000 graduate students.

Students who complete a first degree may apply to a graduate school by taking the nationwide examination that is given once a year. As a rule, admission to higher educational institutions is based on the entrance examination as well as academic, physical, and moral qualifications.

Wise One Says

The most pressing issue facing China's schools is inadequate funding. With expenditures on education totaling only 2 percent of gross national product, China lags behind the world average of 5 percent, and many developing countries outspend it on their schools.

—John Bryan Starr, *Understanding China*

Until recently, university students were given a room in a campus dormitory, free of charge, where they lived and studied during the week. For years, students expressed great dissatisfaction with the quality of the education and with the accommodations; in fact, these issues touched off the 1989 Tiananmen Square demonstration (see Chapter 13). Now, lack of government funding has led to tuition charges as well as major cuts in student aid, putting a postsecondary education out of reach for students from low-income households.

Many students who can study abroad now do so, and not that many are returning to China after they receive their degrees.

Literacy

Before we discuss literacy in China, let's remember just how new an idea it is there. Before the communist takeover in 1949, only 20 percent of the people in China were *literate*.

By 1995, the literacy rate in China had reached 81.5 percent, but there were still 186.3 million illiterates in the country. The claim is that 99 percent of eligible Chinese children are attending school, and if the elderly (the least literate) are eliminated from the sample, less than 7 percent of the Chinese public is now illiterate.

In 2001, the state educational authorities expanded the literacy program to prepare more young people for compulsory schooling. The aim is to keep literacy rates among the young and middle-aged above 95 percent.

Special literacy programs for women have been launched to address the disparity between their literacy rate and that of the men, particularly in rural areas.

Language Lesson

To be considered **literate** in China, a person must be able to recognize more than 1,500 Chinese characters (for a farmer) and 2,000 characters (for an office worker).

Today's Party-State

The early communists in China severely criticized Confucian thinking as old-fashioned and nonscientific. It was banned starting in the 1950s, along with other "religions" and was dealt its greatest blow by the Cultural Revolution. Since Confucianism represented imperial China, and imperial China had been the source of what communist Chinese felt was so wrong with their country, Confucian principles had to come under fire. In their place, Marxist ideals were promoted, first by Mao, then by all his successors. The dominant message, which most Chinese citizens are expected to follow, is: The party knows what is best for its people.

Some, however, including some party leaders, beg to differ with the party-state's maxim. Today's leaders have held power largely by renouncing parts of their Marxist ideology, selectively permitting certain personal freedoms while ruthlessly suppressing any real or imagined challenge to the power of the state. Chinese people by the millions are responding in a new way: They are pursuing wealth and finding areas of personal fulfillment in which the state does not bother to interfere. It goes without saying that they are careful to avoid anything that might be construed as criticism of the government.

Contemporary experts refer to China as a party-state because, just as the Confucian state and society could only function interdependently, the party and the central government are virtually inseparable.

Today, China's government is separated into executive, legislative, and judicial branches. There is only one political party, however, the *Zhongguo Gongchandang*.

Language Lesson

Zhongguo Gongchandang means Chinese Communist Party.

China's current leader, Jiang Zemin, like all the head honchos of the party, wears many hats. He is secretary of the Chinese Communist Party (CCP), president of China, and chairman of the Central Military Commission of the People's Republic of China.

The Central Government

There is a vice president, Hu Jintao, and four vice premiers chosen by the legislature. The central government consists of the following branches:

♦ **The Executive.** The State Council heads the executive branch. Its members are the 29 commissioners and ministers who are at the top of the bureaucratic pyramid that includes 34 ministries and several executive bureaus: the State Economic and Trade Commission, the State Development Planning Commission, the People's Bank of China, and the State Administration of Foreign Exchange.

Han Help

According to Jonathan Spence, author of *The Search for Modern China*, the State Development Planning Commission and the State Commission for Restructuring the Economy rank about as high as ministries. He adds that 22 of the provincial party leaders also hold minister's rank. The number of high-level competing jurisdictions may explain why it's so hard to get big infrastructure projects or policy shifts pulled together.

On the next tier are other key agencies such as the General Administration of Customs (Xinhua), the China Securities Regulatory Commission, and the State Administration for Religious Affairs.

On the third tier are the state-level corporations. They're interesting because they're used by the party to spin off semiprivate companies from known money-makers—most likely to then broker deals with foreign firms. Some of the areas the 26 state-level corporations are involved in are the automotive industry, offshore oil, onshore oil and gas, shipbuilding, aviation, railways, and there are a few competing telecommunications corporations.

- **The Legislature.** The Chinese legislature is made up of the National People's Congress. The congress includes 3,000 delegates who meet once a year in a session that lasts two or three weeks. Between those annual sessions, there are meetings of the Standing Committee of the National People's Congress. The committee consists of 150 members of the congress. The chairman of the committee is Li Peng.

  The National People's Legislative Congress features 2,979 deputies indirectly elected to five-year terms by Provincial congresses. The Chairman of the Standing Committee is Li Peng. All 2,979 were members of the Chinese Communist Party.

- **The Judiciary.** Supreme People's Court is appointed to five-year terms by the National People's Congress. The Supreme People's Procuratorate's president is elected by the National People's Congress to a five-year term. The judiciary's role is strictly limited to applying existing policies and laws to individual cases. It does not have the power to rule on the legality of existing laws and thereby effect changes in the law (as in case law in the United States).

Local Governments

There are 31 provincial governments, or 32 if Taiwan is included as a province. They represent 22 provinces, 4 city governments, and 5 autonomous regions.

- **City governments.** Beijing, Tianjin, Chongqing, and Shanghai are governed directly by Beijing, without an intervening bureaucratic level.

- **Autonomous regions.** Guangxi, Inner Mongolia (Nei Mongol), Ningxia, Xinjiang, and Zizang (better known to the rest of the world as Tibet) are regions originally settled by Inner Asian peoples (see Chapter 1). The designation of autonomous region does not, in practice, distinguish them from the provinces in any way, and is said to be for "historical reasons."

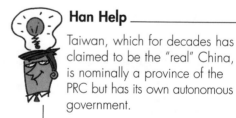

Han Help

Taiwan, which for decades has claimed to be the "real" China, is nominally a province of the PRC but has its own autonomous government.

- **Special administrative regions.** The city of Hong Kong, long under British control, and the former Portuguese colony of Macao recently became special administrative regions of the PRC. What's special about them is that they are outside the ministerial system, and enjoy a great deal of autonomy. Whereas there is friction between Beijing and Hong Kong (mainly a result of the 1989 Tiananmen Square crackdown), Macao, while it has a wait-and-see attitude, changed its flag without seeming to skip a beat.

Han Help

The Portuguese handover of Macao to the Chinese has been quite smooth. Many of the small island's residents, in essence, see the transfer as the end of what was once a vast European empire in Asia—the last gasp of a long-receding colonial rule.

China's massive central bureaucracy (4.5 million) is a cumbersome and unsystematic arrangement in which lines of authority are so sketchily drawn that the only way to resolve disputes is through bargaining— with utmost delicacy, because "face" is involved. Beijing's decentralization policy, if it's to be an improvement, requires a streamlined pecking order and system of communications between the bureaucratic levels—or does it? Corruption remains a huge problem; perhaps the CCP is taking a page from the dynastic book and making the bureaucrats keep an eye on each other.

Modern China Revisits Confucius

Prospects for Confucianism changed when Mao Zedong died, and today more Chinese scholars are becoming interested in relearning its classical texts. On the mainland, where there has been a return to all types of religious practice since the end of Maoism, Neo-Confucianism has re-emerged as a minor movement among bureaucrats and intellectuals. They share with the large segment of Neo-Conservatives an antipathy to Western-type opportunism (especially the economic version), and they seek to bolster a sense of social responsibility while China continues its own economic growth.

Hu Nu?

Confucian thought has actually been through several periods of popularity and rejection. Its high point was during the neo-Confucian (new-Confucian) movement during the Song dynasty. Neo-Confucian supporters did much to popularize the philosophy among all levels of government at that time. Furthermore, they placed heavy emphasis on self-cultivation and social awareness. The writer Xiong Shili (1885–1965) was a very influential Confucian thinker and is considered one of the fathers of modern neo-Confucianism.

Despite Confucianism's weak official status in China, it must be remembered that its ideas have long been integrated into the Chinese culture. The respect still given elders, teachers, parents, and political leaders, as well as the love for one's country are tightly interwoven with Confucian ideals. Ironically, these ideals are so intrinsic in being Chinese that they may not be recognized today as uniquely Confucian, but as part of modern China's ethos.

The Least You Need to Know

- ◆ In imperial China, the Confucian principles of uprightness, decorum, wisdom, faithfulness, and reverence for one's parents and ancestors deeply influenced social relations.

- ◆ The literate gentry were the public servants of ancient China, and its artists, philosophers, musicians, and scientists. They were criticized as class enemies by the communists, and their property and status were taken away.

- ◆ China's current government is ruled by a single party that is organized under three government branches.

- ◆ Families today are more affected by economic change than by Marxist-Maoist ideology.

- ◆ The Chinese family and society have undergone great change since communism, but some Confucian family values remain intact, and Confucian, or neo-Confucian, thought is gaining some popularity again in China, but primarily among intellectuals and bureaucrats.

Chapter **8**

China's Triumphs

In This Chapter

- ◆ China's "four great inventions" change the course of world history.

- ◆ Traditional Chinese medicine gains international recognition.

- ◆ Excavated Bronze Age sculpture is universally considered among mankind's highest artistic achievements.

- ◆ Buddhist influences give rise to the richest period in Chinese art and architecture.

The course of Chinese history has not been all smooth sailing. The great Han dynasty was followed by four centuries of fragmentation; foreigners— first the Mongols, and later the Manchus—ruled China for a total of nearly 400 years; and China faces major challenges today, which we explore in Chapters 15 and 16. Yet even during periods when China's survival seemed precarious, its traditional civic and social infrastructure prevailed—the highly structured bureaucracy and examination system we looked at in Chapter 7 survives in some form today. And the work of scientists, scholars, artists, and writers continued—and even flourished—when the state was at its weakest.

In this chapter we look at what are widely considered to be China's "four great inventions" (the mariner's compass, gunpowder, printing, and paper), and at some lesser-known triumphs of Chinese culture.

Continuity in Change

As we noted in Chapters 1 and 2, during most of Chinese history, dynasties came and went with some regularity, but China was—and remains—China. Han culture's disinclination to absorb other cultures into its own, the tendency of other cultures—including those of alien conquerors—to adopt Han ways, and the Chinese impulse toward unification is what has made China the oldest continuous civilization in history.

A Confucian-based reverence for the past, and a sense of cultural superiority—bolstered by China's isolation from other high cultures—can account for the endurance of the Han idea. But what is most impressive is the balance that China has always maintained—of the Han and the foreign, the old and the new, the secular and the religious.

> **" " Wise One Says**
>
> As a philosophy of life, we have generally associated with Confucianism the quiet virtues of patience, pacifism, and compromise; the golden mean; reverence for the ancestors, the aged, and the learned; and, above all, a mellow humanism—taking man, not God, as the center of the universe ... if we take this Confucian view of life in its social and political context, we will see that its esteem for age over youth, for the past over the present, for established authority over innovation has in fact provided one of the great historic answers to the problem of social stability. It has been the most successful of all systems of conservatism.
>
> —John King Fairbank and Merle Goldman, *China: A New History* (The Belknap Press of Harvard University Press, 2001)

The Four Great Inventions

The four great inventions—paper, printing, the mariner's compass, and gunpowder—took place at different times in Chinese history, and for different reasons.

Paper

About 4,000 years ago, Chinese characters were carved into pottery, animal bones, and stones; they were later written on strips of bamboo, wood, or strips of silk fabric. The bamboo was bundled into "books" that were very cumbersome; the silk was very expensive—even in China where it was made.

At archeological sites in central and western China, rudimentary paper was excavated that was determined to be from the Western Han dynasty (202 B.C.E.–16 C.E.). It was later, in 105 C.E., that paper made with a mix of more substantial ingredients—plant fiber, cloth, and other materials—was officially presented to the Han emperor by the man who developed it, Cai Lun. The emperor was so delighted, he named it "Marquis Cai's paper." There was soon paper everywhere in China, but the first record of its manufacture anywhere else is in Arabia in the eighth century, after which it slowly found its way around the world.

> ### Hu Nu?
>
> Three small towns in Guizhou Province took up traditional paper making about 300 years ago, using the same methods as Marquis Cai used almost 2 millennia ago. It's made from a mixture of bamboo, birch leaves, and water, and has to be boiled for 35 days, and put through several other processes before it's squeezed dry. It sells well everywhere in China.

The invention of paper had a profound influence on the world. Prior to its existence, parchment was the only writing material available, and only the wealthiest could afford to buy books. Paper made knowledge of the wider world available to everyone.

Printing

Once there was paper, the advent of block printing was almost inevitable. Stamp seals that were stamped into clay had been in existence in China since the third century B.C.E. as a means of identifying their owners, and the Chinese had been printing designs and pictures on textiles for some time by carving the patterns into clay or stone blocks, and squeezing the blocks onto the fabric. It wasn't until the sixth century C.E., though, that they began to dip the seals in ink and press them onto paper.

By the sixth century, there were a lot of Buddhist and Daoist monks in China. They had always laboriously duplicated sacred inscriptions and magical images by hand, and they now began to use seals to duplicate them in great numbers. No one knows when someone took the next step and started using larger blocks to print words, but the world's oldest existing printed book is dated 868 C.E.

> ### Han Help
>
> The oldest existing book printed on paper is actually a scroll of a sacred Buddhist text, excavated in the mid-twentieth century. Around the tenth century, the *Tipitaka*, a compilation of Buddhist scriptures, was printed entirely from wood blocks onto squares of paper. It ran to 130,000 pages.

An even greater Chinese triumph of the tenth century was to be the first country to print paper money. It worked well until inflation got so bad that they had to revert to coins until they got a backing system set up, but it certainly impressed the world.

During the eleventh century, Chinese inventor Pi Sheng invented movable type, using baked clay blocks and iron frames, but it didn't come into wide use because the Chinese language requires so many characters—2,000 to 40,000—it's easier to use block type. In fact, China didn't become a beneficiary of this one of its Four Great Inventions until a few decades ago, but in the eleventh century, movable type was a godsend for much of the rest of the world.

Gunpowder

A written formula for gunpowder, a combination of nitre, sulphur, and carbon, appeared in China in 1044, and other formulas appeared after that. Chances are the Daoist penchant for alchemy and experimentation with all things natural contributed to its invention, as it did to dyes, alloys, and other compounds.

Gunpowder is known to have been used by the Song forces in grenades and land mines in the eleventh century, but it very well may have existed a century earlier. The earliest European formula for gunpowder appeared in 1265, and whether it was a Chinese formula that found its way there or an independent discovery remains an open question. In any case, whatever we may think of gunpowder, that it changed life on earth can't be denied.

The Mariner's Compass

There's strong evidence that natural magnets were used for direction-finding during the Han dynasty (206 B.C.E.–220 C.E.), and could quite possibly have been used for building construction a long time before that. The first written reference to magnetism is in a Chinese book dated 240 B.C.E., but the first reference to a magnetic *compass*, that has so far been discovered, is in a Chinese book written toward the end of the eleventh century. A compass designed for sea navigation—a *mariner's compass*—appears in a Chinese book written a few decades later.

The mariner's compass, along with other advances in shipbuilding and nautical technology, put Chinese seafaring ahead of the rest of the world's. The course of history may have been very different if China had been of a mind to take to the sea to extend its empire.

Language Lesson

A **compass** is a magnetized needle mounted on a pivot that points, roughly, toward the magnetic pull of the North Pole (or in China, the South Pole). The magnetized needle of a **mariner's compass** is attached to the pivot through a compass card on which it rests. The compass card turns freely in the compass bowl in a liquid mixture that keeps it pointing toward the magnetic pole and prevents it from swinging from side to side with the ship.

Keeping Records

During the Han dynasty, when the idea of what it was to be Chinese was taking shape, the emperor created an imperial academy (124 B.C.E.) where scholars studied and interpreted the five classic works of Confucius. The Confucian works catalogued China's past and embodied the conceptual foundations of Chinese governance and social behavior. Though there was no hint of religion in Confucius's pragmatic, humanistic philosophy, the Han court does, at this point, begin to sound a little like the Vatican—or the domain of God himself. In fact, distinguished modern scholars of Chinese history—John King Fairbank, Edwin Reischauer, Thomas Metger—found it intriguing that the emperor had absolute power over the imperial library, the academy and its scholars, and Chinese education itself.

Shortly after the founding of the academy, two independent historians, Sima Tan and his son Sima Qian, undertook the project of compiling a complete history of China. When Sima Tan died, Sima Qian continued the work, *Records of the Historian (Shiji)* until his death in 85 B.C.E. Their work was the beginning of a lasting Chinese tradition: the regular collection, organization, and chronicling of events. Sima Tan and Sima Qian are considered China's greatest historians.

In 54 C.E., Pan Piao and his son Pan Ku compiled *Documents of Han*, and it became standard practice thereafter when a new dynasty succeeded that it would publish an official history of the preceding dynasty. The problem was that the *position* of the emperor (past, present, or future) was godlike, so the official histories became riddled with information that was uncritical, distorted, and even untrue.

Han Help

In 99 B.C.E., Sima Qian ran afoul of the emperor, and the emperor had him castrated.

There is some good news, though. The Chinese tradition of record keeping, that had gone on even when there were only bones and shells to write on, took hold in earnest during the Han dynasty. Keeping records sparked significant early developments in China in the fields of astronomy, medicine, and many other sciences.

One of the frustrating things about reading early Chinese history is that the more you go back in time, the more the records conflict in dating events. Astronomy is an example. Scholars may agree that an early astronomer did sight a given heavenly body and describe it accurately, but disagree on whose record of the date is correct. There are historians with an inclination to believe that Chinese astronomy was quite advanced, but if China is hoping to achieve recognition for being the first place a celestial body or event was sighted, well, it has to grapple with statements such as "Chinese records of a 'guest star' we now call Comet Halley can be traced back to at least 240 B.C.E., and possibly as far back as 1059 B.C.E." *The Spring and Autumn Annals* of Confucius records the appearance of what is thought to be Halley's Comet in 613 B.C.E.

There are bone and tortoise shell inscriptions recording five lunar eclipses during the fourteenth and thirteenth centuries before the Common Era. *The Bamboo Annals* records a meteorite shower in 2133 B.C.E. in today's Henan Province.

For a completely reliable source on an astronomical sighting, we have eminent British scientist and historian Joseph Needham, who wrote the seven-volume work, *Science and Civilization in China*, (Cambridge University Press). He and his colleagues maintain that the first sighting of sunspots was in China in the fourth century B.C.E. What we do know for sure is that Chinese astronomers kept very close track of the skies.

> **Hu Nu?**
>
> Mathematics, a major aspect of astronomy, was originally developed in China for purposes of record keeping and land surveying. Early Chinese mathematics is thought to have been quite advanced; mathematician Liu Hui in the third century C.E. calculated *pi* more accurately than it had ever been done. He did it by using a figure with 3,072 equal sides to approximate a circle!

> **Han Help**
>
> *The Bamboo Annals*, written on bamboo slips, were discovered in a grave in 281 C.E. They were lost, then forged, then reconstructed, insofar as it was possible to do so. Many scholars believe that the earliest reliable date in Chinese history is 841 B.C.E.

Traditional Chinese Medicine

Traditional Chinese medicine benefited greatly from the tradition of recording details. Physicians diagnosed patients by asking questions about their symptoms, diet, and previous illnesses, then meticulously recorded their medical conditions. They reviewed treatment options, prescribed remedies, observed the effects of remedies on their patients, and chronicled the results and their conclusions.

Huang Di, the Yellow Emperor, is a traditional personage who is credited with founding China around 4,000 B.C.E., and many legends about him were written down during the Warring States period (circa 403–221 B.C.E.). A book called *The Yellow Emperor's Canon of Medicine* (*Nei Ching*) appeared in its current form in the first century B.C.E., presenting itself as the record of a conversation about medicine that took place between the Yellow Emperor and his doctor. It is China's earliest collection of medical documents.

Han Help

The Yellow Emperor's Canon sets forth the basic theory of internal medicine, based on the Daoist belief in the unity of nature, that the five main organs and orifices of the body correspond to the five parts of the sky: water, fire, wood, metal, and earth; and that the health of an individual is based on the balance of yin (female) and yang (male) forces working in concert with the blood in his or her body (see Chapter 6).

China's first guide to herbal medicine, *Materia Medica* by Shen Nong, was written during the Han dynasty. It presented a theory of pharmacology and summarized the medical and pharmacological knowledge that had gone before in a list of 365 substances and their effects.

Between 1552 and 1578, Li Shizhen, a physician and pharmacologist during the Ming dynasty, assembled and organized 800 pharmacological texts. Over a period of 27 years, he tested the substances they listed, and compiled an updated *Materia Medica*. It lists over 1,800 substances and 11,000 prescriptions, and includes 1,100 illustrations. One famous example of being right on target is the remedy for leprosy, an oil derived from the chaulmoogra tree; it remains the only medication that is known to treat leprosy. Li Shizhen's work, updated many times since his time, is still used by herbal medicine practitioners in China, and is published in several languages, including English. The modern version includes scientific data and features a guide to acupuncture.

Zhang Zhongjing, a scientist during the Han dynasty compared ancient folk medical remedies with his own clinical experiences and wrote a classic work, *Treatises on Febrile and Other Diseases*. It remains a classic work of reference today for the study of traditional Chinese medicine.

In the twentieth century, traditional Chinese medicine and Western medicine began to merge, both in China and elsewhere in the world, including the West. Many physicians today use modern methods to diagnose their patients, and then treat them with traditional Chinese remedies.

There is a growing interest in the United States in what are called "alternative medicines," and Chinese medical methods are among those that have gained dramatically in popularity. Visits to alternative practitioners such as chiropractors, acupuncturists, and herbalists now outnumber visits to physicians in the United States, despite the fact that insurance often does not cover such therapies.

> **Wise One Says**
>
> According to Leslie Tierra, author of *The Nature of Herbal Healing*, "The herb's energies are matched with that of the person, the disease and its cause. Thus rather than making the headache the main treatment focus, we look at the person to see what is occurring in the body to cause the headache."

Arts and Letters

On a generation-to-generation basis, traditional Chinese art seems forever unchanging, but to look at China's historical artistic achievements is to see a wide variety of styles ranging from the Neolithic period to the present day. As most artists and scholars were in the employ of the royal court, their work was conservative, and usually varied in only minor stylistic ways from emperor to emperor, or even dynasty to dynasty. The freelancers (called amateurs or literati) had a wider range, and in many periods of imperial history were the ones to watch. China may not have had much contact with the outside world until recent times, but its diverse inside world ensured an artistic tradition as rich and varied as any on earth.

Historical Chinese art can be divided into seven forms of expression: jade, bronze, tomb ceramics, stoneware and porcelain, sculpture, painting, and calligraphy. There have been lesser achievements, but achievements nonetheless, using lacquer and textiles as the "canvas."

The Bronze Age

Many scholars consider the greatest triumphs of Chinese art to be from the period when bronze was the primary medium—roughly 1800–220 B.C.E. The dynastic courts of the period all revolved around rituals of death and the dead that seemed to have taken up most of their time and creative energies.

Archeological excavations since 1950 have uncovered a wealth of treasures and a great deal of knowledge about the people whose major architectural and artistic efforts were devoted to their underground tombs. The wood structures and the clothing had disintegrated over time, but a plethora of oracle bones, magnificent bronze vessels, jade and ivory carvings, and fine pottery were intact. The bronze containers are decorated with figures of monsters, animals, and birds, real and imagined, but the decorative motif of the greater number of vessels and containers is the *taotie*, or animal mask. There is an astonishing amount of equipment because it was needed for the ceremonies for dead ancestors and nature deities—which included human and animal sacrifice until around the twelfth century B.C.E. There was also all sorts of gear needed by the king, queen, or noble in his or her afterlife.

The most remarkable works of art are of the Shang dynasty (1523–1027 B.C.E.); they're known as the Shang bronzes—vessels unsurpassed in their beauty. Even among man's greatest achievements, they are considered supreme.

The other sublime artistic triumph of the Shang period is its Black (Longshan) Pottery, of exquisite beauty and delicacy.

The Bronze Age architects built tombs, and the painters depicted legendary figures, but toward the end of the Han dynasty, and the Bronze Age, chroniclers noted that landscape painting had come into vogue. The Han dynasty was overthrown in 220 C.E., and a period of disunity followed that lasted four centuries.

> ### Hu Nu?
>
> One of the most remarkable finds was in the province of Shanxi: the burial mound of Qin Shihuang, the first Qin emperor. To protect his domain, there were more than 6,000 terra cotta figures of horses and soldiers, perfectly equipped with weapons and chariots. Human sacrifice was not part of the ritual of the Qin dynasty, but the trappings of the cult of the dead lived on.

The Buddhist Era

Just as Christianity led to forward leaps in Western art during the Renaissance, Buddhism stood behind much of China's great art from the sixth until the ninth century C.E. Great numbers of Buddhist and Daoist monks reached China when it was in a period of fragmentation, and people were dazed and bereft. By the sixth century, Buddhism had had a profound impact on China—especially on its art. Buddhism's influence inspired China's artists and writers to shape their work in new ways that

Language Lesson

A **bodhisattva** is an individual who has achieved enlightenment and vowed to stay in a cycle of birth, death, and rebirth until all sentient beings have achieved enlightenment.

gave rise to paintings, narrative reliefs, architecture, literature, and drama that lifted the Chinese spirit.

A famous ancient work of art is a large stone carving of Shakyamuni, the historical Buddha, that was sculpted in 516 C.E.

During the eighth century C.E., many famous paintings, some made of gilded and painted wood, were of Guanyin, the Buddhist Goddess of Mercy, and the world's best-known *bodhisattva*.

From the Tang to the Qing

In the seventh century, China was reunified under the Tang dynasty (618–907). By then the Buddhism that had come to China from India had been a major influence, but it had bent to Chinese ways and taken on Daoist features.

The Tang Dynasty

As the new Tang dynasty grew stronger and more vigorous, the focus shifted; Confucianism began to reemerge. Majestic, grand scale sculpture remained a feature of Tang art, but painting took on a range of expression. The work of the court painters became simpler, and tended toward serene landscapes (probably an influence of the Daoists) and standard portraits of the emperor and the nobles.

The work of the Taipei painters was distinctly different; it utilized more vivid colors and a looser style than the paintings of the mainland.

The Tang dynasty produced four of China's greatest poets: Wang Wei, Li Po, Tu Fu, and Bo Juyi. Tu Fu is considered the greatest poet in Chinese history:

> Sharp wind, towering sky, apes howling mournfully;
> untouched island, white sand, birds flying in circles.
> Infinite forest, bleakly shedding leaf after leaf;
> inexhaustible river, rolling on wave after wave.
> Through a thousand miles of melancholy autumn, I travel
> carrying a hundred years of sickness I climb to this terrace.
> Hardship and bitter regret have frosted my temples—
> and what torments me most? giving up wine!
>
> —Tu Fu, tr. David Lunde

The Tang dynasty was a rich time for the decorative arts: metalwork, ceramics, glazed earthenware, and silverwork. Porcelain, a Chinese creation, was also perfected during the Tang dynasty after a lengthy period of experimentation. But by the mid-ninth century, the dynasty began to unravel for the usual reasons: corruption in high places and oppression of the peasants. Bandits, warlords, and Turkic interlopers skirmished until, lacking a resolution, North China split into what's known as the Five Dynasties, and the rest of the country was the turf of 10 warlords (euphemistically named the Ten Kingdoms).

What China needed lay just ahead: the Northern and Southern Song dynasties.

> **Han Help** _____
>
> By the ninth century, flower-and-bird painting had taken hold among the "scholar painters" of the court, and edged away from the decorative arts. Plum blossoms, chrysanthemums, and pines, produced with both ink and brush, and an economy of line became its own genre.

The Song Dynasties

The Song rulers were highly cultured, and many of them were artists themselves. The royal painting academy that had fallen by the wayside was reestablished. It became a buoyant and vigorous time in which the art of painting flourished. The literati took on simple subjects—a rock, a tree. The court painters continued the bird-and-flower theme, and the inevitable portraits. They also painted landscapes, and now that Confucianism was in again, family values–type paintings of kids and pets. The imperial style of painting that took hold during the Song dynasties would endure until the present time.

And a whole new school of Chan Buddhist monks were painting in a free and breezy style that was different from that of the courtly as well as the literati schools.

In the thirteenth century, Chinese literature took off. The two most famous plays were written, *The Western Chamber* by Wang Shifu, and *Injustice to Tou O*, by Guan Hanqing.

> **Han Help** _____
>
> Among the most cherished of the later Buddhist works are a pair of 29-foot-long frescos (circa 1279–1368 C.E.) of Tejaprabha Buddha, who protects against natural calamities; and Bhaisajyaguru Buddha, who protects people from untimely death, nightmares, evil apparitions, vicious animals, robbers, and invading states.

Sculpture had still not shrunk back to the size it was before the Buddhist period, but less of it was in stone. The Song sculptors favored the softer, more subtle medium of clay.

The Yuan (Mongol) Dynasty

The Mongols arrived and overthrew the Song dynasties in 1368. They weren't much for court life, so with few portraits and pets to paint, the conservative Royal Painting Academy stagnated. Calligraphy became the genre of the scholar-gentry and was elevated to a form of painting during this period. But the literati painters had a sudden burst of energy and began to produce more dramatic paintings with bolder brushwork.

The Yuan liked massive architecture, curved roofs, and pagodas. They weren't interested in extravagant interiors; they just wanted the wide open spaces of great halls.

In 1368, the Chinese drove out the Mongols and established the Ming dynasty.

The Ming Dynasty

The Ming dynasty is famous for its decorative arts: brightly colored enameled vases and cloisonné, but it also produced some important painters. The Ming established a royal painting academy that drew the bird-and-flower and landscape painters, while the interesting work was going on among the literati. Shen Zhou developed clean-looking genre work of serene people doing ordinary things while Wen Zhengming chose to leave great stretches of blank space in his paintings, with a single tree or boulder as their subjects.

Han Help _____

The classic novels, *The Journey to the West* and *The Golden Lotus,* were written in the sixteenth century and are still popular.

The painter and scholar Dong Qichang took art criticism/history to a new level when, in fine Chinese style, he devoted himself to writing provocative pieces on the history of Chinese painting. They provide valuable insight into the issues of painting in imperial China.

The Qing (Manchu) Dynasty

In 1644, the Manchus (from historical Manchuria) overran the Ming dynasty when it was looking the other way, dealing with political problems. The Manchus happily took on Chinese ways and continued the Ming traditions. They supported a royal painting academy, that had remained stagnant and imitative, and as usual, the literati produced the interesting work. Some of the literati chose to emulate the Yuan masters, or a single master. Others worked on their brushwork and produced edgy, nontraditional paintings that had a vitality lacking in the academy's work.

Perhaps China's greatest novel, *Dream of the Red Chamber*, was written by Cao Xueqin in the eighteenth century.

In 1911, the Qing dynasty and the Qin Empire ended, and China became the Republic of China.

Han Help _____

The Qing built some massive palaces in Beijing that are still in existence.

In 2000, Gao Xingjian, a Chinese writer living in Paris, became the first Chinese author to win the Nobel Prize for literature.

Other Triumphs

No chapter on China's triumphs could fail to note, once again, the Great Wall, and the Grand Canal—two Herculean civil engineering projects that were begun in China's distant past, added to, remodeled, and continue into the future. The Grand Canal, built in the seventh century, was recently linked with a waterway that extended it as far as the outskirts of Beijing. There's even a massive and very controversial project (a la Three Gorges Dam) to redirect the flow of the Grand Canal to the northwest, where the scarcity of water is critical. It's estimated that it would take 50 years to complete!

There are many Chinese ideas and advances that were thought to be European phenomena that were carried to China until Joseph Needham and his colleagues determined that it had been the other way around. A few of them are the following:

- **Second century** B.C.E. Steel produced from cast iron to make farm implements and weaponry.

- **Sixth century** B.C.E. The horse stirrup, and harnessing to advance agriculture.

- **Sixth century** B.C.E. Planting of crops in rows, and use of the iron plow.

And then there's sericulture, to which China has the undisputed claim of originator. Silkworms were cultivated beginning in 1300 B.C.E., or earlier, and the Chinese kept the source and method of processing them into silk a deep, dark secret. In the second century of the Common Era when the Silk Road to the West opened up, Rome became China's main silk customer. The lore is that the Romans spent so much cash on silk that they came close to bankrupting the Roman Empire! Legend has it that some Arabian Silk Road traders eventually captured some Chinese sericulturists and learned how to make silk themselves. Silk is now produced in many parts of the world.

Porcelain, called china for obvious reasons, is another of China's great contributions. Its fragile, translucent appearance is deceiving; it is the hardest of all ceramic products. It was, perhaps independently developed in Europe—after it had been perfected in China.

And then there are ...

- Tung oil, used for varnish.

- Coal, used for heating in China in the fourth century C.E., and not until several centuries later in Europe.

- Zinc, which was used in the eleventh century in coins, along with copper and lead.

Last but not least, two minor triumphs: Playing cards were first used in China at least 1,000 years ago, and the folding umbrella was invented in China in the third century B.C.E.—bamboo frame, of course.

The Least You Need to Know

- China is credited with introducing the mariner's compass, gunpowder, printing, and paper to the world.

- Acupuncture and herbal pharmacology are Chinese medical traditions that are accepted by the Western medical establishment.

- The Shang bronzes and Black (Longshan) Pottery are considered China's highest artistic achievements.

- The Buddhist influence gave rise to China's most accomplished stone sculpture and architecture.

- The Great Wall and the Grand Canal remain mankind's greatest feats of civil engineering.

Part  3

From Mao to the Millenium

These chapters take you from the frenzied days of the beginning of China's communist movement through the period of Jiang Zemin's leadership of the People's Republic of China.

The Long March of the communist revolutionaries produces the leaders of the Chinese Communist Party. Chiang Kaishek's nationalists and Mao Zedong's communists compete for power, form a united front against Japanese aggression, then expand their competition for control of China into a full-scale civil war. Mao becomes the leader of the PRC, and the nationalists flee to Taiwan. Mao's obsession with control brings China some of the darkest days in its history until Deng Xiaoping's leadership brings opening and reform—and the tragedy of the 1989 Tiananmen Square crackdown. When Deng dies, a new team of nonideological technocrats increases the pace of change in China's new economy.

Chapter 9

Mao's Dream

In This Chapter

- ◆ Japanese expansionism poses an increasingly serious threat to China's sovereignty.

- ◆ Chiang and Mao are forced to form a united front against the Japanese.

- ◆ The Japanese invade and occupy China until 1945.

- ◆ Mao develops his concepts for the new communist government he plans to lead.

- ◆ Chiang's forces are defeated by Mao's, and Chiang flees to Taiwan.

- ◆ Mao becomes the absolute ruler of China.

During the early 1930s the Japanese had taken over Manchuria and swarmed through the steppes of Inner Mongolia into China. They set up industries and began to manufacture goods, sometimes with a puppet Chinese industrialist as a front. By the end of 1935, the five northern provinces—Hebei, Shandong, Shaanxi, Qahar, and Suiyuan—were completely Japanese-run. The Japanese even formed a new government near Beijing to run the northern provinces. It was called the East Hebei Anti-Communist Autonomous Government. Including "anti-communist" was a public relations move designed to create the illusion that the Japanese were allies of the

Guomindang government (referred to in the following as "nationalist"), in common cause against the communists. In fact, overpopulated Japan needed China's natural resources, and it was clear that Japanese forces would continue their advance into northern China until they were stopped.

The Japanese Threat

Chiang Kaishek ignored the Japanese threat; he was fixated on eliminating the communists. In fact, he had signed a deal with the Japanese in June 1935, agreeing to withdraw Chinese troops from northern China, leaving the Japanese free to move in. Chiang also promised the Japanese that he would disband the Chinese patriotic societies in the north and ban all anti-Japanese activity.

In the summer of 1935, while Mao Zedong was still on his Long March (see Chapter 5), he appealed to the Chinese people to join with the communists in resisting Japanese aggression. The Chinese Red Army called for an end to Chiang's persecution of the communists and for the formation of a united front against Japan.

The Party vs. the Guomindang

There was mounting public pressure on Chiang Kaishek to fight the Japanese and not the communists. A famous slogan of the period was "Chinese must not fight Chinese."

Chiang resisted the public notion that he had chosen to fight the wrong enemy. His war against the communists continued despite increasing Japanese aggression. He was determined to defeat the communist movement, and had even brought in German military advisers in the early 1930s to help him do it.

Mao was engaged on two fronts: building the Communist Party's rural base and preparing to defend China against Japanese incursions.

Han Help

> The communists wanted a coalition government composed of both communists and nationalists, and a united army. While Chiang was letting the Japanese take what they wanted in the northern provinces, Mao was calling for the confiscation of all Japanese property in China. Opinions differ about the motives behind Chiang's actions, though they were probably mixed; he unquestionably feared the burgeoning power of the CCP, but he also had an affinity for Japan, where he had studied when he was a young man.

Neither the League of Nations nor the United States (which had not joined the league) would commit to defending China against Japanese aggression. There was only one answer—a united front at home.

The Not-So-United Front

In Beijing in 1935, 30,000 students turned out to demonstrate against Chiang's pro-Japanese deal. They shouted "Down with Japanese imperialism!" and "Stop all civil war and unite against Japanese aggression." It was in total defiance of the He-Umezu Agreement banning anti-Japanese activity. Chiang's nationalist police charged the demonstrators and it turned into a riot that lasted until the following day.

Then Chiang Kaishek's generals learned that Chiang had been telling lies about them. To deflect criticism of his pro-Japanese stance he had told each of them that the others were afraid to fight the Japanese. They banded together and vowed to fight the Japanese regardless of Chiang's wishes. When student demonstrations broke out, the military went against Chiang's orders and refused to break them up.

Wise One Says

On December 12, 1936, Chiang was actually kidnapped—in his pajamas—by his own generals when he visited Xian. Zhang Xueliang and other officers captured him, demanded an end to the civil war, and a promise to reorganize the Nanjing government to "save the nation." Stalin still stood by the KMT [Guomindang] leader, thinking he was the only one with a strong enough national presence to instill Marxism, and urged the CCP to negotiate for Chiang's release! It was the heavy hitters like Madame Chiang, her brother T.V. Soong, and Zhou Enlai who forced the reluctant Chiang to give a verbal agreement to redirect his actions.

—Jonathan Spence, *The Search for Modern China*

Eventually, under threat of death at the hands of his own generals unless he agreed to help China unite to resist the Japanese, Chiang called off his war against the communists—at least temporarily.

In December 1936, the nationalists and the communists sat down and talked. The communists pledged to stop trying to overthrow the government. They said they would stop seizing land and would acknowledge that their stronghold in Yan'an was actually part of the same China run by the nationalists. The nationalists pledged to end the civil war and to resist the Japanese.

Even though Chiang and Mao did shift their focus away from one another and concentrate on the Japanese menace, it was only temporary. Both strengthened their military positions during World War II—in anticipation of the full-scale civil war to come.

The Japanese Invasion

On July 11, 1937, Japanese troops crossed the Great Wall into northern China. In response, General Chiang Kaishek ordered the mobilization of the Chinese armies.

Hu Nu?
Japanese troops staged a surprise attack on the Chinese force near a bridge that crossed the Yongding River at Lugouqiao, southwest of Beijing. The attack became known to the world as the Incident at Marco Polo Bridge.

On July 30, Tianjin fell to the Japanese. Beijing fell on August 4. The Japanese went on to bomb Nanjing and occupy Shanghai. They then drove the Chinese up the Yangzi River. The Chinese fought tenaciously, causing the Japanese forces to attack, lose ground, regroup, and attack, over and over again. But by December 1937, the Japanese took Nanjing, the seat of Chiang's nationalist government.

Atrocities

During their six-week assault on Nanjing, it is estimated that the Japanese killed 300,000 Chinese. What's more—and the reason that anti-Japanese sentiment has continued in China to this day—they raped 20,000 of Nanjing's women and murdered many of them afterward.

The recreational use and subsequent murder of the women of Nanjing was an atrocity of historical proportions and is known as "The Rape of Nanjing" (sometimes referred to as Nanking). (It should be noted that there's disagreement in the numbers killed. Ikuhiko Hata, a respected modern historian, asserts that the 300,000 death toll is highly inflated, and that the real figure may be as low as 50,000.)

The soldiers mutilated many of the women before or after killing them. They also raped young children and elderly women. The Rape of Nanjing was heavily documented in journals and eyewitness accounts, and widely covered by the Western press.

Japanese Occupation

It has been said that the Japanese were ordered to treat the Chinese citizens in such a barbaric way so as to better control them as an occupying force, but the reasonable mind refuses to accept this as the only motive. A seething hatred had been released in the most monstrous manner imaginable. Japanese behavior in Nanjing shocked the world, but it did not have the desired effect on the Chinese people. It did not make them meek and subservient before their invaders; rather, it hardened their hatred of the Japanese and bolstered their resolve to get China back under Chinese sovereignty.

Mao Zedong: Social Engineer

During the "lull" in his two-front war against the Japanese and the nationalists, Mao was not idle. At his base in Yan'an he developed new economic, social, and political structures and schemes to put into place when he became China's leader.

He had a stunning capacity to create both long- and short-term plans at the same time, and to put some of his ideas into motion immediately. His policies clearly reflected his first priority: to serve the needs of the peasants. He started rent reduction programs, brought peasants into the political process, and sought to include women, as well. He also planted the seeds of the revolution he would need one day to rule all of China.

Mao's Six Major Campaigns

There were six major campaigns conceived by Mao during the Yan'an era:

- A program to reduce government and army bureaucracy, known as "crack troops and simple administration"

- A program that took intellectuals from the city to the country so that they could meet and mingle with peasants, presumably so that some of that rural goodness would rub off

- Rent reduction

- A "mutual-aid" village economy

- A program called "organizational economy" whereby workers and managers switched positions

- Improvement of education in rural areas

The Three Three Three System

What the communists called the "Three Three Three System" was based on Mao's theory that the government must always rest in the hands of the Communist Party. The theory was put into practice by the communists in the government they were developing in China's communist-controlled areas.

To achieve democracy that gave the peasants a feeling of participation, the government was constructed in traditional pyramid form, with the base being the publicly elected village councils. The councils then chose representatives to the county level, and so forth.

The innovation of the Three Three Three System was that one third of the people elected at every level, by law, had to be members of the Communist Party. This third inevitably comprised the leaders and the directors of the various councils.

Another third were communist supporters but not CCP members, for one reason or another. The remaining third was made up of liberals and the nonaligned. Thus the form of democracy was retained while party control was ensured by the discipline of the communist leaders.

Wise One Says

The importance of peasant support to the communist cause was summed up by its distinctly Chinese slogan: "The soldiers are fish and the people water." The slogan made it clear that the soldiers needed the peasants' help to survive, and that when the enemy attacked, the soldiers would disappear among the peasants.

The communist representatives were a unit; they voted that way, and they maintained control of any issue because they could always find enough non-communist representatives to vote along with them.

It was during the years in Yan'an, a poverty-stricken township in Shaanxi Province, that the ragtag group of communists who survived the Long March were transformed into a force healthy and strong enough to conquer the nation less than two decades later.

Mao was at the peak of his creativity and genius at that time. Those who continue to idolize him, despite his obvious shortcomings in later years, prefer to think of him as he was in the 1930s at Yan'an.

The CCP's Leaders

The first leaders of the Chinese Communist Party (CCP) were not all from common peasant families. In fact, many were from moderately well-to-do families that provided them with early formal education.

Deng Xiaoping

Deng Xiaoping was born in 1904 in Sichuan Province, into a landlord family. At the age of 16, he went to study in France, where he joined a CCP group organized by Zhou Enlai. He then studied in Moscow in 1925, before returning to China in 1927 to work for the CCP's Shanghai office. During the Long March, Deng served as the political instructor for Lin Biao's Red Army First Corps.

Lin Biao

Lin Biao was born in 1908 in Hubei Province, where his family owned a factory. He studied at Whampoa Military Academy in the mid-1920s, and fought with Chiang Kaishek in the 1927 efforts to reunify northern China. Once Chiang began to purge the communists, Lin escaped to the CCP's Jiangxi stronghold. Lin rose through the ranks of the Red Army, and proved to be an excellent military strategist during the Long March. In the 1960s, his claim to fame was compiling *The Quotations of Chairman Mao*, better known as the "Little Red Book."

Liu Shaoqi

The youngest of nine children, Liu was born into a wealthy Hunan family in 1898. He was educated in the Soviet Union in the 1920s. When he returned to China, he proved to be a strong labor organizer and led several workers' strikes in the late 1920s. He was an eloquent and forceful organizer for the CCP, and was known for his philosophy blending Confucian ideals of discipline with Marxism. By the end of the Long March, when the communists were retrenched in Yan'an, Liu had emerged as Mao's right-hand man.

Zhou Enlai the Mediator

Zhou Enlai, like many of the CCP's leaders, was hardly from peasant stock. Born into a gentry family in Jiangsu Province, he was educated at Nankai University. He had also studied in France, where he helped set up CCP branches. During the May 4th Movement, Zhou led the Tianjin students' protests.

In 1937, having proven himself a staunch ally on the Long March, Zhou Enlai became Mao's number one front man for all external relations. Zhou was a natural in the role, as he was a suave and charming negotiator. It was Zhou whom Mao sent to Chiang Kaishek to negotiate the united front in the struggle against Japanese imperialism. This put Zhou in a position of great power since he was the only person on earth who spoke to both Mao Zedong and Chiang Kaishek.

World War II

China struggled on during the last of the 1930s, a period when Chiang's power grew. The country received some aid from the Soviet Union, which knew that Japan had their eyes on Siberia and figured it was in their best interests to prevent the Japanese from getting too strong a foothold in China.

By the end of the 1930s, the war in China was at a stalemate, with the Japanese in control of Manchuria, the coasts, and the lower Yangzi Valley. To advance any farther would have been difficult because of natural barriers such as mountain ranges, which are hard to cross under ideal circumstances.

By 1940, Japan was a member of the Rome-Berlin Axis with Germany and Italy, and the three were waging war on the rest of Europe. Japan proved it was as land-hungry as ever when, after France fell to Nazi Germany, it pounced on France's eastern outpost in Indochina.

Tensions in the rest of the world were heating up, which distracted some of China's potential allies. Nazi Germany, which had been so helpful to Chiang, was threatening Britain and France. The United States was sympathetic to China's cause but was far more concerned with the situation in Europe.

On December 7, 1941, the Japanese inadvertently gave the Chinese struggle its biggest boost when they bombed the U.S. Navy at Pearl Harbor in Hawaii. The move helped the Chinese in two ways. For one thing, it gave the Japanese a new front to fight; defending the land they'd taken in China would prove difficult while they were battling the United States for possession of various Pacific islands.

Japan's bombing of Pearl Harbor also created a new and powerful ally for China—the United States. China and the United States were now at war with the same country. The U.S. Army-Air Force "Flying Tigers" who had been helping launch Chiang Kaishek's air force were reorganized and refortified. The United States instantly gave China a half-billion-dollar loan to help shore up their near empty treasury, along with $630 million in lend-lease supplies. There was no united front when it came to allocating these resources, however; Chiang Kaishek held the purse strings tightly.

In March 1945, as World War II was winding to a close in the Pacific, 914 Chinese counties were said to be under the control of the Japanese. But the truth was that 678 of these counties were actually being ruled by the communist forces of Mao Zedong. Even then, the communists were in control of areas populated by 100,000,000 people. The Eighth Route Army, formerly known as the Red Army, numbered 330,000 men and women; the New Fourth Army, formed initially from the CCP forces Mao had left behind at the start of the Long March, numbered 150,000. Both had been under nominal Guomindang control during World War II, but had veteran CCP officers in command. In South China the communist guerrillas behind the Japanese lines numbered around 30,000.

Han Help

In areas that were controlled by the communists, the new rulers were applying some of the principles Mao had developed in Yan'an. They worked to reduce rents and build a sound representative government. Thus they could present themselves to the world as reformers. It certainly sounded better in the papers than revolutionaries.

With the Japanese vanquished, China had emerged as the number one power in Asia. It was considered one of the Big Five powers in the world, and it became a charter member in a new league of nations—this time called the United Nations.

The Japanese had kicked the Europeans out of Asia, in essence doing China a huge favor, and thus ended 400 years of European colonialism on the Asian continent.

Though the Americans would take most of the credit for the defeat of the Japanese in World War II, the Chinese had certainly done their share. The United States would have had a much rougher time island-hopping their way toward Okinawa if as many as two million Japanese troops had not been needed to fight the Chinese. A greater percentage of the total Japanese war effort went toward the Chinese front than is generally recognized in the United States. More than half of Japan's armed personnel during the World War II fought in China. The Japanese spent the equivalent of $34 billion on their war effort. Out of that, $12 billion was spent on the war in China, in which the Chinese military killed 396,040 Japanese soldiers.

The bulk of the Chinese fighting had been done by Chiang's forces, while the communists had stayed on the sidelines and built party solidarity. The nationalists were so exhausted by the war effort that when peace came they found themselves barely strong enough to rule.

China was in a poor economic state. The war effort had been paid for with borrowed money. To make up for the deficit more money had been printed, but that only spawned crippling inflation.

> ### Hu Nu?
>
> Total number of Chinese troops during World War II: 14,000,000. Of those, 1,319,958 were killed, 1,761,355 were wounded, and 130,126 were listed as missing.

The people were war-weary and unhappy with the way things were. They blamed the nationalists—people always blame those in charge, of course—a point that Mao would not fail to exploit.

The Japanese surrendered to the Chinese in September 1945, and their occupying forces quickly withdrew from mainland China. At the same time the Soviets signed an agreement with China's nationalist government to recognize that government as the one and only government of China, and to supply military support in the event of uprisings. The United States, by the way, signed a similar agreement with the nationalist government—now in Taiwan—but has since reinterpreted its relationship with the island. The United States now claims that it will protect Taiwan if attacked, but that it recognizes the People's Republic as the rightful government of China.

In one short year after the Japanese pulled out of China, Chiang Kaishek had managed to alienate every element of Chinese society. The workers hated him because there was no work. The peasants hated him because they were overtaxed, cheated, and mistreated by his officials. And the middle class hated him because his policies prevented industrial and business profitability.

Civil War in China

Things came to a head in May 1946. The Russians, who occupied Manchuria at the end of World War II, had stripped that land of all it was worth and left. When the Russians left there was a rush to fill the power vacuum.

The nationalists hurried there as fast as they could, but found it already occupied by Lin Biao's communist troops. That May, Chiang sent troops into Manchuria to get the communists out, and the battle was on. The United States had been trying to broker a compromise between the Guomindang and the CCP, but was growing less confident about Chiang's ability to unite and rule a democratic China. To U.S. advisors and envoys alike, corruption was clearly rampant throughout the Guomindang.

On June 17, Chiang ordered the communists to withdraw from an area that started at the Yangzi River and included parts of Manchuria. On June 24, the attack was begun against communist bases in central China. The communists retaliated by attacking the nationalists in Shandong Province. By August 1946, the civil war was going full blast.

Han Help

War by the numbers: When the Chinese civil war began, the nationalist army had about 3,000,000 troops. The communist army had about 1,000,000.

The communists finally crossed the Yangzi in spectacular fashion on April 21, 1949. The riverfront was 500 kilometers long, extending from a point northeast of Jiujiang on the west to Jiangyin on the east.

The Red Army cut through the nationalists with ease, overwhelming their defenses. On May 27, the communists conquered Shanghai. Nanjing was taken on December 4. By the end of the year all of the mainland of China was under communist control, with the exception of Tibet.

Chiang Flees to Taiwan

The nationalists moved south, ahead of the advancing communist armies. At first Chiang went to Guangzhou. He considered moving back to Chongqing to try to hold out as he had against the Japanese, but the communists were another matter. The communists had become so popular, and Chiang so unpopular, that he could expect no support from the people at all.

So Chiang cast his eyes on Taiwan. In 1947, the Taiwanese rose up against the nationalists, whom they detested. The nationalists responded with a bloodbath. In 1949, the Taiwanese were still reeling from the nationalists' punch, so it was no problem for Chiang and his troops to take over the island. They set up a government in exile, the Republic of China, and there it would remain until Chiang could rise up and take over mainland China once again … or so they hoped.

Mao now had more power every day. In June 1949, he ordained the formation of a dictatorship of the proletariat that would be led by the working class through the Communist Party. Reactionaries would be deprived the right of freedom of expression. Only the people could speak. Mao also announced the Communist Party's intention of changing China from an agricultural country into an industrial economy.

First there would be the new democracy; it would evolve into socialism; and finally China would achieve what the Soviet Union had not—true communism, classless, and with plenty for all. A law establishing the Central People's Government was passed by the People's Political Consultative Conference in October 1949. On the mainland, the communists were firmly in charge—but could they govern?

As soon as Mao gained control of China, a China worn out from years of war and economic struggle, he began to put into effect the social plans he had devised in Yan'an during World War II.

His doctrine was labeled the "Mao Zedong Thought" and it was disseminated throughout China. Mao said that the communists' military victory was only the beginning of the story, and it was what they did now that they were in power that mattered.

"The Chinese revolution is great," Mao said. "But the road after the revolution will be longer, the work greater and more arduous."

Mao's New Government

Mao's doctrine represented a sharp change from all of the ruling doctrines to precede it. Previously, the masses had been trained to pursue social harmony. Yet Mao's vision remained revolutionary—full of violence and struggle—even after control was his.

Mao said that if China lived by the rules of the Chinese Communist Party, it would experience unprecedented success in literature, military strength, and political organization.

In September 1949, Mao laid out the new China's constitutional structure. Power would be divided among the party, the government, and the army. The party came under the Central Committee, whose Politburo effectively controlled party direction. The five-member Politburo Standing Committee in 1949 was made up of Mao, Liu Shaoqi, Zhou Enlai, Zhu De, and Chen Yun. In practice, the day-to-day details of running the country were in the hands of the Politburo's Standing Committee.

> ## Hu Nu?
>
> Mao Zedong was the first leader of an Asian communist party to reach that position without the official backing of the Soviet Union. When Mao assumed control of China in 1949, he had never been to Moscow and had had minimal direct contact with Soviet leaders.

China's government structure was led by the Central People's Government Council. Once again, Mao was in charge, with Zhu De and Liu Shaoqi serving as two of his six vice-chairmen.

There was also a State Council, headed by the premier, Zhou Enlai. Under him were several vice-premiers, and 24 ministries.

The State Council had equal power with two other groups: the People's Supreme Court and the Procurator-General's Office. All the top posts were filled by men with considerable CCP and Long March credentials—and considerable loyalty to Mao Zedong.

Originally, China was divided up into six "Great Administrative Areas," each of which was in charge of several provinces. But this turned out to be an unnecessary level of organization, so after 1953, all matters were handled on either a national or a provincial basis.

In 1953, all Chinese citizens were granted voting rights. Only those deemed to be "counterrevolutionaries" and landlords were forbidden to vote. (By Mao's way of thinking, no man could be more evil than he who privately owned land and charged rent to others. Under Mao's system, there would be only one landlord: the State.)

Mao knew that one method of avoiding problems when implementing his new government was to go slow with communist changes in areas where traditions were very old and hard to break. One of these areas was the south of China, where the Guomindang base had been solid.

The first National People's Congress met during the second half of September 1954, and during that stretch, ratified a new Chinese constitution. The constitution consisted of 4 chapters and 106 articles outlining, among other things, the government structure and the rights of Chinese citizens.

China's political and governmental systems seemed more complex than they actually were because there was so much overlap. There were many powerful positions in China, both in the government and in the Chinese Communist Party—but they were held by comparatively few men. Mao wore the most hats of all.

At the same time, for example, Mao was chairman of the following:

♦ Chinese Communist Party Central Committee

♦ Politburo

♦ Central Secretariat

♦ People's Republic

♦ Revolutionary Military Council

♦ National People's Congress

Rule number one of the Chinese Communist Party, then as now, is that there shall be no threat to the absolute power of the Chinese Communist Party. Yet, despite the fact that China is a one-party country and that party is in absolute control, the Chinese maintain the illusion of being a multi-party system like that of the United States, Great Britain, and many other countries.

Other parties are allowed to exist only if they agree with every policy of the Chinese Communist Party. During the early years of Mao's rule, there were six political parties in China besides the communists, but significantly, all of them had existed before the communist takeover and none of them had any power whatsoever. The nationalists were effectively shut out for being "reactionary."

The new Chinese government seemed benevolent enough during its first year. Oh sure, Marxist courses were now mandatory in schools. Chinese newspapers had become organs of the government. But the world saw the communists' revolution as a relatively benign one, certainly less savage than the Bolshevik Revolution had been. And much of that perception was because of the utopian idealism of Mao's words. Marxist philosophy said that society must transform from feudalism to capitalism to socialism, but that couldn't be applied in China because China did not have the form of capitalism Marx was referring to. Mao substituted, in his doctrine, something called the "New Democracy." Only by advancing through this "New Democracy" stage could true socialism be achieved. In the New Democracy, the four classes were expected to coexist and non-communist factions would be allowed to exist.

Mao's Programs and Plans

Mao saw what the rest of the world could not see: Governing China as one single nation, an indivisible unit, was going to be very difficult. It had been centuries since all of China had functioned under a single government. But he had spent years making big plans that he hoped would unify China and solve its problems.

Land Reform

In the countryside it was necessary for the communists to get the landlords to reduce their rents substantially without completely disrupting the rural economy. By the autumn of 1950, the land reform efforts had affected 100 million peasants, with landlords constituting 4 percent of the total. There were "only" 364 million peasants and 10 million landlords left to go.

The destruction of the old agrarian system lasted until 1952, by which time the bulk of the landlords were out of business and most of the land had been redistributed. To rid China forever of landlords, China adopted, in June 1950, the Agrarian Reform Law, which abolished the "land ownership system of feudal exploitation." Land that was privately owned was seized by the state and redistributed among the peasants.

The new law subdivided China's rural population into five categories:

◆ Landlords who owned land that was worked by others

◆ Rich peasants who owned land and worked it themselves with the help of poor peasants

◆ Middle peasants who owned land but worked it entirely by themselves

◆ Poor peasants who had to rent land from others

◆ Hired hands who owned no land and lived on the wages from their labor

The top two categories did not fare well under the new law. Most often they were rounded up and executed—or at least forced to confess their evil ways. Though Mao's concepts often seemed benign and even utopian on paper, they were being implemented by the same corrupt system that had plagued China for hundreds of years.

Language Lesson

A **mou** is a unit of land equivalent to approximately one sixth of an acre.

The communists' agrarian revolution was complete by December 1952. During that time, 700 million *mou* had been distributed to 300 million peasants.

Agricultural Collectivization

The drive toward the collectivization of China's farmland began in 1953. The object of the program was to increase food production so that China would be able to continue to feed its people, even as its population grew dramatically. The program also discouraged the existence of "rich peasants" and encouraged agricultural specialization.

The Chinese farmers were eased into the collectivization program in three stages:

1. Peasants pooled their resources, both tools and labor, to accomplish planting and harvesting in what were known as "mutual aid" teams.

2. Peasants pooled not only their labor and their tools, but their land as well. Each peasant still owned his own land, in theory, but the lines of ownership were blurred.

3. All members of the community collectively owned the land and worked together for the common good. These farm units were called "socialized cooperatives."

The program was accomplished with remarkable speed. In three years, 96 percent of all peasants in China were members of a cooperative. By 1957, that figure was close to 100 percent. More than three quarters of a million cooperative farms were set up during the agricultural collectivization, each with about 160 families, or 650 persons.

Han Help

The only privately owned farmland allowed was small plots that could be owned by an individual for the purpose of growing vegetables for private consumption.

Industrial Development

According to Mao, capitalism was not totally without its place in the new system. Some businesses were allowed to remain privately owned.

In 1953, China announced its first "Five-Year Plan" to expand industry. It turned out that the leaders didn't know where to begin to implement the plan, and the first couple of years were frittered away as they tried to determine a suitable first step.

The plan called for the construction of 694 factories and plants across China. Of them, 156 were to be built with financial aid from the

Wise One Says

Mao's guidelines went like this: "In this period all capitalist elements in the cities and countryside which are not harmful but beneficial to the national economy should be allowed to exist and expand."

Soviet Union. Despite the slow start, the Five-Year Plan turned out to be a smashing success. In 1956, industrial output in China increased by 25 percent, while capital investment increased by 60 percent. Grain output, coal production, steel production, and electricity production were all above the goals that had been set. The first Five-Year Plan was such a success that another one was called for immediately.

Hu Nu?

As industrial productivity grew rapidly during the 1950s, the government revamped China's education system to meet the growing need for technicians and engineers. Liberal arts were discouraged and some general universities were replaced by technical institutes. The leadership also welcomed thousands of Soviet technical advisers in the 1950s to help build up China's industries and infrastructure.

New Foreign Policy

Domestic concerns were not the only things on Mao's mind during his first months as the ruler of China. He had foreign affairs to think about as well, and relations with the Soviet Union and the United States were high on his priority list. Mao believed that the United States and the Soviet Union were preparing for war against one another. He also believed that the United States held the key to a peaceful settlement of China's problems. In order to bring about such a settlement, Mao believed, the United States would have to abandon its support of Chiang Kaishek.

Although the United States might not have liked to think so, the Chinese could get by without U.S. help in any form. Mao might have liked the aid, but he would not have liked the strings that would have been attached. Mao had no intention of having anything to do with the United States—certainly not as long as they were giving military support to his archenemy.

Besides, the communists had taken over in China in the midst of the Cold War. It was a world in which it was difficult to be friends with both the United States and the Soviet Union, so Mao's choice was easy. He would be friends with the Russians. They had a history of supporting Chinese revolutions. They had helped the Chinese revolutionaries in the Revolution of 1911, and back in the 1920s, Russia had sent advisors, guns, and money to the infant Republic of China.

The moment the communists conquered China, the Soviets recognized them as China's official government. When Mao made his first foreign visit as Chinese leader, he went to Moscow.

Wise One Says

Mao was disdainful of the Americans as well as Chiang Kaishek. He called them "paper tigers" and said that their power would erode with time. "Take the case of China," he said. "We have only millet plus rifles to rely on, but history will finally prove that our millet plus rifles is more powerful than Chiang Kaishek's airplanes plus tanks. Although the Chinese people still face many difficulties and will long suffer hardships from the joint attacks of U.S. imperialism and the Chinese reactionaries, the day will come when those reactionaries are defeated and we are victorious. The reason is simply this: The reactionaries represent reaction, we represent progress."

In February 1950, China signed the Treaty of Friendship and Alliance with the Soviet Union. The Russians promised to return the Manchurian railways and Port Arthur, but the Chinese had to give up their desire to have Outer Mongolia returned to the Chinese fold.

The parts of China along the Manchurian-Siberian border that Russia had snipped off years before were not returned either, and incipient disputes ran almost all the way along the common border.

The real test, though, came on the Korean peninsula. On October 8, 1950, Mao Zedong said, "The Chinese and Korean comrades should unite as closely as brothers, go through thick and thin together, stick together in life and death and fight to the end to defeat their common enemy."

That common enemy, of course, was the United States, which had just signed on to help South Korea in its civil war against the communist- and Chinese-backed North Koreans. The international balance of power—and China's fortunes—were about to change dramatically.

The Least You Need to Know

- Japan's aggression was a constant in the history of modern China.
- The Rape of Nanjing perpetrated by Japanese forces was one of the greatest atrocities in history.
- Chiang Kaishek and Mao Zedong had diametrically opposed ideas of how to unite and reform China's government.
- Mao built a communist base and a set of principles that were powerful enough to drive out Chiang's nationalists.
- Once it finally climbed into the driver's seat, the CCP had a long road ahead of it to reform the Chinese people and restructure the economy.

Chapter 10

Mao's Disaster

In This Chapter

- ◆ The Chinese Communist Party establishes control of the Chinese people through mass campaigns.
- ◆ The Hundred Flowers Campaign encouraging free expression proves a harsh blow to China's scholarly and professional classes.
- ◆ The Great Leap Forward establishes the commune system to improve the rural economy.
- ◆ The Gang of Four and the Red Guards launch the Great Proletarian Cultural Revolution, one of the darkest times in twentieth-century China.
- ◆ Chairman Mao loses his grip, and then dies, precipitating a struggle for succession.

The communists had not been in power for long when it first became apparent that Mao's theories, which looked great on paper, did not always work in the real world.

For one thing, Mao's new approaches to solving China's problems needed intelligent and devoted people to set up and run the enormous new government and its colossal number of programs and plans. They were being steeped in Communist Party ideology and trained for the job, but there weren't enough of them yet. Meanwhile, the whole ambitious structure was still, in great part, in the hands of the corrupt and jaded bureaucrats of the old regime.

After the successful revolution, the people were giddy with the idea of all the new possibilities that had been opened up to them through Mao's programs. They had higher aspirations and more energy. It quickly became clear that the survivors of the Long March would have to share their power with younger and less predictable men and women who would lay the imprint of their own character on Mao's programs.

Mass Campaigns

By 1951, the Communist Party cadres were joined by an increasing number of young people who were instructed to observe the class structures of the villages and become more familiar with the local people. Then the cadres organized the peasants into village associations. The associations chose delegates to county congresses and these, in turn, sent delegates to congresses at the provincial level.

Solving class struggle was Mao's mission, and anyone who was not completely committed to it was a "class enemy." As the dynastic rulers of China had done, Mao set in motion his plan to establish a firm foundation for his government. The cadres held continual meetings to indoctrinate the locals in party ideology. Informers identified those who undermined the party, and appropriate punishment was meted out. Control was the order of the day.

Special people's tribunals were established by the party, and those who rose in the hierarchy were the ruthless and cruel.

Mass campaigns were one of the tools the CCP used to teach Mao Zedong thought, and also identify dedicated potential leaders. The CCP had already learned during the Yan'an period how "self-rectification" and group pressure could be effective ways to strengthen party unity. Thus, in the 1950s, a series of mass campaigns were initiated to investigate foreign companies, the bourgeoisie, landlords, and anyone associated with the Guomindang—as well as the party itself. At the same time, the CCP was quietly collecting all the weapons that were left over from the many years of fighting. There would be no room for armed insurrection in the New China; nor would there be a return to a China ruled by competing warlords.

Han Help _____

While the countryside was being cleansed of "class enemies" Chinese troops were fighting U.S. and UN forces who were trying to prevent communist northern Korea from taking over southern Korea. By the end of 1950, there were few foreigners left in China, other than Soviet advisers. Those who had run schools, orphanages, companies, and other businesses had fled. The Chinese associates they left behind would later pay a heavy price for their foreign connections.

Mao soon removed from the village councils the power to sanction arrests and executions and put that power back into the hands of the prefectural authorities. Cadres settled in among the workers in factories and businesses to put the pressure on "bourgeois" employers.

Han Help _____

In Shanghai, hundreds were harassed to the point of committing suicide, but even if they confessed to crimes against the state they were not killed. Mao's instructions were to harry the bourgeoisie but not to eliminate them; the bourgeoisie were to be rendered subservient.

In 1953, the Communist Party of China declared that the cities and towns of China were now corruption free. Of course nothing could have been farther from the truth; now the corruption was merely less visible than it had been before.

Thought Reform

In order to teach the people the ways of Chinese communism and to prevent dissent, several programs were put in place. Semi-governmental organizations were formed so that every citizen would have an outlet to receive the government's and the party's teachings. Among the organizations that citizens were expected to join were the following:

- ◆ All-China Federation of Democratic Youth
- ◆ All-China Federation of Trade Unions
- ◆ All-China Democratic Women's Federation
- ◆ Young Pioneers
- ◆ Democratic Youth League

The lessons that citizens learned at their weekly meetings involved forging a new lifestyle *(zuo feng)*, that is, becoming a "New Socialist Man." It required more than just maintaining socialist habits; it also involved squealing on anyone who *wasn't* maintaining good socialist habits.

Language Lesson

Xi nao means brainwashing.

Those who didn't get with the program were given a thorough *xi nao*, a program of psychological coercion lasting from several months to a year. An individual was isolated with only the works of Marx, Lenin, Stalin, or Mao to read, in order to be slowly convinced that the communist way was the only way.

In these first years of communist control of China, the number of people killed for voicing their negative opinions of the party was, by friendly estimate, around three million. Unfriendly estimates are much higher. Dissenters were arrested, executed, or told "You are sick, Comrade," and subjected to brainwashing.

And it soon became clear that even those in the top ranks of the CCP leadership were vulnerable. Two members of the Chinese Communist Party's Central Committee, Gao Gang and Rao Shushi, disagreed with some fundamental economic policies of the party and began to campaign for new members of the committee to be chosen from those who thought as they did. Mao quickly made the point that he saw any dissent as a threat to his leadership that could not be tolerated; he then ejected six committee members, including Gao and Rao. From then on, party members who didn't agree with Mao kept their mouths shut. Those who didn't hold their tongues often found themselves fired from their jobs or harassed into subservience in other ways.

China's intellectuals—most of whom had received foreign training, or had been associated with the Guomindang government in some way—had been working hard to prove their loyalty to the new regime. Many intellectuals had taken special courses in 1950 and 1951, spending months studying Mao Zedong's theories, as well as standard Marxist-Leninist principles. Of course, they also prepared "self-criticisms" of their most obvious "flaw," as a group—their privileged class background. Significantly, though, there were hundreds of Chinese intellectuals who chose to return to China after 1949, and were eager to play their part in the formation of a new Chinese society.

Mao, no intellectual slouch himself, was smart enough to see that intellectuals in all fields could help with his overall goals. Zhou Enlai, Lin Biao, and Deng Xiaoping all agreed with Mao that tolerating a little criticism was acceptable, given the contributions being made by the intellectuals. But others within the party leadership—notably those in charge of military affairs, such as Zhu De and Peng Dehuai—felt the party was threatened by the winds of dissent.

The Hundred Flowers Debacle

This was no delicate difference of opinion within the party, but the beginnings of heated debate within the leadership. Events outside of China had an impact on the inner workings of the CCP leadership. Did the Hungarians revolt against the communist regime because the Soviets had been too harsh? That was Mao's view, it seems. In February 1957, reiterating the theme of a little-heralded speech he had made some months earlier, Mao urged unity, and less repression. His phrase, "Let a hundred flowers bloom together, let a hundred schools of thought contend ..." prompted many intellectuals to voice their opinions, once he finally got the party to agree with him. Students and intellectuals took Mao up on his invitation to speak their minds, criticizing everything—including Mao Zedong and the Chinese Communist Party. At Beijing University, students created huge posters of their criticisms and mounted them on a "Democracy Wall" for all to see.

Within a matter of weeks, the party leaders in several provinces, with the backing of the hardliners in Beijing, went on the counterattack. Mao quickly saw that he could not win the fight, and retreated to revise his initial speech. Lo and behold, the revised document was suddenly much more critical of intellectuals who did not support the socialist cause. The Hundred Flowers were crushed just as fast as they had bloomed. The teachers and students who had been responsible for the wall posters were hunted down. Leading scholars in many different fields were labeled as "rightists," and many were punished by being sent to labor camps or to the countryside to work. All told, some 300,000 intellectuals were denounced, their lives and careers ruined. Others, not so fortunate, were executed. In hindsight, the Hundred Flowers debacle is still puzzling. Many scholars of Chinese politics feel that Mao had been shaken by the events in Hungary. Fearful that this type of mass dissatisfaction would result in the downfall of the Chinese Communist Party, he had perhaps hoped his rhetoric would let a little bit of steam out of the pressure cooker.

Cynics would counter, perhaps, that Mao allowed dissidents to speak up for a brief time simply so that they could be identified and subsequently "purged." After all, he was known for his cunning; intellectuals were the enemy and it was a good way to smoke them out and destroy them.

Or it is always possible that the Hundred Flowers Campaign was launched with the intention of hearing and responding to the criticisms that would follow—but that Mao

Hu Nu?
When Mao took a vote among those on the Central Committee of the Chinese Communist Party to revoke the "Hundred Flowers" policy, all but one voted with Mao. The lone dissenter was Deng Xiaoping, who would one day lead China himself. Deng was a good follower who bowed to Mao's wishes and accepted the new policy.

had no clue how loud and widespread the attack on the CCP would be. This would make Mao a brilliant philosopher—but a tragically poor administrator.

Whichever the true reason for launching the campaign, it was a particularly short-lived one. After a mere six weeks, China's experiment with free speech was quickly curtailed.

The Great Leap Forward

The political tensions that led to the Hundred Flowers Campaign didn't end there. Another big debate within the CCP leadership had to do with the economy. Mao's first Five-Year Plan had been a huge success, and there were immediate plans for a second one, this one even more ambitious and aggressive. While the first Five-Year Plan had resulted in many new, large state-owned factories that were now up and running, agricultural production had not increased as fast. Once again, Mao's theory of "continual revolution" won out over more moderate plans for both agricultural and industrial reforms.

Zhou Enlai, for example, was in favor of increasing production by increasing financial incentives for farmers, and making fertilizer and other inputs more affordable. Mao was in favor of another mass campaign.

The second Five-Year Plan was announced by the National People's Congress in February 1958. The communists proclaimed that through the development of Chinese industry, great economic growth would be accomplished.

China wanted to catch up to the rest of the modern world as an industrial nation. Mao, for example, wanted to surpass Great Britain as a producer of steel. And there were more than just lofty goals at stake: China had borrowed heavily from the Soviet Union to launch new industries, and needed some huge grain crops to repay its debt.

The plan called for the following:

+ 19-percent increase in steel production

+ 18-percent increase in electricity production

+ 17-percent increase in coal output

And they wanted to do it all as fast as possible. In fact, "More, faster, better, cheaper" was the slogan. But as usual, there were problems. It took an enormous amount of capital to industrialize, and the funds just weren't there. In the factories and plants that did exist, workers didn't have a chance of getting ahead, or even of getting paid fairly, so it was difficult to get them to work harder. This was particularly true because the government, their employer, couldn't afford to pay them very well.

Mobilizing the Peasants

The CCP began experimenting again, this time with massive engineering projects designed to boost irrigation. People power was what was needed, along with some good slogans, a few model workers, and socialist principles. In early 1958, according to CCP claims, over 100 million peasants had been mobilized to work on a series of irrigation projects.

But taking this many men out of the fields meant that the women left at home would have to take up the slack. Or, as the popular slogan went, the women of China would have to "hold up half the sky." Party leaders soon realized that it would be possible to put even more women to work in the fields and in the new industries the CCP was starting up in many rural areas. There was one catch though: To get women working outside the home, it was necessary to centralize their domestic duties such as cooking and caring for children.

The organization of "people's communes" *(renmin gongshe)* was the next step in the quest for increased agricultural and industrial output. The transformation of China's cooperatives into larger communes was quick. By the end of 1958, over 90 percent of the rural population was now part of a people's commune. Communal dining, laundries, schools, health care, and other services were all lauded by the party as "leading peasants toward a happier collective life."

At the peak of the Great Leap Forward, China had 26,000 communes. Communes consisted of an average of 30 cooperatives of about 5,000 households, or 20,000 people apiece. They were designed to be large enough to be efficient, yet small enough to adapt quickly to changes in the local weather and the countryside. After the first year, everything pointed to the success of the Great Leap Forward.

In a typical people's commune, men and women went to work in the fields every day. Households were separated; it was thought that the nuclear family discouraged communal thinking. A good commune, said Mao, should be *da* (large) and *gong* (public). Mao's theories on communal living were adapted from those of Kang Yuwei, who wrote during the Qing dynasty that in a utopian land there is no private property, ownership, commerce, or industry. But there would be public hospitals, education, and welfare.

A good harvest in the summer of 1958 helped fuel the euphoria about the Great Leap Forward. From the commune leaders' reports, Chinese officials proclaimed that China's agricultural difficulties were in the past. The country could now produce as much grain as it needed. Some officials, however, warned that the commune leaders were eager to please and that there was exaggeration in productivity figures across the board.

China Falls Back

As it turned out, warnings that the figures were exaggerated reflected the reality. Grain production for 1958 had not been 375 million tons as the commune leaders had claimed, but only 250 million tons. The peasants, by Great Leap design, had increased crop cultivation and the crops had been planted as usual. But there was so much local political activity and so many party study sessions going on that many crops were left unharvested. Storage and transportation problems resulted in further losses. The commune leaders, in an effort to make the Five-Year Plan appear successful, had "cooked the books." The inflated figures were happily passed up through the party bureaucracy to Mao. The Great Leap Forward had been a failure; the cover-up was primarily for the purpose of keeping Chairman Mao happy.

By 1959, the problems worsened considerably. Widespread floods in 1959 and 1960 made for dismal harvests. Grain production was off so much that China was forced to purchase 10 million tons of wheat from other countries. By 1960, there was bad weather, a drought, and famine.

It is estimated that as many as 20 million Chinese people starved to death during the famine. Children were the hardest hit. (When your mother told you to eat your lima beans because there were kids starving in China, this is the famine she was talking about.)

Agriculturally, the Great Leap Forward was a disaster. Industrially, the "backyard furnaces" that had sprung up in commune after commune certainly boosted China's steel production. Unfortunately, most of the output was poor quality, and had few uses.

Socially, the Great Leap Forward produced a new group of communist heroes—and a host of patriotic songs and stories about these brave men and women who risked life and limb to boost production. And there were tangible economic benefits for several of China's poorer interior regions, which now had some industrial facilities.

Wise One Says

Liu Shaoqi, second to Mao in the Chinese Communist Party after 1949 and later president of China, said, speaking of the Chinese famine: "The problems were not caused by natural calamities. They were man-made." Perhaps this sidebar should be called "Truthful One Says," as the wisdom of Liu's making such a statement was highly questionable. It's not surprising that he was imprisoned in 1968 and died there the following year.

Politically, the Great Leap Forward opened the door for criticism of Mao and his vision of a happy and productive socialist society. There was no choice but to abandon the policies of the Great Leap Forward; the movement had actually set the Chinese economy back several years. Most of the party leadership felt that the country needed to return to central planning and allocation as quickly as possible. Even before the famine of 1960, some communes were disbanding in favor of a much smaller unit, the production brigade.

But Peng Dehuai was the only one within the top party ranks to criticize Mao directly for the failures of the Great Leap Forward. Mao's response was a quick counterattack in which he labeled Peng a "rightist" and an "opportunist." Peng was stripped of his position.

While Mao may have been able to oust Peng Dehuai, it was now clear that he was not the undisputed leader of a unified Chinese Communist Party. The party was, in the early 1960s, split into factions that fell into two wings. Mao believed that the class struggle could only be solved through a state of continual revolution by the peasants. The bureaucracy of party officials and activists he had built had taken on an enfranchised life of its own, and party leaders Liu Shaoqi and Deng Xiaoping were more concerned with improving the local-central government structure that was in place than in perennial revolution. Zhou Enlai was, as always, calming troubled waters and negotiating agreements. (See Chapter 12 for more about Zhou, Liu, and Deng). In another setting they would have led the loyal opposition; in Mao's China they could survive only by being yes men. Mao, of course, controlled the most powerful wing of the party.

Readjustment and Recovery

Yes, the Great Leap Forward was a mistake, Mao finally conceded, but the country could move on. To recover, Chinese leaders, even Mao, knew that the industrialization and modernization of the country would have to wait; they would have to focus once again on producing an adequate amount of food to feed the people of China.

The idea was not to betray Mao's concepts, but rather to apply them to undertakings that were feasible. Some industries were still encouraged, particularly those that supported agriculture. The production of chemical fertilizer, for example, increased rapidly. Agricultural recovery would take some years, so millions of people began to be relocated to rural areas to help out.

New programs to modernize agricultural techniques were put in place. Irrigation and water conservation programs were installed for dry areas. Privately owned lands, previously for privately consumed vegetables only, were enlarged, and citizens were now allowed to sell some of the vegetables. By the end of 1962, the worst was over and China appeared to be on the road to recovery.

Han Help

After years of strained relations over doctrinal differences, in 1963, China and the Soviet Union, the Goliaths of communism, formally parted ideological company. The last of the Soviet advisors was escorted out of the country. Mao became more convinced than ever that China needed to develop its nuclear capability fast—and go on the nuclear defensive by locating high-tech industries deep within the Chinese hinterland.

In 1965, the United States began its intervention in the Vietnam conflict, giving Mao yet another thing to worry about. (China's relations with Russia and the Soviet Union are covered in Chapter 17. Chapter 19 is about China and the United States.)

The Great Proletarian Cultural Revolution

As the more moderate arm of the party moved ahead to patch up the economy, Mao began to feel even more frustrated. The gap between urban and rural workers was too great, and China's intellectuals had failed to understand the nature of socialist revolution.

A new fuse was lit by historian Wu Han, who wrote a series of articles and a play about a Ming dynasty official who criticized his emperor. Wu Han had actually been asked by Mao to write about the same Ming official, cast as a selfless hero who battled the Ming bureaucracy to protect the poor peasants. Other thinly veiled criticisms of the CCP followed, and the leadership began to debate how to handle the situation.

The party moderates, led by Peng Zhen, criticized Wu mildly, but chose to characterize the offense as a "problem of academic contention." But others within the party, most notably Mao's wife, Jiang Qing, saw Wu's writings as an all-out attack on Mao and his views of a socialist society. Backed by Lin Biao, who had been put in charge of the PLA after Peng Dehuai's fall from grace, Jiang and three of her colleagues—with Mao's approval, of course—helped launch a new campaign to save Chinese society from being corrupted by bourgeois, anti-Maoist art and literature. It was known as the Great *Proletarian* Cultural Revolution. Jiang Qing, Yao Wenyuan, Wang Honhwen, and Zhang Chunqiao, more commonly known as the Gang of Four, were about to unleash forces they ultimately would not be able to control.

Mao's ideology was based on Marxism, which was the underpinning of the communist government in the Soviet Union. But China and Russia were very different societies, and while Mao used Marxist terminology in his ideology, it played out differently in Chinese communism. In Russia the proletariat—the masses—had revolted against the oppression of the Russian Empire's feudalism; the oppressor of the Chinese peasant masses was the landlord—not the Chinese Empire itself—and the foreign imperialists along with the bourgeois capitalists who did business with them. The *mass line* in China came from, and returned to, the peasant class.

Language Lesson _____

The term **proletariat** in Russia meant the urban industrial working class who constituted the major segment of the population. China was an agrarian society, so it was the rural peasants who, in Mao's adaptation, were the **proletarians.** The Marxist notion that the proletariat originates the revolution and benefits from it is called the **mass line.** Chinese Marxism had acquired a wide following of Western intellectuals who were inspired by Mao's initiative to liberate the proletariat. Many of them were unaware until years later that Mao's utopian vision had become a brutal police state.

The rallying cry behind the Cultural Revolution, which was launched officially by the Central Committee in August 1966, was Mao's ideology. The divisions within the top leadership could not be mended, and Mao was ready for one last big mass mobilization against those within the party who were taking "the capitalist road." At the ripe old age of 73, he was ready to strike against anyone trying to shut him out of the top party decisions. And there were new tensions and new players, too, as Jiang Qing and her Shanghai colleagues looked to discredit the old Beijing clique.

Mao's Last Stand

Mao prepared to rid the Chinese Communist Party of those who had betrayed the revolution by …

◆ Placing the People's Liberation Party (PLA) under the control of the chairman of the CCP—himself.

- Weeding out the enemies of the party and replacing them with those he knew were loyal to him.

- Using the new education program to indoctrinate the youth in party ideology.

Even though Mao had fallen in stature in some quarters following his disastrous Hundred Flowers and Great Leap Forward initiatives, years of indoctrination in his utopian ideology had had the intended result: He had developed a cult following. He was now ready to utilize their devotion.

The Red Guards

In 1966, groups of high school students known as the Red Guards, armed with copies of *Quotations from Chairman Mao*, began to hold rallies throughout China to proclaim Mao's greatness and revile those who clung to the old ways. By the fall, all schools and universities had been closed. Mao encouraged the Red Guards, and their rallies soon turned into rampages.

The goal was to attack the "four olds"—old customs, habits, thinking, and culture. For two years, 10 million adolescents terrorized anyone that could vaguely be considered "bourgeois." Anyone who had a bourgeois class background, or had been connected with the Guomindang or foreign companies in the past, was an obvious target. Intellectuals were defenseless, and forced to wear dunce caps on their heads as the Red Guards paraded them through the streets. Given the split with the Soviet Union, anyone in China known to have a collection of Russian novels could be at risk. Red Guards destroyed homes, libraries, houses, stores, and factories. They destroyed cultural treasures and houses of worship throughout the country.

Han Help _____

Particularly hard hit were cultural sites far from Beijing—and far from the moderating influence of Zhou Enlai and other party leaders. In Tibet, Red Guards destroyed all but 10 of the 1,600 or so monasteries. When reports came in of archaeological discoveries in Xian, Zhou Enlai is said to have quietly ordered the terra cotta army of Emperor Qinshihuang reburied before the Red Guards got wind of the cultural treasure. Full excavation of the site did not begin until 1974.

The Red Guards had seemed to be a spontaneous rebellion against the moderates of the CCP. In reality the movement to cleanse the party was staged by the Gang of Four and the Central Cultural Revolution Group—and millions of impassioned young actors jumped at the chance to play their roles.

It was soon clear that the Red Guards were not easy to restrain. Mao also grew increasingly suspicious of his wife's plans. He depended heavily on Lin Biao and the loyalty of the PLA—but seems to have misjudged his protégé. A bizarre story of intrigue and betrayal was about to unfold.

As the Red Guards grew in power their acts became increasingly barbarous. They were now a rabid, bloodthirsty mob that no longer discriminated in their choice of targets. They soon became factionalized and, like the northern warlords of the past, directed their savagery at each other. By 1968, Mao had had enough; he disbanded the Red Guards and turned to the PLA to marshal regional activists to replace the teenage gangs. It was the signal for the military to assume tremendous power in the Chinese Communist Party; soon, even Mao would be unable to control them.

Lin Biao had been a favorite of Mao's since he joined the Communist Party in 1928. He had been a general in the Civil War. Lin was Mao's choice to succeed him as chairman of the party and chief of state. At the Ninth National Party Congress in April 1969, Lin Biao was named the vice-chairman of the Chinese Communist Party, which quickly installed many of the leaders of the Red Guards in positions of power.

It was also at the Ninth National Party Congress that Mao's little red book of quotations was made the official book of the Chinese Communist Party. It was rather ironic because Lin, who had assembled the quotations, was becoming a problem. He had maneuvered the troops under his command into too many key party positions, and had urged his PLA troops to take a heavy hand in investigating party cadres—too heavy a hand, in Mao's eyes.

Mao began sending signals that Lin had fallen out of favor. In 1971, after a plot to assassinate Mao had been linked to Lin, he and his wife and son disappeared and were never heard from again. The party line was that Lin had panicked and tried to escape to the Soviet Union in a military jet. The plane, which had no navigator and insufficient fuel, crashed in Mongolia. The real truth may never be known, but Lin Biao was certainly out of the picture.

Mao, at the center of the maelstrom he had created, seemed to have no concept that he was destroying China. Like so many emperors before him, he lost any sense of the chaos into which he had plunged the country.

The Gang of Four

The hardest of the hardliners when it came to orthodox communism were the Gang of Four. They had been the major ideological force behind the Cultural Revolution. Now, with Mao in a weakened position, they were poised to impose their will on the Chinese Communist Party.

The Gang's agenda was nothing less than the complete destruction of Chinese culture. Among other objectives, they advocated replacing all school textbooks with books of communist doctrine. Movies, operas, and even songs had to represent the purest socialist ideals. At the zenith of the Cultural Revolution, the party outlawed all theater productions that were not revolutionary operas or ballets, with revolutionary heroes and a clear message about class struggle. "The Red Detachment of Women" and the "White-Haired Girl," for a time, were *it* for entertainment.

Because members of the Gang were already in powerful positions in the party, their radical theories gained support—at least for a while.

Han Help

In 1972, President Richard M. Nixon announced to a stunned world that he would make a visit to China. It was not an imperialist adventure; in the middle of the Cold War, Nixon saw the Sino-Soviet split as an opportunity to pursue trade talks with China on an equal basis. It was a high point in his presidency that was for a time overshadowed by his resignation from office over the Watergate break-in.

They made their big move for power in January 1974, when they presented an allegorical criticism of Confucius which was a thinly veiled attack on Zhou Enlai. The allegory heaped great praise on the empress of the period, thinly disguised as the power-hungry Jiang Qing.

The Gang of Four's power did not go unchallenged. Zhou Enlai and Deng Xiaoping were working hard to keep them from taking over China completely, and they, too, had their supporters: In January 1975, Deng was elected vice chairman of the Central Committee; less than a week later Zhou was named premier. None of the Gang was given a formal position of power within the party. (See Chapter 11 for more about the demise of the Gang of Four.)

In 1975, Zhou became ill with cancer, and Deng, his heir apparent, took over his duties in the party and the government. Mao, sensing an opportunity to get some of his power back, launched a verbal offensive against Deng.

Death and Succession

Deng might have been in real trouble but something happened that greatly pushed public opinion in his favor. Zhou died on January 8, 1976, and everyone became sentimental and talked about what a great man he had been. At the state funeral, which

Mao did not attend, Vice-Premier Deng gave the eulogy, and praised Zhou's moderate temperament and model conduct. A lot of the widespread admiration rubbed off on Zhou's replacement, Deng—to the chagrin of Mao and the Gang of Four.

The glorification of Zhou launched an anti–Gang of Four movement, which was of course by inference an anti-Mao movement. The Gang moved to prevent an official period of mourning, but millions of mourners gathered in Tiananmen Square bearing wreaths for Zhou and poems denouncing the Gang of Four.

The army, which was still under Mao's control, was sent in to break up the gathering. Many people were killed, wounded, and arrested. (See Chapter 14 for more about this and other Tiananmen Square demonstrations.) Deng Xiaoping was the scapegoat for the mass demonstrations that had gotten out of hand.

Hu Nu?

Deng Xiaoping had the distinction of being purged twice during the Cultural Revolution. During the early years of the Red Guards, Deng was removed from office for being a "capitalist roader"—his economic policies were just too pragmatic—and placed under house arrest. His family suffered terribly, too: His son Deng Pufang was permanently paralyzed after being pushed out a window by Red Guards. But Zhou Enlai managed to protect Deng, and bring him back as vice premier in 1973. When the Gang of Four attacked Deng in late 1975, Jiang Qing accused him of not liking model revolutionary operas. Mao stripped him of his titles, and accused him of trying to restore capitalism in China. Purged from power once again, Deng went to live in Guangdong Province. When he returned to Beijing, he would open the floodgates to full-scale economic reform.

Mao had Deng removed from all government and party posts, and replaced him with his own man, Hua Guofeng. It was his last official act: In September of 1976, Mao also died—though he remained a godlike figure in China and his little red book continued to be the bible of the Chinese Communist Party.

The Gang made one last move to seize power, but failed. Then Deng made his move, and Hua Guofeng, the only other logical candidate around, was afraid to oppose him.

The Least You Need to Know

◆ In its first years the Chinese Communist Party established control through mass campaigns to teach the war-weary Chinese population about socialism.

◆ The Hundred Flowers Campaign ended the careers of many of the scholars and professionals who could have helped build a better society.

♦ The Gang of Four and the Red Guards destroyed the lives of millions of Chinese who appeared to be less-than-perfect socialists.

♦ Chairman Mao died in 1976, leaving the radical Gang of Four and the more moderate party leaders in a struggle for control of China.

Deng's Doers

In This Chapter

- ◆ Deng Xiaoping wins the succession struggle and becomes China's leader.

- ◆ The government retreats from Maoist ideology and puts the economy on the front burner.

- ◆ Deng presents his plan to transform the Chinese economy and raise the standard of living for everyone.

- ◆ Students and other protestors demonstrate in Tiananmen Square for more reforms and less inflation and corruption.

- ◆ The army massacres the demonstrators, and Deng later addresses some of the reform issues.

Hua Guofeng was not much competition for Deng Xiaoping but Hua—an obscure provincial functionary—had been named by Mao as his heir, a replacement for Deng after he was dismissed for his part in the 1976 Tiananmen Square demonstration. If Deng and Hua battled one another, the Gang of Four would surely take over—Jiang Qing's ambition knew no bounds—and everyone knew that that would mean a new kind of dictatorship in China. The Gang of Four was arrested, and the party leaders easily brought Deng back into the fold.

Deng's leadership of China began another kind of revolution—one that slowly dismantled many aspects of Maoism, moved the country toward a market economy, and opened China to the world.

The End of the Gang of Four

After the Gang was arrested, its four members were sentenced to death. The sentences were later reduced to prison terms. A final profile of each member of the circle is provided:

- **The Ringleader.** In Chapter 10 we introduced the leader of the Gang, Mao's wife, Jiang Qing. She had been an actress in Shanghai in the 1930s, but not a very successful one. She joined the Chinese Communist Party in 1937 and became Mao's companion. Jiang became active in culture and the arts in the early 1960s, and she came up with the idea of writing communist operas to replace the nonpolitical operas that were being performed. Her ability to move through Mao to the top echelon of power made her a force and a formidable adversary.

  Jiang Qing hanged herself in prison in 1991.

- **The Writer.** Born in 1917, Zhang Chunqiao was a writer in Shanghai during the 1930s. He joined the Communist Party in 1938. In 1949, Zhang became a prominent journalist for a paper called the *Liberation Daily*. Zhang joined the Central Committee in 1969 and became the second deputy prime minister in 1975. He was arrested in 1976 and died in prison under unknown circumstances in 1991.

> **Hu Nu?**
>
> Zhang Chunqiao was called the Father of the Cultural Revolution.

- **The Baby.** The youngest of the Gang was Wang Honhwen, who was born in 1933. He fought in the Korean War and later was a member of the Red Guards. He was elected to the Central Committee in 1969, and became deputy president of the party in 1973.

  Wang died in prison in 1992 of liver cancer.

- **The Critic.** A former writer and propaganda official, Yao Wenyuan began his career as a literary critic in Shanghai. In that capacity, Yao campaigned against writers whom Mao considered "bourgeois intellectuals."

  Yao criticized a new play by Wu Han, claiming the playwright was actually taking a stand against Mao Zedong's thought. Yao's article, published in 1965, was said to have launched the Cultural Revolution. Yao was sentenced to 20 years in prison. He was released in 1996, is still alive, and is said to reside in Shanghai.

Deng Xiaoping Leads

Hua was the official chairman of the party, but the leadership brought Deng back as vice chairman of the Central Committee and vice chairman of the Military Commission. The appointments placed Deng in a very powerful position. From that time on, even after his retirement in 1989, he was the undisputed leader of China until his death in 1997.

Deng took over the government of a country that had just lost 30 million people to famine and the purges of the Cultural Revolution. The economy was at a standstill. People were hungry, and they feared what the future would hold. Morale was at a new low.

Deng was a party man through and through. He was a survivor of the Long March and he had held high positions in diverse branches of the party and government. Post-Mao China had a lot of problems, and Deng had plans to solve them.

Reversals of Policy

The party, with Deng unofficially at its helm, immediately began to excise major aspects of Maoist doctrine. The first thing they did was to recall old party leaders who had been victims of the Cultural Revolution; they needed their help. Intellectuals were once again welcomed back into the Communist Party—something unthinkable during the Maoist era.

Class struggle—the heart of Maoism—was no longer emphasized. There was still the occasional rail against the upper classes but most people had tired of the rhetoric; what they wanted were concrete improvements in their lives.

 Wise One Says

Mao said, "We should support whatever the enemy opposes and oppose whatever the enemy supports."

With the Cultural Revolution dead and gone and the Gang of Four in jail, the government would curtail its interference in social and cultural matters.

Maoism was seen as a thing of the past. Even the way Mao was portrayed by the party changed. He was no longer considered flawless. He was remembered as a great strategist and revolutionary theorist who had made gross errors in judgment during the Cultural Revolution.

 Han Help

Workers were still portrayed in propaganda as heroes, but they were no longer the sole role model. Intellectuals were now thought of as workers who worked with their brains.

Paradigm Shift

Deng acknowledged the failure of the Chinese economic system. In the early 1980s he said, in essence, that there was no point in everyone having the same amount if everyone was poor. His dictum was "Socialism means eliminating poverty."

Hu Nu?
There was one area in which the government now took a much stronger position: birth control. Mao did not believe in birth control, but with Mao gone, the new government seriously addressed the overpopulation problem. The result was that families were strongly discouraged from having more than one child.

Deng promised a new kind of socialism that he called "socialism with Chinese characteristics." It favored economic growth as long as the government—the party-state—remained in control. Economic reforms would lead China not toward capitalism as the Gang had feared, but toward a higher standard of living.

A less-ideological, less-politicized China would open itself to the world's ideas and technology. A decrease in officialdom's control over people's lives (the old *danwei* system) would give them greater freedom to make personal choices and express their views.

A Market Economy

Deng committed himself to transforming China into a modern state through economic reforms. The planned, or government-controlled, economy would eventually result in what he called a "socialist market economy."

At the core of his vision were the "Four Modernizations" China had to undertake. Industry, agriculture, science and technology, and national defense were the four targeted areas for rapid development. Deng believed that the time had come to look abroad for the technologies needed in these four areas, in an abrupt shift from the Maoist principle of self-reliance.

Hu Nu?
The "Fifth Modernization," the emerging class of dissidents argued, had to be democratization of China.

One of Deng's first official acts was to visit the United States in 1979 to discuss his economic plan. Foreign investment was on the agenda, and Deng made a big hit wherever he traveled. U.S. investors were eager to get into the world's biggest undeveloped market. Deng also tapped Chinese investors living outside of China, particularly those in Hong Kong—still China's main source of investment capital.

Deng's government also studied the highly successful economies of its neighbors (Taiwan, Hong Kong, Japan, and others) to identify economic strategies that could be successful in China. A reorganized, decentralized government mandated reforms that would support local collectives, encourage private enterprise, and gradually privatize state-owned industries.

Some of the most sweeping reforms took place in Guangdong and Fujian Provinces. The choices were anything but random, as these two provinces were closest to two huge pools of foreign cash: Hong Kong and Taiwan. In 1980, the two provinces were given the freedom to handle foreign trade and financial matters. And Beijing set up special economic zones (SEZs), where provincial officials could offer foreign investors special deals such as holidays and preferential land deals. From 1979 to 1992 the Guangdong SEZs (Shenzhen, Zhuhai, and Shantou) and the Xiamen SEZ in Fujian Province accounted for nearly 50 percent of China's foreign investment.

Hu Nu?
Deng Xiaoping saw his reforms as a slow, gradual transformation of China's economy. This would be no "Great Leap Forward." Instead, Deng urged that the reform process meant "crossing the river while feeling for the boulders." Trial balloons would be launched, and the results examined carefully before the particular reform would be instituted nationwide.

Gradually, as the economic progress in these provinces clearly outpaced growth in other regions, many of the reforms were adopted elsewhere.

Reform on the Farm

In the countryside, meanwhile, Mao-style collectives were being phased out. Deng's collectives were to be administered locally. They would send less in taxes to Beijing, and not be burdened with the costs of worker benefits that drove up the operating budgets of traditional state-owned enterprises.

The Household Responsibility System that had been attempted during Mao's regime would become officially adopted throughout China. The system permitted individual farmers and farm communes to sell their products and services locally and keep the profits.

By the 1980s, the greatest change in farming was automation. Many workers had been moved off the farms, replaced by machines, and agricultural productivity rose dramatically. That gave the rural population the opportunity to develop light industry and service operations under local administration.

Privatization

Deng was deeply committed to increasing non-state-run business and industry.

◆ By 1986, 18 million individuals were engaged in private enterprise in China.

Han Help

In the mid-1980s small, privately owned restaurants seating six to eight people began to spring up in the cities.

◆ A long-term plan was initiated to convert unprofitable state-run industries to private ownership. This area of economic reform proved particularly difficult and slow to achieve; state-enterprise reform is still a top agenda item for the Chinese government.

The New Government

Hua Guofeng was replaced in 1980 by Hu Yaobang as party general secretary, and Zhao Ziyang became prime minister. They would figure prominently in Deng's government.

Deng promised the Chinese people a government that would improve their lives in every way. It would be accomplished through decentralization, depoliticization, and democratization. Many of these reforms were spelled out in the new Chinese Constitution, which was adopted in March 1978:

◆ **Decentralization.** As the leader of China, Deng faced the same problem Chinese leaders have faced throughout history: The size and diversity of the country makes it impossible to rule from the center. The alternative—decentralization—had its problems, too, but it would give the government more flexibility in delegating important administrative tasks to official state offices closer to the source of local needs.

◆ **Depoliticization.** Indoctrination in party ideology was out; individualism was in.

◆ **Democratization.** People could have access to the world's information, literature, art, and entertainment—at least up to a point. Government leaders would have fixed terms of office instead of life tenure, the legislature would have more decision-making power, and local officials would be elected directly by the people. The brutality of the Mao regime would not be repeated.

Hu Yaobang, in his powerful new position, brought many intellectuals and professionals who had been purged back into favor and gave them high-level jobs. China looked like a nation that was heading toward democracy. The world watched with admiration.

New Issues

The new economy and government brought with them a range of new issues and problems for Beijing:

- **Less tax money.** Decentralization, along with the privatization of state-owned industry, resulted in less taxes going to the central government. That meant virtually no central funding for public health, education, or public works.

- **Corruption.** The bureaucracy of the decentralized government, combined with the temptations that went with an opening economy, created a surge of corruption at every level.

- **Social stratification.** China's perennial problem of social inequity resurfaced in a new way. The government that no longer exercised total control over people's lives no longer provided the cradle-to-grave supports they were used to. The wealth of the enterprising grew as workers in previously state-run enterprises became unemployed.

- **Drug use, prostitution, and female infanticide.** Isolated resurgences were documented in these and other social behaviors the party had sought to eliminate. Drug use and prostitution were on the upswing because the central government had done a poor job enforcing laws consistently. Female infanticide, in contrast, was on the rise because of the one-child policy. Rural workers, desperate for a son, might be tempted to let an infant daughter die so the parents could try again to conceive a son.

- **Regional imbalances.** Regions with resources flourished while others remained backwaters that were barely aware of the reforms.

- **A weaker Beijing.** Decentralization of the government made control and security a major concern within the party.

The government also lacked the banking and currency regulatory systems that are essential in a market economy.

Tiananmen Square, 1989

At the Thirteenth Congress held in 1987, Deng said that his generation was preparing to step back and turn the government and the party over to younger people. They took him at his word.

Student demonstrations had started to break out around the country. With the changes came a call for more changes. Many wanted the government restructured to provide a more frequent turnover of representatives. The people of China had always lived in a controlled society. They were used to submitting to authority, but now that they'd had a taste of democracy, they wanted more.

The older contingent of the party had watched the rise of powerful dissident movements in Eastern Europe with trepidation. They enjoined Deng not to dilute the party's political power any further. They blamed Hu Yaobang and the intellectuals he'd nurtured for giving the students the impetus to take to the streets. No one was executed or imprisoned; Hu and the dissidents weren't even removed from their jobs—but they were stripped of the power they had been given. Hu was replaced by Zhao Ziyang.

A New Reform Plan

A whole new plan for reform was established under Zhao Ziyang as party leader and Li Peng as government leader. It was known at the time that these men represented opposite ends of the political spectrum when it came to the Communist Party. Zhao Ziyang came from the liberal element. Li was a Moscow-trained moderate who had not, like Zhao, survived the Long March and the heady, revolutionary period that followed.

> **Wise One Says**
>
> An unidentified woman from Shanghai, during the days of the democracy movement in China, said, "We have just gained some peace after the Cultural Revolution. Is the suffering brought about by the Cultural Revolution not enough?"

Zhao and Li did the best they could, but none of their reforms stuck. China had appeared to the world to be making great strides toward democratization, but the people who lived there knew better. The China the world saw was a facade.

- The Chinese had little freedom to travel, even within their own country. And travel abroad was for the very privileged—a passport in China was very difficult to obtain and very easy to revoke.

- The books and periodicals allowed into the country were scrutinized for inflammatory materials. Anything pornographic was forbidden, but so were many classics of Western and Chinese literature.

- The media were still strictly controlled; television was a state institution.

- Authorities opened mail whenever they liked.

- People who practiced unapproved religions (Christianity, Islam, Tibetan Buddhism) could be persecuted.

The people had a long list of complaints, but there were two overwhelming—and growing—problems that disturbed the entire Chinese population: corruption and inflation. The rising economy should have been producing a much greater effect on the standard of living. The reform team that hadn't gotten anywhere with lesser issues couldn't hope to address issues of such enormity.

Han Help _____

It was the very contrast between Deng's rhetoric of massive reform and the reality of continued repression and censorship that so infuriated the young people of China.

Those who had their hopes and dreams kindled by Deng's words now felt betrayed, frustrated—and angry.

The Death of Hu Yaobang

Hu Yaobang, who had sparked the student movement in 1987, died suddenly on April 15, 1989. Beijing's Tiananmen Square, the symbol of the Chinese Communist Party's conquest of China, was instantly flooded with student demonstrators, then teachers; then the city's intellectuals and journalists arrived. Energetically, but peacefully, they called for freedom of expression and an end to censorship in the media. By the end of May, they had been joined by millions of workers and peasants who demanded the reform of the corrupt Chinese government and Communist Party, and a solution to the inflation problem.

The atmosphere on Tiananmen Square was initially calm, even lighthearted at times. For example, the Beijing acrobatic students, demonstrating along with the others, would entertain the crowds with their feats. The students continued to demonstrate for weeks, and their rhetoric rose in pitch: Some of them called for the overthrow of Deng and the leaders, who now feared a full-scale rebellion. The students were joined by thousands of government workers, including staff from key ministries. The government threatened military force. The demonstrators would not be intimidated.

Zhao Ziyang went to Tiananmen Square and promised that the reforms they wanted would be made. He asked the students to go back to their classes; they stood their ground. For three days students and leadership spokesmen engaged in a dialogue on television. It produced nothing; the Chinese leadership was split between those who supported action on the demands of the demonstrators and those who were unwilling to make any concessions.

The demonstrations continued, and grew in size. The government made an official announcement that there would be no concessions. They demanded that the protestors clear Tiananmen Square. The protestors held on. The demonstrations were still peaceful, but they were losing their point and going nowhere. And within the leadership, Zhao Ziyang's support had withered because he hadn't succeeded in bringing the demonstrations to an end.

Deng Xiaoping, furious that he had become the villain of the piece, cast his lot with the party hard-liners he had previously been working hard to control.

Li Peng now came forward and demanded in the harshest language that the demonstrators disband. He was ignored. He threatened. He was still ignored.

As a result, Li Peng declared martial law. The protestors refused to back down. Now Deng and Li felt they had no recourse: They called in the troops—and even *that* did not go well for them.

In Beijing, rumors were running rampant. A week before the crackdown, for example, there were widespread fears that government troops were parachuting into the sports stadium. Anyone with a radio and the ability to understand the BBC news was considered a source of valuable information. In the university district, located in the northern part of the city, students armed only with bandannas against the anticipated tear gas attacks would march out each night to guard the entry routes into the city. And truckers would be persuaded to let the air out of their tires on the major roads, to be a roadblock against enemy troops.

Wise One Says

In the days before the Tiananmen Square massacre, China's vice minister of education, He Dongchang, said, "God allows young people to make mistakes."

The Thirty-eighth Army, located in the Beijing vicinity, reportedly refused to move against the demonstrators. Seven retired generals and field marshals, in a letter to the editor of a popular Chinese newspaper, cautioned the government against killing its own people.

The Massacre

Deng and Li had gone too far to back down. Now they brought in the Twenty-seventh Army from the Mongolian steppes. Reportedly, the troops were told that a small number of rebels were threatening national security. On the grisly night of June 3-4, 1989, the Twenty-seventh Army marched into the center of Beijing and began firing on the demonstrators and anyone unlucky enough to be in the wrong place at the wrong time.

The government succeeded—on the face of it. The leading agitators for reform were removed from their jobs, imprisoned, or exiled. The popular rebellion went underground. The shock of what had happened hung in the air; it felt like the Cultural Revolution all over again. But Deng and his colleagues couldn't hide what had happened as Mao had done. The massacre had been covered by television for all the world to see, and the truth could not be denied. (In Chapter 13 you can find some thoughtful perspectives on this and other significant Tiananmen Square demonstrations and what meaning they may hold.)

China Moves On

Foreigners began to move out of China. Within two weeks, foreign confidence in China had been badly shaken. The Chinese government blustered at international criticism. They accused the United States and other nations who formally protested the massacre of interfering with China's internal affairs.

The Chinese government threatened to purge anyone in China who spoke out against the massacre, but it was counterproductive. China began to lose its diplomats to defection. Perhaps a whole generation of Chinese students who were abroad would also be lost to the nation. In the United States, tens of thousands of Chinese students were allowed to stay on indefinitely.

Abruptly, the official line changed. Threats of more executions and harsher punishment gave way to a plea for reconciliation and a promise of amnesty for the surviving demonstrators.

The party began to look inward, all the while denying that the demonstrators had any real reason for complaint. Some officials were dismissed and trials were promised—and all this within a month of the attack.

So, though some of the activists were dead and most of their leadership was underground, the protestors had won a victory. Their demands for change were being addressed.

By the end of the summer of 1989, foreign businesses—not as starry-eyed as they had been about China—were nevertheless starting to move back. But it would be months, even years, before the damage done by the guns at Tiananmen Square could be undone.

Deng Xiaoping retired, and Jiang Zemin was installed in the country's highest office. The Chinese Revolution was unfinished—but at least it was still in progress.

> **Hu Nu?**
>
> After the Tiananmen Square massacre, the United States cut off all sales to China of any arms-related technology. That meant such things as airliner communications systems. World Bank loans for anything other than basic human needs were also suspended.

The Least You Need to Know

♦ Deng Xiaoping succeeded Mao as the leader of the People's Republic of China.

♦ The new government discarded many of Mao's concepts and practices.

♦ Deng's agenda was to raise China's standard of living by transforming its economy.

♦ The Tiananmen Square massacre revealed the depth of China's problems and the government's fear of rebellion.

♦ Deng retired in 1989, but continued to be in control of China until his death in 1997.

Chapter 12

Jiang's Gang

In This Chapter

- ◆ After Tiananmen Square, economic reforms become the name of the game.

- ◆ Jiang Zemin steers a steady course as president, while seeking to solidify the Chinese Communist Party's power.

- ◆ Zhu Rongji creates China's economic reform program.

- ◆ Jiang Zemin's "Three Representatives" concept, opening the CCP to wider membership, gets a mixed response.

In the immediate aftermath of Tiananmen, China was in as much shock as the rest of the world. Its student leaders, for the most part, had fled Beijing. Some managed to escape to Hong Kong and then to the United States; others, not so lucky, tried to hide in the countryside, and were turned in to authorities.

The government appealed to the nation to resume order and calm. Stability was a powerful message in a country that had a significant older population—anyone old enough to remember the Cultural Revolution of the 1960s. The momentum for political change that had developed in Beijing, and also to some extent in Shanghai, Chengdu, and other cities, seemed to have been stopped in its tracks.

After Tiananmen Square

Li Peng was widely despised for spearheading the military crackdown. Deng Xiaoping was ailing and largely absent from public view. When he did surface, his message was that China was to focus on being economically strong. In 1992, for example, Deng launched a big campaign to speed up economic reforms. Other parts of the country, Deng argued, should learn from the example of Guangdong Province and its special economic zones.

Luckily for the Chinese leadership, the economy was cooperating. Inflation had been tamed, for the most part, and urban incomes were shooting up fast. From 1989 to 1997, urban incomes grew almost 70 percent in real terms, a vast improvement over virtual stagnation from 1985 to 1989.

Han Help

Foreign investors took Deng's encouragement of economic reforms as a sign of strong government support, and went on an investment binge. Contracted foreign investment in China, which shrunk to about $12 billion in 1991, surged to $111 billion in 1993.

And the Soviet Union, China's old enemy, probably helped secure the government's stability in those first post-Tiananmen years. The collapse of the Soviet Union in 1991 and the rapid disintegration of the Soviet economy was a stark lesson for the Chinese population. Those who had demanded, during the heady days of the 1989 Tiananmen protests, "democracy, just like they have in the Soviet Union," could now see where Gorbachev's *glasnost* policy had taken the now-defunct Soviet Union.

The New Beijing Team

Deng Xiaoping had retired in 1989, but remained a powerful voice behind the Chinese government until his death in 1997. Deng's goal was to continue the economic reform program he had set in motion more than a decade earlier. He himself knew little about

Han Help

When Deng Xiaoping died in February 1997, he left an impressive track record. Foreign trade in 1978 was about $20 billion, and soared to $289.9 billion in 1997. Foreign investment in China went from a paltry $600 million in 1983, to more than $40 billion a year at the time of Deng's death.

economics, but he had hand-picked party leaders who would carry out the reform program. With Hu Yaobang and Zhao Ziyang out of the picture, Deng had to pick a few new heirs.

Deng named Jiang Zemin to the top leadership office in the party and government. Jiang is secretary of the Chinese Communist Party, president of China (elected by the National People's Congress to a five-year term in office, and confirmed by the National People's Congress), and chairman of the Central Military Committee of the People's Republic of

China. Jiang is due to retire in the fall of 2002 and has named the current vice president of China, Hu Jintao, as his successor. (See Chapter 21 for more on Hu.)

The premier is Zhu Rongji, nominated by the president and confirmed by the National People's Congress to a five-year term. Jiang Zemin and Zhu Rongji are the two most powerful men in China today.

Jiang Zemin

Jiang Zemin was born in 1926 in Jiangsu Province. His father and grandfather were local scholars. Jiang studied electrical engineering at Shanghai's Jiaotong University, where he joined the CCP and participated in student demonstrations against Chiang Kaishek. Jiang worked in a Shanghai factory for six years, spent a year working at Moscow's Stalin Auto Works, and went on to hold various posts in the government's industrial administration.

From 1983 to 1985 he was minister of the electronics industry, and in 1985 he was elected mayor of Shanghai. A year later he attracted national attention by peacefully ending the social unrest in Shanghai. After the Tiananmen Square debacle, that was surely a factor in Deng's choice of Jiang as his successor.

It also didn't hurt that Jiang had some solid reform credentials. Jiang, after all, had been the first planner of the Shenzhen Special Economic Zone, and had helped the SEZ idea get off the ground. In Shanghai, Jiang raised $3.2 billion in foreign capital, $1.4 billion of which was for several huge infrastructure projects, including a new subway, bridge, and water treatment facility.

Hu Nu?

The sons and daughters of the top CCP leadership, known as the "princelings," traditionally looked for plum party jobs. Nepotism in the 1990s meant getting in on the economic action, rather than a party post. Jiang Mianheng, one of Jiang Zemin's two sons, is involved in a $1.6 million joint venture between the Shanghai Grace Semiconductor Manufacturing Corporation and Formosa Plastics. The new venture will produce .25 micron silicon chips used in the microelectronics industry.

In June 1989, in the wake of the Tiananmen Square uprisings, Jiang became general secretary of the Thirteenth Chinese Communist Party Central Committee. He replaced Zhao Ziyang, who had been purged by Deng Xiaoping for having sympathized with the protestors.

Deng groomed Jiang as his heir-apparent and he took over many duties as Deng's health deteriorated. In March 1990, he was elected chairman of the PRC Central

Military Commission, and in March 1993, president of the PRC. He had established a network of connections with rising political stars (later dubbed "the Shanghai faction"), which he used to extend his power base after Deng died in 1997.

Zhu Rongji

Zhu Rongji was born in 1928 in Hunan Province. He graduated from Beijing's Qinghua University as an electrical engineer. He joined the Communist Party in 1949 and was sent to work for the State Planning Commission.

> **Han Help** _____
>
> In 1957, when Zhu was working for the State Planning Commission, he criticized Mao Zedong's "irrational" high growth policies. He was labeled a "rightist" and sent to a cadre school as a teacher. He was rehabilitated in 1962, and worked as an engineer until 1970, when he was purged again during the Cultural Revolution and was sent to work at a "May Seventh Cadre School," where he underwent reeducation until 1975.

After the Cultural Revolution, Zhu spent some time working for a pipeline company under the Ministry of Petroleum Industry. He also served as director of the Industrial Economics Institute of the Chinese Academy of Sciences. In 1982, he joined the powerful State Economic Commission, which was overseeing the reform program.

Zhu's next posting took him to Shanghai, where he served as mayor from 1987 to 1991. Zhu was popular with the foreign business community, who liked his no-dithering, no-nonsense approach to project approvals. A natty dresser, Zhu has a good command of English. He was also instrumental in attracting foreign investors to the massive Pudong New Area, an industrial and financial zone roughly the size of Singapore.

Zhu was named vice premier of the State Council and director of the State Council Production Office in 1991. He also served as governor of China's central bank, where he helped modernize the financial oversight of China's banking regime. He has a reputation of being quick-tempered and resolute in his drive to push through with the economic reforms.

In the past decade, Zhu has spearheaded many deep and significant reforms in industry, finance, and agriculture. In 1992, he wasn't afraid to take China's runaway economy by the horns. By reining in the money supply, Zhu was able to keep prices under control and lead the economy to a "soft landing."

The one area where he may have met his Waterloo, though, is state enterprise reform. Closing down the struggling state enterprises is proving harder than it looked on paper.

Hu Jintao

Deng Xiaoping had a finger in many pies for many years. Picking out who would lead the "Fourth Generation" of Chinese leaders into the new millennium was something Deng did in 1992, even though he was supposed to be in retirement.

Like Zhu Rongji, Hu is a graduate of Qinghua University, where he studied hydraulic engineering. He joined the Communist Party in 1964, only to get "sent down" to build houses for workers in Gansu Province, one of China's poorest regions. Bouncing back from the Cultural Revolution may be replacing Long March survivor status (now that the Long Marchers are all dead) as the ticket to political power in China.

Hu was named head of the Communist Youth League in 1982 and soon came under the wing of Hu Yaobang. (The two Hus are not related.) Hu Jintao was also posted to Guizhou and Tibet, where he had to call in troops to put down a Tibetan revolt in 1989. Deng brought him into the inner circle of the party leadership in 1992, where he began his training in earnest.

On his first trip to the United States in the spring of 2002, he impressed reporters with his firm command of economic data. If the succession plan goes ahead as scheduled, Hu will take over Jiang Zemin's post in the fall of 2002.

The New Economy

In the aftermath of Tiananmen, economic reforms continued apace, almost as if nothing had happened that June night. One of the first milestones was the reopening of the Shanghai Stock Exchange, which had been closed for more than 40 years. A second stock exchange also opened in free-wheeling Shenzhen.

Deng Xiaoping was taking the experimental approach once more by letting the exchanges open up so speculators could have a field day, even before there were any finalized laws to regulate stock transactions. A decade later, China stocks are traded on both exchanges, as well as on the Hong Kong and New York exchanges.

Hu Nu?
Zhu Rongji in 1999, a new book reportedly written by one of Zhu's former aides, tells a story of backstabbing to rival any intrigue in past dynasties. Zhu may be in charge of the reform program and other tough tasks, but Jiang Zemin holds the cards. The book claims that Jiang Zemin uses Li Peng, Li Lanqing, and other party members to "hold Zhu Rongji in check."

Jiang Zemin, like Deng, relied heavily on Zhu Rongji to implement the Chinese economic reform program.

Zhu has been the architect of China's current economic reforms:

♦ He orchestrated the soft landing of China's overheated economy in 1994, by devaluing China's currency and other measures while maintaining a high rate of economic growth.

♦ In the Asian financial crisis of 1997, he resisted devaluation pressure, and helped countries hardest hit by the crisis.

♦ In March 1998, when he became premier, he launched the streamlining of China's government, depriving half the bloated bureaucracy of their posts, and promised to pull the country's state-owned sector out of debt in three years through layoffs.

He began privatization of housing and education, and movement toward a commercially viable banking system while luring Western investment and increasing market competition, forcing Chinese firms to become more efficient.

Han Help

It was Zhu who succeeded in making an agreement with the United States, ending the last barrier to China's entry into the World Trade Organization on November 1, 1999.

Zhu seems unlikely to sponsor political liberalization to eliminate bureaucratic resistance to his economic reforms. He remains committed to the supremacy of the Chinese Communist Party, but unlike his colleagues, he has not aligned himself with any faction. His independence allows him to launch anti-corruption campaigns, and may account for his political resilience.

The Wild Card—the PLA

For Jiang Zemin, having a successful economic "czar" like Zhu Rongji was important. So was forging close ties to the PLA (People's Liberation Army). Jiang had no previous ties to the PLA, but quickly developed a close relationship. He knew all too well what happened in the Soviet Union when the army and government were no longer on the same page.

The PLA of the 1990s bears little resemblance to the grizzled fighting force of the Yan'an period. The first and second generations of military leadership in China following the communist takeover were revolutionaries and experts in guerrilla warfare. They fought the Japanese and they fought the nationalists. Since then the leaders have been concerned with the creation and implementation of the "military region" system, which was designed to provide security from foreign threats. Along the way, China's PLA became entrepreneurs as well as soldiers.

Wise One Says

According to John Bryan Starr (*Understanding China*, Hill and Wang, 2001), the PLA's sales of weapons to foreign purchasers probably generates up to $1 billion annually, and the sale of civilian products produced in military-controlled factories "may until very recently have contributed as much as an additional $4 billion per year to PLA revenues. The armed forces are responsible for some 10,000 factories that employ about 700,000 workers."

How the PLA moved from fighting force to maker of cosmetics, ice cream, and untold other goods and services is complicated. Part of the answer is simply defense conversion, the same post-Cold War process going on in the United States, Russia, and many other countries that once felt the need to maintain significant arsenals of nuclear and conventional weapons.

In China's case, Deng Xiaoping left the PLA little choice but to look for profits elsewhere to cover its military expenses. From the late 1970s, Deng cut military spending sharply, while ordering the military to be responsible for producing the country's weapons. He also pushed the PLA to convert many of its military facilities to civilian production.

But Jiang Zemin inherited some new problems from Deng's actions. First, he had to make sure the military was closely aligned with the party, and not out getting rich at the expense of the country's military readiness. Second, he had to face the hard reality that state enterprise reform could not work if the military enterprises were not also subject to market forces.

Hu Nu?

It's recently come to light that many of the ailing state enterprises are indeed military factories. Most likely, these include factories located deep in the hinterland, a legacy of Mao Zedong's "Third Line." Fearful of invasion from Taiwan or the Soviet Union, Mao relocated thousands of defense-related factories into the interior, especially in Sichuan and Guizhou Provinces.

In 1998, Jiang Zemin initiated a big shake-up of the defense industry. Some 20,000 factories employing over 16 million workers are now being run by a civilian organization, the Commission on Science, Industry and Technology for National Defense. In return for divesting itself of money-making as well as unprofitable ventures, the PLA got a sharp boost in government outlays.

Corruption within the PLA and its commercial enterprises is also part of the reason Jiang ordered the divestment. According to a report in the *Christian Science Monitor*, "The military has been implicated in extensive smuggling, thought to cost the Beijing government $12 billion in customs revenue annually. Profit-seeking has enmeshed top officers in a web of corruption. All told, the PLA is less effective because of its business activities."

The State of Jiang's Party-State

With the economy in good shape, the PLA being reeled back into line, and some major reforms to brag about, Jiang Zemin launched a new initiative. China-watchers love a good puzzle, and this latest twist is proving to be just that.

What Jiang did was start a new campaign called the "Three Representatives," in essence an attempt to shore up the Chinese Communist Party's image. It's a classic move, right out of Mao Zedong's book—promote ideology, get everyone to study it in widespread Marxist-Leninist study sessions, and build the country's unity behind the party, once more.

Jiang Zemin's *san ge dai biao* (Three Representatives) was launched in February 2000, when he visited Guangdong Province. The party was no longer the voice of the working class and the agricultural workers in China, but now represented the "most advanced mode of productivity, the most advanced culture, and the interests of the majority of the population."

What Jiang is hoping to achieve is a revitalized and more united Chinese Communist Party. Some analysts view his message as a step toward democracy. If the CCP were truly to represent the interests of the majority of the population, that would be democratic thinking. Others dismiss the move as a naïve and desperate ploy by a leader to hold a dying CCP together—and make sure he still wields some power after retirement.

Whatever the outcome of this move, be it months or years down the road, Jiang seems to have been able to get the government on board pretty quickly. In 2000, there were more than 300 papers and commentaries printed in the *People's Daily*, the main newspaper of the Chinese Communist Party. One theme that was repeated several times was the importance of studying Marx, Mao, and Jiang to keep the Washington-led Western alliance from turning China into a "vessel of capitalism."

From agriculture to customs, the "Three Representatives" concept is now part and parcel of the official goals and policies of China. Hu Jintao has echoed Jiang's call, which is hardly surprising.

Wise One Says

In November 2001, Wei Jianxing, the president of the All-China Federation of Trade Unions, called for trade unions to "uphold the great banner of Deng Xiaoping Theory, follow President Jiang Zemin's 'Three Representatives,' and implement the Law on Trade Unions." The Ministry of Agriculture has built the "Three Representatives" into its Tenth Five-Year Plan goals, to "further strengthen the fundamental position of agriculture."

Perhaps new thoughts on Marxism are in the works. In the year 2000 the Chinese Academy of Social Science organized a two-day international symposium that brought together 80 foreign and domestic philosophers from Australia, Britain, Germany, Italy, and Japan to look at the new Marxist philosophy. Li Tieying, the Politburo member in charge of the intelligentsia, told the symposium that "new conditions require an enrichment of Marxist philosophy."

For the first time, the works of French academic Jacques Derrida, German Marxist Jurgen Habermas, and younger theoreticians like Britain's Antony Giddens are being translated into Chinese.

The new ideas and new directions the CCP seems to be taking are a reflection of the vast societal changes China as a whole is undergoing. China's intellectuals, embraced by Jiang as valuable contributors, not anti-revolutionaries, cover the political spectrum from left to right. Nationalism and anti-Americanism seem to be common themes among neoconservaties and leftists alike.

Wise One Says

In a speech marking the Chinese Communist Party's eightieth anniversary in 2001, Jiang Zemin said "the party must expand its popular support and increase its social influence." He said there is no fixed truth or meaning even in communist tenets such as the Communist Manifesto. "The party must not cling dogmatically to theses and specific programs formulated for special situations by authors of Marxist classics," taking cognizance of changes in historical conditions and present realities.

It remains to be seen if China will adopt more liberal views. Continued crackdowns on those who are too openly critical of the government suggest that the tight hand over political thought is not about to relax. Jiang's advisors are reportedly split on whether China should allow the activities of nongovernmental organizations, or encourage people who would join these groups to become members of the Chinese Communist Party. Jiang's decision to allow capitalists into the party suggests that the issue has been decided in favor of keeping all interest groups inside the party.

The Least You Need to Know

- ◆ Chinese Communist Party secretary, Jiang Zemin, also the president of China, is expected to retire in 2002.

- ◆ Zhu Rongji, premier of the People's Republic of China, is the architect of China's economic reforms.

- ◆ Controlling the powerful People's Liberation Army has been key to Jiang's political control.

- ◆ China's economic reform program has been an astounding success in some areas, though there are some tough problems still to solve.

- ◆ The jury is still out on Jiang Zemin's "Three Representatives" initiative.

13

The View from Tiananmen Square

In This Chapter

- ◆ Find out what people think about the Tiananmen Square crackdown of June 4, 1989
- ◆ Follow the trail of the student leaders of the demonstration
- ◆ Learn what groups are mounting organized protests now
- ◆ Understand how the forces of economic and social change threaten China's stability

Tiananmen means "Gate of Heavenly Peace," and Tiananmen Square takes its name from the gate that overlooks it. The square, a huge expanse of 440,000 square meters, is bounded by the Great Hall of the People (where China's National People's Congress meets) on the west, the Forbidden City to the north, and the Museum of the Chinese People's Revolution on the east. On the south end, near the Qianmen Gate marking the southern entrance to the square, is the huge mausoleum containing Chairman Mao's body. In the center is the tall obelisk known as the Monument to the People's Heroes.

This central part of Beijing was once known as the Imperial City, a large area that included the Forbidden City—the home of China's imperial rulers since the Ming dynasty. Just to the west of the Forbidden City lies Zhongnanhai, the new "forbidden city." Off limits to the general public, this enclave houses the current leadership and other high officials of the Chinese Communist Party.

Much of the history of the Chinese Empire and of modern China was played out in this part of Beijing, so it seems fitting that arguably the most memorable event in China's recent history took place in Tiananmen Square on June 4, 1989.

Thirteen years have gone by, and China has become a major economic power with a growing middle class. Yet the Tiananmen Square crackdown is still a subject of analysis and debate, and a recurrent theme in general articles and books on modern China—as it is in this one. Well, it *was* the largest demonstration in Chinese history, and the government's reprisals did shock people everywhere who had fully expected continuing political reforms. But interest in these events remains high because there are lingering questions and concerns about the significance of the crackdown. In this chapter we do something different; we sample a range of perspectives on the suppression of dissent and how it may affect China's modernizing society.

The Square

The 1989 demonstration was the largest but not the first one to take place in Tiananmen Square. You may remember from Chapter 5 that a demonstration on May 4, 1919, by a cross-section of Chinese society, was followed by an intellectual revival, a burst of nationalism—and the birth of Chinese communism. Over the longer term, the May Fourth Movement, as this intellectual awakening came to be known, would be a recurring theme in China. To understand Tiananmen in 1989, you have to understand the precedent of the May Fourth Movement, for this is why the 1989 students saw themselves as patriotic heroes, and why they had the government over a barrel—until it was impossible to defuse the situation peacefully.

Han Help

On October 1, 1949, Mao Zedong looked out from the Tiananmen Gate to declare that "[t]he Chinese people have stood up" and proclaim the formation of the People's Republic of China.

On April 5, 1976, a group defied the Gang of Four and gathered in Tiananmen Square to memorialize the Gang's enemy, the deceased party leader Zhou Enlai (see Chapter 10).

> **Wise One Says** _____
>
> For China, 1999 was the eightieth anniversary of the May Fourth Movement, when the Chinese intelligentsia first advocated the adoption of Western science and democracy. But it was also the fiftieth anniversary of the establishment of communism in China. And the twentieth anniversary of the beginning of the era of economic reform under Deng Xiaoping. And the tenth anniversary of the Tiananmen Square democracy movement and massacre.
>
> —Trevor Corson (*The Atlantic*, February 2000)

April 15–June 4, 1989

Mao's successor, Deng Xiaoping, had himself been kicked out of the party twice by Mao for being soft on intellectuals. Deng had tolerated the Democracy Wall movement begun by Wei Jingsheng in 1979—until Wei criticized him personally. The movement was banned and its leaders imprisoned.

Ten years later on April 15, 1989, pro-reform leader Hu Yaobang died. Students in Beijing, Shanghai, and other cities gathered to memorialize him. Memorials turned into protests for an end to corruption, increased personal freedoms, better treatment of intellectuals, and stronger political reforms. The students denounced Deng and other party leaders. Wei was still in jail, but his pro-democracy platform was alive and well in the squares of China's major cities. Students were joined by workers. Ignoring the government's order to end the demonstrations, on May 4, 100,000 converged on Tiananmen Square.

Martial law was declared on May 20. Hundreds of thousands more students and workers crowded into the square and then spilled out into the surrounding areas. Ordinary cadres—the working drones of China's many ministries—joined in the demonstrations. Droves of unemployed workers poured into Beijing. By June 4, there were one million people in and around Tiananmen Square and an estimated two million more clogging the city's streets.

> **Wise One Says** _____
>
> Terms such as prodemocracy may have helped to fuel the idea that demonstrators were trying to create a Western system and overthrow the Communist Party government. In fact, most of the demonstrators wanted to do no such thing.
>
> —Rob Gifford, BBC News (June 2, 1999)

PLA troops and tanks rolled toward the center of the city on June 2 and 3. The world saw the indelible image of a solitary man who stood his ground with his fist raised in defiance at a massive oncoming tank.

By early morning, the lights went out on Tiananmen Square and the tanks rolled in. The crowd ran for cover, but hundreds are estimated to have been killed on the square.

The tanks and troops charged through the streets, killing hundreds—perhaps thousands; everyone has a different estimate—and injuring several thousand more. Beijing officials have never released a credible accounting of the number of casualties in Beijing.

The ensuing crackdown was wide-ranging and brutal. The arrests, summary trials, and executions shocked a world that had warmed to the idea that China was on its way to becoming a free and open society. Dissent was out—and still is.

The party propaganda machine was put into action to do some serious damage control. One story shown over and over again on television was the fate of the hapless PLA soldier who was beaten and burned by the unruly "rabble." This was the story told to the rest of the country. In a previous era, it might have worked, but post-Mao China had better sources of information, and the true course of events was quickly known throughout the country. Fax machines played a large role in transmitting information throughout China.

In January 2001, official Chinese documents detailing the events leading up to the crackdown were leaked, and published in *The Tiananmen Papers* (Public Affairs Press, New York). In *The New York Times* (January 6, 2001), Richard Bernstein summarized the process by which Deng and the CCP leaders made the decision to order the PLA to clear Tiananmen Square:

> The documents indicate that the officials who formally held the top posts—the members of the Politburo Standing Committee—were split two to two, with one abstention, over whether to use force to end the protests. Without a majority, the hard-liners lacked standing to call in the troops. But, according to the documents, the deadlock was broken by Deng and his octogenarian comrades, who had retired from most of their official posts but still held ultimate power. In this sense, the papers suggest an important conclusion, surmised before but now emerging more forcefully; that had it not been for Deng and the other elders, the moderates might have prevailed in the power struggle, averting bloodshed and inaugurating a period of greater political openness and economic liberalization.

The Media

In the Maoist era, everything of major importance that happened in China—mainly purges—was kept secret for as long as possible. When the PLA swept through Tiananmen Square on June 4, 1989, contingents of international press rolled tape, clicked cameras, and scribbled furiously in notebooks. They had arrived in May to cover a summit meeting between Deng and Soviet leader Mikhail Gorbachev, and they stayed right through to the bitter end.

Rob Gifford, in a series of pieces he wrote for the BBC News on the tenth anniversary of the crackdown, describes a fragmented student movement that lacked experience in activism and reduced complex issues to banal slogans. But, as he and other media-watchers observed, they knew just what to do for the television cameras.

They carried banners with quotes in English from Patrick Henry ("Give me liberty or give me death") and a copy of the U.S. Constitution. They erected a statue, the Goddess of Democracy, in Tiananmen Square. By the end of May, they were denouncing the CCP in increasingly harsh terms.

Their live worldwide audience was captivated. In the United States, hearts were melting for them. In the inner sanctum of the Politburo, the party was moving toward the decision it made on June 4.

Certainly the demonstrators had real concerns and frustrations, but it's hard not to wonder if, without all the media coverage, the students who had gathered to memorialize Hu Yaobang on April 15 may have just gone home as usual.

> **Wise One Says**
>
> The lessons that China's leaders learned from Tiananmen Square were from their own history. They knew that, as in the past, many of the demonstrators were more concerned about economic conditions than about freedom per se. They also knew that anarchy in former times, from the Ming rebellions to Mao Zedong's Great Cultural Revolution, cost millions of lives.
>
> —Robert Kaplan, *The Atlantic* (August 1999)

The World Reacts

President George Bush, the elder, had once been the U.S. ambassador to China. He, like many Americans, felt dismayed by the events of June 4. In Congress, both the House and Senate held long debates on the appropriate U.S. response. At times, particularly in the House of Representatives, the bombast of anti-Communist Party sentiment was reminiscent of U.S.-China relations in the bad old days. The House called for a breach of all but diplomatic relations with China—with some of its more strident members pushing for a complete break.

Multilaterally, the United States and Europe were determined to take a strong stance against the Chinese crackdown. With the United States and several European countries at the lead, the global community began to slap at Beijing's wrists with limited economic sanctions and cancellation of scheduled high-level visits.

 Wise One Says

DECLARATION ON CHINA

July 15, 1989

We have already condemned the violent repression in China in defiance of human rights. We urge the Chinese authorities to cease action against those who have done no more than claim their legitimate rights to democracy and liberty.

The repression has led each of us to take appropriate measures to express our deep sense of condemnation to suspend bilateral Ministerial and high-level contacts, and also to suspend arms-trade with China, where it exists. Furthermore, each of us has agreed that, in view of current economic uncertainties, the examination of new loans by the World Bank be postponed. We have also decided to extend the stays of those Chinese students who so desire.

—Excerpt from the official statement of the G-7 meeting in Paris, July 1989

The question of American policy toward China arose again in the summer of 1989. Would the progress that had been made in Sino-American relations be reversed? Fortunately, that did not turn out to be the case.

China's international relations were fractured for a time, but by the mid-1990s, its economic growth had made China a country impossible to ignore. In 2001, China's entry into the World Trade Organization said it all.

The View

While China's diplomatic and trade relations were soon proceeding apace, the people who had lived through the crackdown; the international press who had covered it; and the world's human rights organizations, think tanks, China scholars, and journalists were just beginning to consider its origins and implications. And 10 years later, in case anyone had stopped thinking about what happened on June 4, 1989, in Tiananmen Square, international media attention to the anniversary brought forth a whole new wave of analysis and speculation. Many of the people we quote in this chapter, whenever their thoughts were published, reached back into China's history for insight into the actions of Deng Xiaoping's government. It's not an unreasonable thing to do; after all, modern China has only recently emerged from almost three millennia of dynastic rule. So before we move ahead to the issues, we take a brief look back at the principles and challenges that shaped governance in imperial China.

Until the Chinese Empire ended less than a hundred years ago, the emperor, and the bureaucracy that represented him, had the mandate of heaven to reward and punish his subjects—that is, if he was a worthy emperor who had the good of the people at heart. It is the rare scholar of Chinese history who does not see aspects of the Han emperor in the leaders of the Chinese Communist Party. As John Bryann Starr, author of *Understanding China*, points out, "In fact, among the politically conscious citizenry [in China] there is widespread skepticism about democracy. Many of them argue that democracy is ill-suited to China, either because of its history and culture or because of its size and ungovernability."

If Starr is correct (he is not alone in his opinion), and the endemic problems of corruption and inflation and unemployment continue to dog one segment of the population while enriching another's, will frustration simply evaporate?

If the government manages to get the problems under control, an increasing, and increasingly modern middle class at some point will want to exercise influence on its government. How far ahead that day is would be anyone's guess.

The '89 Dissidents

After the massacre, those political dissidents who were known to have participated were tracked down and imprisoned, even tortured and executed in some cases. Those who lived to tell about it have started new lives. What have they done lately?

- **Chai Ling.** She inspired the hunger strike that galvanized the pro-democracy movement and received two Nobel Peace Prize nominations. She got her MBA at Harvard, and is CEO of her own Internet startup.

- **Li Lu.** Chai Ling's deputy and one of the last students to leave the square, Li also sought refuge abroad. Like Chai, he has moved on to other things. Li recently started his own New York-based hedge fund. While he has remained a member of human rights organizations, Li admits he has moved to the sidelines of political activism.

- **Wang Dan.** One of the student leaders, he was sentenced to 11 years and later freed and exiled to the United States shortly before President Clinton's 1998 visit to China. He was one of the five plaintiffs in a lawsuit filed in New York in 2000 against Li Peng for "crimes against humanity; summary execution; torture; arbitrary detention; and violation of the rights to peaceful assembly and the rights to life, liberty, and security of person."

Han Help

The "Tiananmen Mothers," a group of more than 130 families who lost a child or other family member during the Tiananmen crackdown, has begun documenting the deaths of hundreds in Beijing in June 1989. This group faces government persecution, yet continues to call for a public inquiry into what really happened on that particular June 4 and the days afterward. The government maintains that only about 200 people, all of them "lawless citizens," lost their lives. The group's main spokesperson is Ding Zilin, whose son was killed in the crackdown.

- ◆ **Wang Juntao.** A journalist who played a key role in the movement, he was sentenced to 13 years in prison, and was sent into exile in 1994.

- ◆ **Wuer Kaixi.** A Uyghur student, Wuer got his 15 minutes of fame on Chinese television in May 1989, where he argued heatedly and articulately with Premier Li Peng. After June 4, Wuer escaped to France and later studied briefly at Harvard. He was granted permanent residence by Taiwan, where he has worked in public relations and as a talk-show host.

And the old man of Chinese dissidents, Wei Jingsheng, also found refuge in the United States—eventually. The originator of the 1979 Democracy Wall, and a major influence on the pro-democracy movement, he spent nearly 20 years in prison and was allowed to emigrate to the United States, shortly before Jiang's visit to Washington. It's thought that Wei Jingsheng received an extremely severe prison sentence for leading the Democracy Wall movement because he was not a student, but an electrician.

It's not known what happened to all those who were arrested after the 1989 Tiananmen demonstrations. It is estimated that there were perhaps hundreds of executions of those accused of leading the protests in Beijing. Hundreds more were arrested, and some no doubt executed, for participating in demonstrations in Shanghai, Chengdu, and several other cities. Some China analysts believe that China's student leaders were largely spared the death penalty because the leadership was afraid of making them martyrs.

On the March

More than a decade after Tiananmen, many of the issues that inspired the young protesters still remain. Party corruption is still a major beef with the common Chinese—and the theme of recurring internal party crackdowns that don't seem to have much lasting effect on the problem. Stories of graft, corruption, embezzlement, and other excesses of officials at all levels of government continue to trickle out. If we're hearing these in the West, you can bet the rest of China knows the scoop, too.

And new pressure points are growing. The "iron rice bowl" is empty for an estimated 150 million unemployed workers, many of whom are on the march in great numbers. It's likely that China's unemployment problem will get worse before it improves. Officially, there are only about 6.8 million unemployed. But then there are millions of furloughed state enterprise workers, and untold millions of agricultural workers. Joining the WTO, for instance, will mean that Beijing will have to let more and more state enterprises stand on their own two feet, as the WTO rules limit how much a government can protect its industries.

Wise One Says

In China's northeastern rust-belt provinces, unemployment remains high as state-owned companies continue to shed workers. The newly unemployed typically have trouble finding jobs and are dependent on a minimal safety net provided by the government and their former employers. Many workers accept the fact that industries which were unprofitable must be restructured, but when they don't get the benefits they were promised and suspect that corrupt officials are plundering these funds, they often take to the streets in protest. Two weeks ago as many as 20,000 people protested in the oil-drilling center of Daqing, and this week the iron-working city of Liaoyang saw crowds of up to 10,000 on the march.

—The *Asian Wall Street Journal* (March 21, 2002)

One way to relieve some of the demands of these people would be to give them greater autonomy over some decisions. But there is no legal means for workers to organize outside the Communist Party structure. Independent trade unions are not permitted. And the limited local elections now going on in many villages in China stop short of allowing villagers to elect their representatives to the provincial assemblies and National People's Congress, where the real decisions about taxes and benefits are made.

For the average Chinese worker, having some say in the political process might be something of a pressure valve. But it isn't happening, not just now. The party seems bent on controlling a lot of things in China, and not too keen on relinquishing power. Seen in another light, the CCP motto today might be "If you can't beat 'em, make 'em join." One theory is that the reason Jiang allowed businessmen to join the CCP last year was that he assumed they would try to grab political power if they weren't included in the top echelons of the party.

Protests continue today in Beijing, too. In March 2002, demonstrations broke out all over Beijing, but they were not made up of the usual suspects.

> The marchers were people who have gained the most from economic reforms, members of the emerging middle and upper classes.
>
> More than 600 homeowners had come together in the upscale residential compound of Wangjing New City to oppose a developer who is trying to erect a 33-story building instead of the three-story building that had been described to them …. The conflict at Wangjing began last year when residents complained to the city planning bureau about the decision to construct the 33-story tower. After officials failed to respond homeowners used vehicles to block the construction site, prevent workers from entering.
>
> 'They don't want to solve the problem for us because they have a relationship with this developer,' said Jason Wang, one of the protest organizers, who like most people in the city says the local government and developers are enmeshed in a web of corruption.
>
> Middle- and upper-class property owners have not been strong proponents of political change. They have been major beneficiaries of the Communist Party's economic reforms; many property owners support the path of economic openness and tight political control.
>
> —Frank Langfitt, the *Baltimore Sun* (March 8, 2002)

The Falun Gong

There are political protests, too, or at least this is what the party would call them. For the past few years, global press attention has focused on the Falun Gong, a group that says all it wants to do is raise people's spiritual awareness and strength through traditional Chinese exercises. Why is the Chinese Communist Party taking such a hard line on the Falun Gong, a group that was outlawed in 1999 as being a subversive cult?

The easy answer may be simply the legacy of Tiananmen. The Falun Gong have attracted too many followers in China and have staged too many public demonstrations on or around Tiananmen, and the party leadership is running scared.

The more complex view would look at parallels between the Boxer Rebellion, which started as a martial arts group and had a cultlike following. Jiang Zemin is reported to have called the recent demonstration of 10,000 Falun Gong followers outside the CCP leaders' Zhongnanhai complex "the most serious incident since the political turbulence in 1989." Thousands of Falun Gong followers have reportedly been arrested, and there are new reports that many of the leaders are being executed.

The Legacy of Tiananmen

Tiananmen is not a name that is easily forgotten. How can it not evoke horrific visions so far removed from the idea of "heavenly peace"? In a year that saw the Berlin Wall crumble and the newfound freedom of jubilant Eastern Europeans, Tiananmen was a stark reminder that China's leadership was not interested in moving the country any closer toward democracy.

For those in China, Tiananmen can mean a lot of different things. For some, especially the older generation, the events of 1989 took China perilously close to chaos and anarchy. To these people, the price of democracy is too high. Better to prosper as a nation under strict party rule, they would argue.

For the many thousands of Chinese students studying abroad in 1989, the brute force of the government crackdown must have been terrifying. Many of them will never feel comfortable about returning to work in China, and China will be the worse off for the brain drain. For those brave few who stayed in China and continue to voice pro-democracy sentiments, Tiananmen will always be a turning point. Tiananmen was when the army fired on its own people, and hundreds of unarmed civilians died.

 **Wise One Says**

Tiananmen has become a word that fits in politics, like Hiroshima, the Berlin Wall, and Pearl Harbor.

—Professor Lucian W. Pye, Department of Political Science, MIT (January 24, 1989)

For the party leadership, the legacy of Tiananmen is perhaps a lesson in survival. Be strong, be resolute, and stomp out any opposition that looks like it might attract a large following—if you want to continue in power.

So many of modern China's significant protests have taken place in April, May, and June that the party leadership probably has their anniversary dates printed in red on their annual calendars. Let's face it—it's pretty darn near impossible to keep everyone happy, and even more so when your constituency is a whopping 1.4 billion people.

We don't know what will spark off the next demonstrations in Beijing, but it's a good bet that the action will be on Tiananmen Square.

The Least You Need to Know

- ◆ The brutal Tiananmen Square crackdown of June 1989 is a cloud over China's new prosperity.

- ◆ Many of the demonstration's student leaders now live outside of China.

- ◆ Organized protests by factory workers and the Falun Gong continue despite the danger of reprisals.

- ◆ Maintaining control of an opening and changing society is a dilemma for the party.

Part 4

Inside Today's China

In these pages you can find out what's really new in China: the growing middle class and the cosmopolitan urban youth; and what's not so new: ongoing issues with the Taiwan government, the inequities between the urban and rural population, government corruption, environmental crises, government repression of dissent, and discrimination against unofficial religious groups.

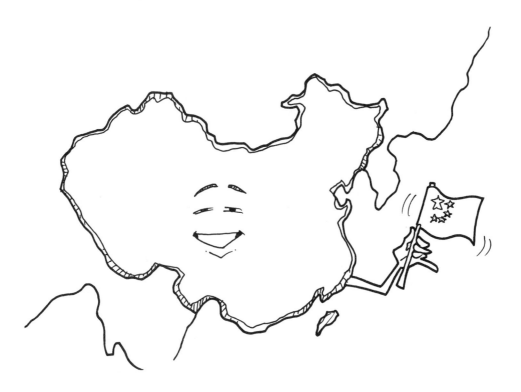

Chapter 14

The New Generation

In This Chapter

- ◆ President Jiang Zemin gets high marks for China's economic success.

- ◆ Farm workers, particularly women, are worse off than they were.

- ◆ Internet access encourages freedom of expression—within limits.

- ◆ NGOs spring up to address social needs.

> Within the Party, opposition and struggle between different ideas occur constantly; they reflect the class contradictions and the contradictions between the old and the new things in society. If there were neither contradictions nor ideological conflicts through which the contradictions were resolved, the Party's life would come to an end.
>
> —Mao Zedong, *On Contradiction* (1937)

Sixty-five years after Mao Zedong wrote these words, contradictions and conflicts are plentiful in China, both inside the party and out. It's a well-worn cliché to say that China is at a crossroads. How the history of China unfolds in the new millennium is anyone's guess. The seeds of democracy have been planted, but is the next generation of leaders going to make significant strides toward an open and democratic society? Or will the rising middle class, or the intellectuals, or other groups in China take the lead on pushing for change?

Absent a crystal ball, we can at least take a closer look at some of the groups, both old and new, that will shape China's future.

What's New?

When the subject is China, the term "New Generation" has a specific meaning. Also called the "Fourth Generation," it designates the CCP leaders who were children or young adults during the early days of the Cultural Revolution and are now in mid- to late middle age. They matured during a period of disillusionment with Maoist ideology, and many of them look with admiration—and perhaps some envy—at the thriving economies of Taiwan and Hong Kong. They are pragmatists, and many of them are technocrats like Hu Jintao, who appears slated to step into Jiang Zemin's shoes in late 2002. We look at Hu Jintao and some of the other "New Generation" party-state leaders in Chapter 20. In this chapter, we take the liberty of extending the metaphor to Chinese society as a whole—a society that is being transformed as China emerges as a global economic power to be reckoned with.

Jiang's "Cultural Revitalization"

Deng Xiaoping's reform and opening plan is a clear success. China's Gross Domestic Product (GDP) is now greater than $1 trillion a year, ranking the country sixth in the world. China is now the world's largest producer of coal, fertilizer, televisions, chemical fiber, and steel. Total imports and exports are on the order of $400 billion each year, according to *People's Daily*.

What's next for China? Jiang Zemin, the current president, deserves kudos for steering the boat through some rough political and economic seas. Somehow, over the last decade, he has managed to juggle the economic reform program and loosen up some of the political and societal restraints just a little, all the while keeping a firm hand on the party, the People's Liberation Army, and the populace.

Jiang is a smart cookie, and has had some lucky breaks, too. The Chinese economy continues to expand in giant steps, but Jiang and his economic head honcho Zhu Rongji have managed to keep inflation in check. Urban incomes have risen, along with new opportunities to spend money on better housing, automobiles, imported goods, and other things. Politically, Jiang has been able to harness new feelings of national pride to work for the party, not against it. The scars of Tiananmen will always be there, but Jiang has done a lot to move the country forward. Just where Jiang is steering China next, though, is a good question. The "Three Representatives" campaign he launched in February 2000, seems a throwback to Maoist times, when the idea of perpetual revolution was part of the political culture. Jiang Zemin's initiative is clearly aimed at revitalizing the party. (For more on the "Three Representatives" see Chapter 12.)

One of the things going in Jiang's favor is the renewed sense of national pride. It also didn't hurt the party to see this national pride erupt into demonstrations against the United States when a NATO plane accidentally bombed the Chinese embassy in Belgrade in May 1999. And the collision between a U.S. Navy spy plane and Chinese jet in April 2001 reinforced the rising anti-American sentiment in China.

Han Help

Wang Wei, the Chinese pilot who died in the crash, became a national martyr. Chinese hackers retaliated against some 1,000 U.S. websites, defacing the U.S. web pages with nationalistic slogans such as "All Chinese must be united and battle for the honor of our homeland."

The "Workers with High Incomes"

The Chinese Communist Party, being a staid organization, doesn't use the phrase "middle class" in any of its official communications. When necessary, they refer to "workers with high incomes." The Chinese Academy of Social Sciences also will not use the seemingly forbidden term. They say that it has negative connotations, and they've been known to refer in their publications to the "middle stratum."

Only during the last years of the twentieth century was private enterprise mentioned in the Chinese constitution as something that was allowed. The very thought of private enterprise for personal gain would have been unheard of when Mao Zedong was alive.

According to the government-sponsored Chinese Academy of Social Sciences, 15 percent of the work force in China is what we would call middle class. When Jiang Zemin suggested in 2001 that private businessmen be allowed to join the CCP, there was quite a fuss. So, the CCP may want to deny that the middle class exists, but that isn't going to make that ever-growing segment of the population go away.

In his speech commemorating the eightieth anniversary of the Chinese Communist Party, Jiang Zemin said, "The Party must expand its popular support and increase its social influence… It must not dogmatically cling to some individual theses and specific programs of action formulated for a special situation by authors of Marxist classics in the specific historical conditions, in spite of the changes in historical conditions and present realities."

Han Help

Just who is in China's middle class? Foreign investors may dream of selling to 1.3 billion consumers in China, but know that only a small fraction of the population will have enough disposable income to buy imported luxury goods or joint-venture products. The Gallup Organization's subsidiary, Gallup China, has been conducting polls in China for several years. Gallup China defines the middle class in China as those people with low fixed expenses and small families. According to *The China Business Review*, Gallup polls reveal that China's "emerging middle and upper classes encompass people from all walks of life, from entrepreneurs, employees of foreign-PRC joint ventures, and taxi drivers, to senior-level government officials, tour guides, celebrities, and chefs."

Long Yongtu, who was China's number-one negotiator during China's accession talks with the WTO, predicted that China would have as many as half a billion middle-income consumers by 2012, a number that would give that country a larger middle class than the United States. A more conservative estimate from the Chinese State Information Center says that there will be 200 million members of the Chinese middle class by 2005.

Others are not nearly as optimistic about the future of China's middle class, saying that their numbers will be held in check by unemployment long before they get to 200 million or half a billion.

Certainly the hard-liners in the CCP do not want to see the middle class grow anywhere near that large. Affluence, they believe, will inevitably lead to a desire for more political influence. Jiang's softening of the CCP's requirements for membership, under the "Three Representatives" policy, was seen by some observers as a transparent maneuver to co-opt the perceived threat represented by the growing entrepreneurial class.

Shen Mingming, director of Beijing University's Research Center for Contemporary China, was quoted in the *Economist* (February 5, 2002) as saying that the only groups in China "with collective political consciousness are those traditionally recognized by the party: workers, peasants and 'intellectuals,' as graduates are known." Of businessmen who wanted to try to change the system, Shen said, "During this transitional process, these people are direct beneficiaries, they are getting a free ride, so why should they bother?"

In 2002, four private business owners were given the title of "model workers" and presented with May 1 Labor Medals by the government's national-level labor organization, the All-China Federation of Trade Unions. The awards had traditionally been given to workers in state farms and factories.

Wise One Says _____

Fred Hu, an economist with Goldman Sachs in Hong Kong, was quoted in *Business Week* as saying "This growing middle class is really the foundation of social stability in China. As they become richer, they will have natural aspirations for greater social and political freedom and pluralism. They will have a strong interest in building the rule of law in China. They will want to protect their property rights, just like Americans. This will enhance the rule of law in China."
—Bruce Einhorn, *Business Week* (October 16, 2001)

The Rural Picture

Down on the farm the economic picture isn't nearly so rosy. Initially, the reforms of the 1980s gave rural residents far greater autonomy over what they grew and where they sold their agricultural goods. And the township and village enterprises that sprang up around the country helped increase rural incomes significantly. From 1979 to 1984, the average income of Chinese rural residents grew by 15 percent a year, a huge increase. But rural income growth then slowed to as little as 1.7 percent in 1991. Declining market prices in the past five years have meant a decline in the real income of agricultural workers. Many have left the farms, looking for work of any kind in China's cities, where they've joined a growing pool of migrant labor.

At the same time, the tax burden on rural residents has increased sharply. Less income, more taxes—it's not a pretty picture. In some areas, taxes and miscellaneous fees (many of them bogus and illegal) imposed by local officials amount to 20 percent of gross annual income. Technological improvements—one of Deng Xiaoping's "Four Modernizations"—mean that fewer bodies are needed to work the same amount of land. And with so many state enterprise workers being furloughed throughout the country, there haven't been enough jobs created in other sectors to absorb the excess agricultural workers.

The list of rural woes goes on and on. Corrupt local officials increasingly try to squeeze more money out of the peasants. And many villages, led by corrupt officials or not, are deeply in debt. Schoolteachers and other service providers are not paid, and schools can't stay open enough to educate children. Rural health care, once served by the proud "barefoot doctors" Mao Zedong sent all over China in the 1960s, is on the decline. Rural hospitals can't afford to operate if rural residents can't pay for their services. And the "social safety net" envisaged by Jiang Zemin and Zhu Rongji really doesn't help rural residents, who usually have to pay out-of-pocket for medical and other services.

A 1999 book by Ren Zhi, *Chinese People Suing Officials*, gives a fascinating look at some of the excesses of local officials. In Hebian township in Sichuan Province, local officials were keeping two sets of books to hide the fact that they were charging the 67,000 local farmers illegal fees. Several hundred of the farmers took the case to court in 1997, but most dropped out after being harassed by city officials. And the lawyer bringing the suit nearly lost his license.

Ren Zhi's commentary is remarkably harsh for a book published in China. He says:

> Ignoring the burdens placed on farmers, ignoring what they need to survive in the end is like planting a time bomb at your own feet. All people in government should be conscious of this. The Communist Party grew so quickly and won because it liberated and brought benefits to the people. It won the support and protection of the people. If it were to do the opposite and ignore the people, well what would happen in that case is obvious and goes without saying … The Party Center and the government sent down strict orders on reducing the tax burden on the farmers and on allocating to them land on a thirty-year lease basis. But what local officials do in practice is very worrying ….

The Status of Women

Here's a quick look at women in China, the group that Mao labeled during the Great Proletarian Leap Forward as "holding up half the sky."

- Almost all urban women and the majority of rural women work outside the home.
- Women account for 44 percent of the total number of people employed in China (the international average is 34 percent).
- Their jobs are lower-paying.
- Only 62 percent are literate (compared with 90 percent of men).
- The majority of unemployed are women.
- China may have as many as 20 million prostitutes.
- China is the only country in the world where more suicides are reported for women than for men.

A 2001 survey by the All-China Federation of Women found that women in China actually fare worse now than they did a decade ago. There are fewer women in all levels of government and party, for example, and women tend to work in the lowest-paid jobs, often in factories where working conditions are less than ideal.

On paper, China offers its female citizens far more benefits than the U.S. government promises U.S. women. China's Labor Law provides specific guarantees for maternity leave. In practice, though, there is just too much cheap labor available in China, and factory owners tend to fire women who become pregnant. Somewhat ironically, these problems tend to be worse in Guangdong and Fujian Provinces—the wealthier provinces—where the long arm of Beijing has trouble reaching.

One particular burden in China falls heavily on women—birth control. Since the 1980s, women in China have been harassed and bullied into having tubal ligations after having their one child. The one-child laws have relaxed somewhat, or maybe we're just not hearing the type of horror stories of a decade or two ago. Nevertheless, women are generally expected to have an IUD inserted and checked each year, or have a tubal ligation. Those in the countryside can often have a second child, especially if the family is involved in agricultural work—and if the first child was a girl.

In practice, China's one-child policy today means that the rich can often afford the heavy fine for having a second child. They can also afford to have a sonogram to determine the sex of the fetus, even though there are strict penalties for using sonogram equipment for this purpose. Poorer couples, particularly in the less-affluent provinces and autonomous regions, may not have the same options. While there is no hard data on female infanticide and the number of abandoned babies in China, the census data suggest that there is a serious problem with missing or undercounted female babies.

Hu Nu?

According to the BBC World: Asia-Pacific service (January 7, 1999) "the sex ratio of Chinese babies at birth is now 120 boys to 100 girls. This is fueling concerns that millions of Chinese boys are destined to become life-long bachelors ... Rural couples who discover that they are going to have a girl often choose to abort, especially if the child in question will be the second—and therefore subject to heavy fines for exceeding one-child family planning restrictions."

The plight of women is particularly acute in rural areas. Suicide rates, one strong indicator of a country's mental health, are on the rise. Unlike the typical suicide pattern in other countries, the majority of China's suicides are rural women. Overall, the number of suicides in China has tripled in the past decade. One delegate to the March 2001 National People's Congress called on education officials to ease up on students to prevent suicides among young people aged 15 to 35, as this is the next highest group of suicide victims. But little has been published on the rural women, who tend to be poorer, and they feel their lives and futures are so hopeless. Increasingly, the suicide method of choice among these women is ingesting Paraquat, a powerful pesticide.

Women in China also have a better chance of being unemployed, which is leading to another major problem: prostitution. Not surprisingly, there are no national statistics on the number of prostitutes, as this is a social problem that was supposedly resolved when the Communist Party took over in 1949. "Open the door, and the flies come in," as conservative party members would likely warn. And if you open the economy, you can pretty well forget about controlling what businesses start to flourish. The government is trying, though. In 1999, the State Council issued the "Regulations on the Management of Places of Entertainment."

The *Singapore Straits Times* did some analysis of China's prostitution problem in 2000, basing their estimates on the reported anti-vice campaigns in 1999. In Beijing alone, over 6,000 hair salons, baths, and other establishments were raided, and 4,100 patrons were arrested. The Singapore newspaper estimates that Beijing has at least 300,000 prostitutes.

The number of prostitutes is likely to be much higher in cities far from Beijing. In Fuzhou, Ghangzhou, and Shenzhen—all thriving cities with a great deal of foreign investment—according to the *Straits Times*, "prostitution is closely tied to organized crime, corrupt local officials, and underground vice marketing organizations that use hotels, places of entertainment and other semi-public locaux to provide sexual services."

Wise One Says

How did China's sex industry get to be so big? Over the past two decades, economic changes have been too great and have come too fast. Morals have been changing, and the population pressure is more and more apparent. When everybody was poor, being rich was seen as evil.... From a situation where everyone lived in abject poverty to a situation where some people ate fish and traveled around in cars. People lost their moral bearings. The old attitude "People laugh at poor people but don't laugh at prostitutes" reemerged. Many traditional Chinese values were lost during the rapid development of the economy. The reconstruction of a new morality still lies quite far often at the end of a long, dark tunnel.

—Zhong Wei, *Singapore Straits Times*, (October 2, 2000)

For many young women in rural China, prostitution is a profession of last resort. Globally, prostitution tends to rise where women are marginalized, and have few options. In southern China's Pearl River delta region, where many foreign factories are located, there are twice as many female migrant workers as male migrant workers. Young women leave their villages for work, and are expected to send much of their earnings back to their families. The Chinese Academy of Social Sciences reports that women in the delta earn 20 to 30 percent less than men do. Women tend to work in factories making shoes or clothes, where long hours, poor working conditions, and low pay are the norm. Zhang Ye, China country director for The Asia Foundation, notes, "Salary levels have stagnated since the early 1990s. Given inflation and increases in the cost of living, salaries have fallen in real terms." (*The China Business Review*, May–June 2002).

China's Youth

What about China's youth? The younger generation in any country, after all, are the hopes and dreams of their parents and grandparents. For now, in China the urban-rural divide is harsh. Young people in the countryside simply don't have the same access to education, particularly higher education, that young Chinese living in the cities do. And families employed by state enterprises are also being left behind, as the furloughed workers are not likely to be able to educate their children to compete for jobs in the new China. And without a real change in the economic outlook for China's poorest regions, it's hard to see a particularly bright future for these youngsters. The temptation to get rich quick by engaging in organized crime, smuggling, prostitution, and other means is high.

One scenario, admittedly extreme, envisages a China where the division of haves and have-nots leads to an "economic cultural revolution." One essay appearing on the Internet, an increasingly popular place to voice political and social concerns in China, argues that the growing economic divide will inevitably cause rising frustration among those left out of the economic boom.

Wang Lixiong, author of a book on Tibet, *Tianzang*, that was banned in China, says that the growing difference between rich and poor in China leaves serious cracks in the foundation of stability of Chinese society. Wang argues that the next economic setback in China could actually lead to a "Maoist-inspired movement that would attack the Party and State."

For those in the cities, the outlook is considerably brighter. China's gilded youth are those in cities, particularly those in Beijing and Shanghai. They are educated, cosmopolitan, and have plenty of cash. Mobile phones and pagers are their status symbols, and they like to keep track of their stock earnings with these devices. Many have studied abroad, and have returned to work as managers for foreign firms in China, where salaries are far higher than they could ever have earned in a state-owned enterprise a decade or two ago.

> **Han Help** _____
>
> China's younger crowd is commonly referred to as "Generation Yellow." (The older fogys are known as "Generation Red.") By some estimates, nearly 80 percent of China's 20 million Internet users fall into the Generation Yellow group. Bulletin boards, chat rooms, instant messages—this group has it all, and has access to just about anything on the Internet, despite Beijing's very stringent efforts to control the flow of information in China. Etang.com, one of China's leading web companies, estimates that at least 15,000 Internet start-up companies have been founded by these young entrepreneurs.

Is this group into politics and political reform? The events of Tiananmen would suggest that the answer is yes, quite strongly. But it remains to be seen how and when those with money in the new China seek to translate their economic power into political power. This is the generation that grew up at the tail end of the Cultural Revolution, or later, and the group least likely to have any loyalty to the Chinese Communist Party.

Intellectuals

Generalizations are always risky when it comes to China, as who can really generalize about the mood and motivations of 1.3 billion people? When it comes to China's intellectuals, the only generalization that probably holds true is that this is a group to be watched closely.

Recent analysis of Chinese survey data by Wenfang Tang, an associate professor of political science at the University of Pittsburgh, suggests that intellectuals in China are generally supportive of reform. Intellectuals—a group Tang defines as those with a university or junior college degree—are a relatively tiny fragment of Chinese society, accounting for just 2 percent of China's workforce. Surprisingly, perhaps, Tang found that intellectuals within the Communist Party "seemed to show more political activism, were more supportive of reform, and more critical of their government than non-party intellectuals."

China's intellectuals come in all shapes and sizes. Western-trained managers are highly sought after, both by joint ventures in China and by Chinese enterprises. It's not inconceivable to imagine the fifth generation of Chinese leaders a decade from now including some U.S.-trained MBAs-turned-politicians. Education, whether in China or abroad, is a distinct social marker.

> ### Hu Nu?
>
> The U.S. Embassy in Beijing reports that China's recent census data shows there are about 600,000 more people claiming college and advanced degrees than were ever awarded in China. Bogus IDs, college diplomas, and physician credentials can be purchased readily in open-air markets in Beijing and other cities.

China's scientists, too, are a valued bunch. Science and technology, after all, was one of the key pillars of Deng Xiaoping's "Four Modernizations" policy in 1978. Many of China's best and brightest scientists are studying abroad. In an encouraging development, nearly 50 percent of the 50,000 or so students who leave each year to study in the United States are now returning to work in China's new research institutes and other facilities. The attraction is not the pay scale, which is significantly lower in China than in the West. The real bonus, many of these returning scientists say, is getting to head up their own research projects on many of the new frontiers of science, including genetic coding and biotechnology.

Intellectuals who write about politics and democratic reform are finding China a fertile, but potentially dangerous, place to voice their opinions. At no other time in China's recent history have so many been able to disseminate their opinions so freely—at least not since the very short-lived Hundred Flowers Campaign in 1957.

The Internet is an increasingly important vehicle for the dissemination of ideas and articles. Though the CCP information control mechanisms have tried to clamp down on who uses the Internet and what information is available, China's savvy surfers easily find ways to circumvent the firewalls. Books that are banned in China are often serialized on the Internet, and accessed by jumping through other Internet sites. As fast as the government can identify and shut down these portals, new sites spring up. For the Chinese leadership, it's a losing battle.

It's hard to say just how tolerant the leadership is of criticism. The critics, after all, come from both within the party leadership and outside, at China's universities. Anyone advocating government overthrow would be pushing too hard, of course.

There are a wide number of new publications available on the street and online. Certainly, for anyone in China with a computer and Internet access, more information is available than ever before. It's astonishing to see the range of official information available on each ministry's website—much of this information would have been considered state secrets only a decade ago. Now, it can be easily accessed in Chinese, and often in English as well.

But criticism from outside of China is still common, an indicator that intellectuals don't really trust the party not to crack down hard. In October 1998, a group of Chinese intellectuals formed an independent organization called China Development Union in Beijing. Peng Ming, director of Research Institute for New Strategy of the Development of China, was elected the first secretary of the council. The meeting also elected a monitor committee composed of seven members.

The organization registered in Hong Kong rather than in mainland China where the registration of such a group was bound to cause trouble. There was hope among the intellectuals that this level of organization was merely a beginning and that this was the birth of intellectualism as a force in China's social reform.

According to the Hong Kong Voice of Democracy, a Hong Kong-based organization promoting political freedom, "The principle of the Union is to study the political, economic, and social problems that will occur in different developmental stages of China, so as to promote political reform. In the first plenary meeting of the Union, the representatives called for the approval of the registration made by civil groups and the promulgation of the Political Party Law.

"Political analysts believe the formation of the Union signifies the emergence of the Chinese intellectuals as a social force of political reform." But such optimism as was experienced at the birth of the China Development Union soon faded as the realities of the Chinese Communist Party's grip on Chinese thinking emerged. In September 2001, four Chinese intellectuals who had formed a discussion group that proposed reforms were arrested and charged with attempting to overthrow the government.

The four arrested intellectuals were 27-year-old *Consumer Daily* journalist Xu Wei, 29-year-old software developer Yang Zili, 25-year-old geologist Jin Haike, and 27-year-old freelance writer Zhang Hongha. Apparently the four participated in the study group's events and members sent e-mails to each other and posted material on a website, articles with titles like "Be a New Citizen, Reform China" and "What to Do."

Social Responsibility: NGOs

One last group to watch is the non-governmental (NGO) sector in China, a group that didn't exist even a decade ago. Now, NGOs are springing up in many parts of the country, and with agendas that cover a broad range of social and other issues. That the NGO sector even exists is a testament to China's decentralization. NGOs in health care and social services, for example, are taking up some of the welfare burden previously borne entirely by the government.

NGOs now cover everything from agricultural support to environmental standards and women's aid. The Expert Committee of the China National Committee on Care for Children (CNCCC), for instance, was founded in 1991 and now oversees some 2.4 million members in 400,000 grassroots organizations spread across 30 provinces and municipalities. A national education NGO, the "Hope Project," has built a number of new schools and raises other funds to help hundreds of thousands of rural children whose parents can't afford to pay school fees. In Ghangzhou, where women migrant workers face a plethora of problems, there are NGOs aimed at enhancing women's legal rights, health, and education.

The Chinese Communist Party is still boss, but is retreating fast from some of its previous areas of control. Many of its quasi-governmental organs such as the All-China Federation of Labor and the All-China Federation of Women are now helping to spin off these NGOs. At the local level, there are fascinating new alliances of local entities and Western foundations and companies to bring in outside information and capital. In Guangdong Province, for example, the Levi Strauss Foundation and The Asia Foundation are working with the Guangdong Women's Federation to help female migrant workers get the social services they need. One of the successes, according to a *China Business Review* article in May 2002, is that local governments have now endorsed minimum labor rights standards for Guangdong's large migrant worker pool.

Hu Nu?

In several parts of the country, civil affairs bureaus have contracted out the management of orphanages to international charitable organizations. Education and health authorities in some areas are reportedly exploring similar arrangements with private service providers. In many cities, nonprofit and private service providers—though there is seldom a clear distinction between the two—have established retirement homes with varying degrees of local government investment and support.

China has yet to develop clear standards and an adequate inspection system for institutions and services of this kind. It is, however, evidently pursuing an American model of private and nonprofit provision, backed by private and public insurance schemes, rather than a European model of mainly state-delivered social services.

—Nick Young, *The China Business Review* (January–February 2002)

Government controls over the scope of activity and where these groups can operate are still quite stringent. It remains to be seen whether the NGO sector becomes a force for social change in China. Certainly grassroots organizations have the potential to relieve some of the pressure on Beijing to provide necessary services and support to the

Chinese population. But the CCP has long been wary of opposition groups gaining too much power. And by nature of their mission, many of these groups are quietly critical of the party. Environmental groups, for instance, help focus attention on the lax and inadequate monitoring and enforcement of environmental laws in China. Inevitably, these groups will come into conflicts with local and national officials.

For now, the CCP seems cautiously tolerant of the NGOs in China, as long as they don't pursue what the CCP thinks is an overtly political agenda. The Falun Gong, for instance, is not tolerated. In contrast, the YMCA, a group that was very active in the 1920s, has reemerged as a provider of neighborhood social services, and that seems to sit just fine with the CCP.

The Least You Need to Know

- ◆ Deng Xiaoping's plan for reform and opening has succeeded.
- ◆ Women and rural youth have fewer opportunities than ever.
- ◆ The Internet has had a positive effect on the free exchange of ideas.
- ◆ Without a mandate from the party, NGOs are addressing social needs.

Pressure Points

In This Chapter

- ◆ Economic reform creates a new set of economic and social problems.
- ◆ Disparities in rural and urban income make rural poverty a major pressure point.
- ◆ Privatization and decentralization create increased opportunities for corruption.
- ◆ Runaway environmental pollution reaches critical proportions.
- ◆ New laws encourage international investment and trade but do not benefit the society as a whole.

Let's start with the good news—the results of China's war on poverty: China has put together an impressive record in reducing human poverty over the last 50 years. During that time period there has been a dramatic increase in life expectancy in China, a decline of infant mortality, and a rise in literacy. From 1949 to the present, China's life expectancy at birth almost doubled, rising from 35 years to 69 years. The adult illiteracy rate went from 80 percent in the early 1950s to the current rate of 20 percent.

According to *China Daily*, since Deng Xiaoping began his economic reform program in 1978, the market-based economy has grown 9 percent per year, reducing the number of people below the poverty line (currently around $63 per capita income) to about 50 million in 1999.

Recipe for Conflict

Inevitably, there is a price to pay for unleashing the market economy; you could call it the dark side of economic liberalization. Fundamentally, of course, free-market economics are at odds with the goals of socialism: In the new China, wealth is not shared equally, and in China's case, the newly rich are leaving many of the country's residents in the dust. It's also becoming abundantly clear that many of China's fat cats got where they are by using their "back door" connections—or in some cases, by outright graft, corruption, bribery, pyramid schemes, and any number of other illegal activities.

The fast-paced economic reform program has placed new burdens on Chinese society. Those who are left behind—farmers, rural workers, migrant laborers, and increasingly, women—put new strains on the central government's resources. Economic reform has meant loosening central-level control and putting more and more decision-making power in the hands of provincial and local authorities, who also have more fiscal obligations. The opportunities for corruption have increased almost as fast as the country's economic growth.

China's leadership is walking a fine line all the time. Maintaining the hulking, inefficient state-run industries, for example, would be an impossible drain on state resources. Privatizing them means putting millions of poorly trained workers out on the streets. To liberalize the economy too far and too fast leaves the very real threat of massive social unrest—and potentially, revolution—at a time when the Maoist view of "perpetual revolution" is no longer on the CCP agenda.

These new economic freedoms, perhaps inevitably, also tend to erode the willingness of the Chinese people to submit to continued *political* restraints. In the new China, those who are left behind economically may be replacing the peasants as China's oppressed class. Will they rise up, in good Marxist-Leninist fashion, and demand a more egalitarian society? And what would be the response of the party leadership? From what we've seen so far, maintaining control and keeping chaos at bay will continue to be CCP priorities.

Old Government, New Economy

Changing the mindset of a billion or so people—and changing the economic infrastructure of such a huge country—did not happen overnight. There were no tried and true blueprints in 1978 for Deng Xiaoping's economic reform program. Instead, Deng began to use the CCP's considerable propaganda machinery to promote the quiet successes of some initial experiments in market economics. In the mid-1970s, in Sichuan Province, the up-and-coming Zhao Ziyang had been expanding the amount of private acreage that farmers were allowed to farm, and increasing the number of free markets where they could sell their crops. Grain production in Sichuan, Deng's home province and China's breadbasket, jumped 24 percent between 1976 and 1979. Other incentives such as bonuses for extra production helped boost Sichuan's industrial output a staggering 80 percent during the same period.

Behind the scenes, at party headquarters, the process was anything but smooth. Deng Xiaoping was the man of the hour and had a vision. Hua Guofeng and Zhao Ziyang (who Deng had elevated to vice premier in 1980) were all in favor of opening the economic floodgates quickly. Other party leaders, including many Soviet-trained technocrats, a new breed of party cadre, were more cautious about the pace of reform and more vigilant about the need for central-level controls. Given the complexity of the economic overhaul, the party leadership came to rely heavily on China's many government ministries and research institutions. This traditional bureaucracy had to contend with competing provincial interests, as the more populous and influential provinces made increasing demands for investment funds.

> **Han Help**
>
> Throughout the country, the party-controlled newspapers sprang into action. Stories began to praise little ventures in the restaurant business, small-scale industries, and other entrepreneurial pursuits. The message was becoming clearer: Capitalism isn't such a bad thing anymore.

Initially, the party had wanted to introduce market economics through controlled experimentation. Special Economic Zones (SEZs) were set up to be little pockets of free enterprise and free trade, where local officials were allowed to strike deals with foreign firms and offer foreign investors tax breaks and other perks. By 1984, the Shenzhen SEZ had racked up over 2,000 agreements with foreign firms and nearly $2 billion in foreign investment. Customs duties were abolished for products coming in from Hong Kong, which led to a flourishing import/export industry—legal and illegal.

Legal Reforms

Flush with early successes, by the mid-1980s the party leadership ran into some nasty problems such as inflation, unemployment, and trade deficits. The proponents of fast-paced reforms won out again, and the economic reform program continued, but it was clear early on that massive legal reforms would be needed to bolster the economy for Deng's *Four Modernizations* to see the light of day. Without laws to protect contracts, for instance, new deals struck with foreigners or even among Chinese companies could quickly turn sour. And it was no secret that engaging with the outside world would require China to adopt a whole body of international law. Law schools, not surprisingly, were among the educational institutions that sprang up quickly in the 1980s.

Language Lesson

Deng's **Four Modernizations** were for agriculture, industry, science and technology, and the armed forces.

For the most part, the broad legal reforms that began in the 1980s are still a work in process. "Trial" laws are issued experimentally, as was done with the SEZs and other development zones. There would be a substantial period for study and commentary, and often some provision for inviting input from foreign legal experts before the passage of the final law.

New foreign investment laws, for example, were absolutely necessary if China was to compete with South Korea, Thailand, Indonesia, and other Asian nations for the foreign dollars and technology needed to jump-start the economy. But the CCP was not about to let foreign companies do whatever they liked in China. The history of being bullied by foreign governments in the past century had left a strong legacy. So the new investment laws put limits on the extent of foreign ownership in a Sino-foreign joint venture, and made the venture responsible for balancing its own foreign exchange. In translation, if you are a foreign investor: Don't expect to own the majority share in a China joint venture, and don't come running to Beijing if your venture isn't turning a profit fast enough. And don't think that every area and industry in China is open to foreign investors. The CCP was, and still is, intent on not giving away the keys to the kingdom.

Han Help

The leaders also tugged and pulled over banking reforms. To qualify for World Bank loans and credits, as well as satisfy foreign investors, China had to put its financial house in order—and fast. At stake initially was some $2 billion in World Bank/International Monetary Fund monies—once the People's Republic of China was able to oust Taiwan from its World Bank seat in 1980. The projects that China was able to push through these institutions in the 1980s were no small potatoes; land reclamation, university science programs, and transportation initiatives were among the first World Bank projects in China—which was eager to claim its share of investment funds.

But make no mistake in assuming that these early legal reforms suggest the emergence of an open society or that they were aimed at protecting individual freedom. The individual rights taken for granted in the West, such as the freedom of assembly, or the freedom to protest, were not what the CCP had in mind. Instead, the types of laws that were passed reflect the leadership's twin goals of loosening the economy enough to encourage the modernization Deng sought for his country, while making sure that the party still had the upper hand, and would not get cheated out of its share.

Growing Economy, Growing Inequities

There are large disparities in income between rural and urban residents and among urban residents of different regions. Some of the free-wheeling Special Economic Zones are flush with money; other regions, usually far inland, are struggling to feed their growing populations.

Continuing privatization of state industry and the encouragement of private enterprise have made it difficult for the government to maintain shared prosperity. China's largest population segment can be considered its "working poor." These people may earn upward of $1,000 per year, but they have little security or few prospects in the new China. Some, still employed in struggling state enterprises, saw their secure wages whittled away by inflation and a gradual decrease in the number and variety of state subsidies. They were also hit hard by the state's "iron rice bowl" of cradle-to-grave benefits. Foreign investors in the 1980s, for instance, were astonished to find that they were expected to begin covering a wide range of expenses for each employee they inherited when they joined forces with a state-owned enterprise. Vacation, maternity leave, and sick days were to be expected, but who knew they would also be paying fees for each employee's housing, education, and recreation—even, if the factory were in a hot climate, an ice cream subsidy during the warm summer months.

State-owned enterprise workers were not the only ones left out of the glory days of economic reform. Rural workers with little to do on the increasingly privatized and mechanized farms were also at loose ends. And entire groups of people, including many of the "sent-down youths" dispatched into the Chinese interior during the Cultural Revolution, found themselves with no education or skills to compete with in the new economy.

Migrant Workers

Since 1949, each person in China has been required to carry a household registration card, or *hukou*. The leadership tried to control who could go where in the country. Further tabs were kept on workers through their work unit, or *danwei*. As mentioned in Chapter 7, the *danwei* determined where an individual could work, when he or she could get married, where a worker could live, and so on. For rural residents, including all those sent-down youths from the Cultural Revolution, these restrictions meant that they were effectively tied to the land.

By the early 1980s, though, official controls began to ease—and officials looked the other way to get cheap labor. The bait of plentiful jobs in construction and industry in China's cities proved to be very powerful. Urban areas were soon awash with illegal migrant laborers. Unfortunately, they enjoy few of the protections of the economic safety nets set up by the central leadership. Migrant laborers tend to work upward of 70 hours a week, with no day off. China's Labor Law, in contrast, guarantees workers 40-hour weeks with one or two days off each week. Migrant laborers, who rarely have a work contract, don't usually receive medical insurance or services, or even the minimum wage.

Hukou or no hukou, more than 200 million rural Chinese migrated to the cities between 1982 and 2000. Better jobs and better schools continue to attract more and more rural residents to the cities. The official compromise solution on the hukou seems to be allowing more migrant laborers to qualify for a hukou near or around the city if they have a stable job and have been living there for at least a year. The State Commission on Restructuring the Economy claims that 600,000 rural residents were granted urban hukou in 2001. The word from the State Council is that all cities with populations of less than 100,000 should now begin granting urban hukou to those who qualify. But local officials really have had little incentive to welcome the migrant laborers as residents. In the wealthy Shenzhen SEZ, migrant workers contribute cheap labor but don't count when it comes to social services. And migrant workers actually have to *pay* special fees and taxes for the right to live and work temporarily in the SEZ. By some estimates, local governments in Shenzhen and elsewhere in Guangdong Province earn up to 70 percent of their income from these fees!

Hu Nu?

There's a dirty little secret to the successes of many export-oriented factories in China. Behind all the shoes, textiles, apparel, toys, and other products made in southern China, for instance, are a lot of underpaid women. In 2000, one report by the Chinese Academy of Social Sciences noted that the average monthly salary for a woman migrant worker in Guangdong province is between $37 and $62. And the never-ending stream of young women looking for work makes it easy for employers to fire sick or pregnant workers rather than uphold the protections supposedly guaranteed in labor regulations. In Guangdong Province, women migrant workers outnumber men two to one. The women are expected to send most of their earnings back home to support their families.

Rural Poverty

Mao Zedong's agricultural workers, the backbone of the Great Proletarian Revolution, are decreasing rapidly. In 2000, by government tally, only about 355 million people in China were actually working in agriculture. Another 145,000 were working in rural industries. More striking, perhaps, is the small contribution agriculture now makes to China's overall GDP. Fifty years ago, agriculture accounted for half of China's GDP; now it is a mere 16 percent.

The decrease in agricultural workers may simply be a natural side effect of the transition to a modern industrial economy. But the signs of income disparity began to show soon after the PRC government granted conditions to certain regions and individuals to enable them to get rich through preferential policies. Those tied to the land got richer, too, but only up to a point. Those in cities could get as rich as their skills and connections would allow. The Chinese government carried out a special investigation into rural poverty in 1978, and declared it had found 260 million impoverished rural Chinese. One third of the rural population of China lived beneath the poverty line. To make it above that line, a Chinese family had to make more than the equivalent of 60 cents a day.

Between 1978 and 1985, the number of people living beneath the poverty line declined from 260 million to 97 million. The number of rural poor decreased to 96 million, while the urban poor population decreased to less than one million.

Today, by World Bank estimates, 270 million people in China live on less than $1 a day, which is the poverty line set by the Bank and the United Nations. In China, according to the government, anyone who earns less than 16 *cents* a day is defined as poor. By Chinese calculations, 42 million Chinese live in poverty.

Official statistics don't tell the whole story though. On average, urban residents earn easily two to three times as much as their country cousins. Pensions are rare among rural residents; most will rely on their children to look after them in old age. Health care in rural areas is rudimentary at best, and nonexistent in some areas. Collective farms used to provide some rural health cooperatives, but these were dismantled along with the collectives. Rural residents account for about 75 percent of China's population, but consume only about a quarter of the medicine consumed in China each year. Unless a rural resident happens to work for the local government, he or she usually has no health insurance.

The party leadership in Beijing knows it has to do something to eliminate poverty. A National Seven-Year Plan for Poverty Reduction (1994–2000) was launched, with considerable loans and funds distributed from wealthier regions to the poorer ones. In early 1997, President Jiang Zemin pledged government spending (including loans) aimed at poverty reduction would top $1 billion per year. Other central-level initiatives focus on mandatory education for both boys and girls in the poorest parts of China. New small loan programs were also announced to provide start-up funds for family businesses throughout the poorest areas.

Increasingly, the initiatives are launched by Beijing, but the provincial, municipal, and local authorities are expected to provide some of the funds and much of the actual administration. Decentralization, once again, is leaving much of the actual funds and the power to distribute them in the hands of officials far from Beijing. It's not clear that these initiatives will actually put the money where it's needed most—or whether the funds will be skimmed off by local officials.

China is also looking for all the help it can get. The World Bank has funded 31 projects related to poverty reduction in 23 provinces in China in the past decade. These projects target rural education, agricultural development, rural industries, and other solutions to China's poverty. In June 1997, for example, the Bank approved a loan package totaling $180 million for poverty reduction in the Qinba Mountains of northern China. The project promoted rural development in several sectors, increased labor mobility, and environmental solutions.

Corruption

Absolute power corrupts absolutely, a saying that holds true for just about any political or economic system, and China in the early days of reform was no exception. In the first six years after 1978, there were thousands of criminal cases involving economic crime. Embezzling cash, taking bribes, cheating on taxes—all of these crimes were now possible, especially in the SEZs and other areas cleared for economic takeoff. The punishments were harsh by Western standards. China had no country-club prisons for white-collar crime; the courts tended to execute the worst offenders, and lesser offenders were sentenced to hard labor.

> **Wise One Says**
>
> "Corruption is the greatest legacy and the greatest challenge for China's next generation of leaders," said Hu Angnang, an economist who also characterized China as the world's most corrupt society.

There are also huge corruption schemes that have come to light. On Hainan Island, one of the designated SEZs, for example, a scheme to import cars and other goods duty-free was discovered. Hainan Party officials were using their clout and the SEZ's liberal import regime to sell luxury vehicles to government officials throughout China.

Corruption in Shenyang

A look at one Chinese city, Shenyang, a city of eight million people and the capital of Liaoning Province, reveals the extent of the corruption problem China faces.

Shenyang's mayor, Mu Suixin, was investigated for corruption. Investigators raided his house and found $6,000,000 in gold bars hidden in the walls, 150 Rolex watches, and computer files documenting many years of criminal activity. Mu was a dynamic leader and succeeded in gaining many grants from the central government for his city. When the city government hired a Hong Kong construction firm to build a beltway around the city, Mu's wife sold faulty construction materials to the contractor, and the result was a highway marked with cave-ins and potholes six months after completion.

When Mayor Mu decided to beautify Shenyang with better lighting and billboards, his daughter Mu Yang won the contracts. Investigators discovered she had a Hong Kong bank account with $3,000,000 in it. She fled to the United States where she is now a fugitive.

The Shenyang government was so corrupt that in the middle of the investigation in 2000, Mu's wife managed to bribe Mu's way to freedom for several months and almost got the probe quashed. Other major figures were tipped off and fled to Canada and the United States with millions of dollars. Ma Xiangdong, the deputy mayor, made 17 trips in one year to Macao and Las Vegas, and squandered $4,000,000 in public funds. He was executed in 2001.

Mayor Mu was not a fly-by-night politician, but a respected man, a graduate of Qinghua University, China's major technical university. He received a United Nations citation in 1999 for improving housing in Shenyang. He apparently had a bright political future ahead of him. He had achieved international fame for a plan to save China's faltering state-owned industries.

He was given a sentence of death, which was later suspended to life imprisonment because he is suffering from lung cancer.

Chinese experts on corruption are casting a critical eye on the party's attempts to eliminate sleaze. In Shenyang, for example, the Chinese authorities removed 15 top government officials and 500 others, but left the party structure intact. Two whistle blowers were jailed and punished for telling the truth. Many escaped prosecution because of party influence, and the corruption remains. Bo Xilai, the man picked as provincial leader to restore confidence in government, is now under investigation for corruption in his former post as mayor of Dalian.

Prime Minister Zhu Rongji spoke of the extent of the problem at the National People's Congress convention in Beijing in early March 2002. "Festivals and ceremonies of every conceivable description are celebrated during which the hosts vie with one another for lavishness. They use public funds for wining and dining, extravagant entertainment, and travel abroad."

But the prime minister did not offer any new ideas to battle this corruption. It is the bane of China, the single most common factor offered in polls, surpassing concerns over unemployment.

Hu Nu?
According to economist Hu Angang, from 1999 to 2001, the cost of corruption was approximately 14.5 percent of China's GDP (gross domestic product).

Affairs have reached a point where many citizens have no confidence in their local authorities, and seek relief from the National People's Congress, which holds its annual meetings in Beijing. The meetings are surrounded by security guards whose ostensible duty is to prevent disturbances, but who seem equally bent on preventing petitioners from getting a hearing on their grievances.

Yu Baozhong's Case

The case of Yu Baozhong is not atypical. Yu was 1 of 50 elected village heads in Shandong Province who resigned after the Communist Party stymied their efforts to investigate corrupt village finances. He had made four previous trips to Beijing, without success in getting a hearing—and despite a story in *The People's Daily* which outlined his case.

Why had he come this time? He knew that officials from Shandong might catch him and bundle him off back home to be tried for some imagined offense. "This is the only time when the higher ups might pay attention to us," he said. "I knew it was dangerous to do so, but this is the only road open to us."

"If delegates raise questions about a case and call for action it is hard for the People's Congress to ignore them," said another petitioner.

In 2001, the state petitions and appeals bureau received 160,000 petitions, each representing some claim of wrongdoing by officialdom. It isn't unusual for the petition to trigger the arrest of the petitioner, and his forcible return to his native place to face charges. But it is the last resort of those courageous enough to stand up against corruption and malfeasance.

The Communist Party argues that all the corruption is the fault of a few bad eggs, but the stories from Shenyang and elsewhere suggest that the problem is as widespread now as it was in the Qing dynasty. In many parts of China, the corruption is systemic and virtually out of control. Prime Minister Zhu called for "moral standards based on honesty and moral integrity." "But what will they tell the legislature now?" asked economist Hu. That is perhaps the question of the new millennium to a Communist Party apparently unable to keep its far-flung cadres true to the goals of Marxism-Leninism Maoism.

Environmental Crises

As China changed from an almost exclusively agrarian society into a industrial one, it began to suffer the environmental difficulties—air and water pollution—that are common to industrial nations around the world.

In 1989, a Chinese law was passed that required regular environmental reports by all levels of Chinese government. Despite that fact, local governments routinely kept information about their environmental conditions secret. And the central authorities were not about to let the economic engine stall out while everyone figured out how to pollute less. Modernization of China's industry—one of Deng's Four Modernizations—did not extend to buying and installing the latest energy-efficient and pollution-control devices. By the late 1990s, though, the party leadership began to make more noise about environmental problems. Twenty-seven cities began to make weekly air pollution reports. (Although, even today there is a suspicion that some of those cities are more honest about the condition of their air and water than others.)

Air pollution was cited as a major problem with serious health side-effects in several major Chinese cities, including Jinan, Chongqing, and Beijing.

China's environmental problems are continuing to mount at a troubling rate. Check out these statistics presented by both Greenpeace (August 27, 1999) and a BBC News report (November 17, 2000):

> **Han Help**
>
> The 1989 PRC Environmental Law stipulates "The departments with administrative responsibility for environmental protection of the State Council, each province, autonomous region and municipality directly subject to the central government should periodically publish reports on the environmental situation."

China is the second-largest emitter of greenhouse gases. (The United States is first and has much higher per capita emissions than any other country.)

Seventy-five percent of China's energy production still comes from coal, an inefficient and "dirty" energy system.

Five hundred major cities in China do not meet World Health Organization air quality standards.

Beijing, Shenyang, and Xian are 3 of the top 10 most polluted cities in the world.

Acid rain, from the burning of China's high sulfur coal, causes $2.8 billion of damage to China's forests, agriculture, and industry every year.

On June 4, 1996, China issued a white paper on Environment Protection. It reminded the people that China faces an uphill struggle in developing the economy without crippling the environment. Pressure on resources, it noted, is becoming greater and greater. China's 1.3 billion people survive on only 7 percent of the world's arable land. Enormous damage has come from pollution, brought about in the past decade by swift growth and negligence.

Under the Tenth Five-Year Plan, the Yangzi and Yellow Rivers, along with the Bohai Sea, will be cleanup targets. The plan also includes environmental industries for the first time, a sign that Beijing is beginning to shift from end-of-the-pipeline fixes to putting environmental controls in from the beginning. In 1999, the State Development Planning Commission prioritized the development of sewage treatment plants, cleaner electricity generation facilities, and sanitary landfills.

Air Pollution

China, with its unlimited coal supply, has become one of the world's prime air polluters. Every day hundreds of steam locomotives speed across the railways, belching smoke, soot, and noxious gases over the countryside. Thousands of factory chimneys spew smoke, soot, and gases into the air. Every day millions of motor vehicles send gaseous emissions along the streets and highways. In Beijing, 1.12 million cars and trucks pollute the air every day. It is the same story in all of China's cities.

Five of China's cities are among the world's 10 worst in terms of pollution: Beijing, Shenyang, Xian, Shanghai, and Ghangzhou. Coal-burning is responsible for 70 percent of the smoke and dust in the air, and 90 percent of its sulfur dioxide emissions.

The city of Beijing is doing something about its pollution problem. Beijing burned 27 million tons of coal in 2000. The city is cutting its coal consumption, hopefully to less than 15 million tons by 2008. Priority is given to development of cleaner energy, such as electric power and natural gas. These should constitute 80 percent of the energy consumed by Beijing in 2008. Since 1990, Beijing has taken a number of measures to control air pollution, reduce auto emissions, and increase green space by building parks to improve the air quality. Many of these moves were taken in part to beef up the city's proposal to host the 2008 Olympic Games.

Acid rain has occurred most seriously in Sichuan Province and Tibet, and south of the Yangzi River. Pollution has led to cancer, and respiratory diseases have become the leading cause of death in rural areas.

Xie Zhenhua, director of China's National Environment Protection Agency, has warned that environmental pollution with cities at the center is gradually extending to the countryside, the scope of ecological destruction is intensifying, and eco-environmental problems have become major, affecting overall social and economic development in some regions.

Water Pollution

Nearly all of China's major rivers are badly polluted. The Yellow River is heavily polluted even though much of its long course is through farmland and grassland, without industrial development. The Yangzi River is nearing the ecological disaster phase, and fighting that threat is the great concern of Chinese ecologists, particularly with the building of the Three Gorges Dam, the world's largest hydroelectric project. The Yangzi flows from Qinghai Province in the northwest through southwest China's Sichuan Province, and empties into the East China Sea near Shanghai. It forms the backbone of China's major economic activity and population. But industrial sewage discharged into the Yangzi now is more than 15 billion tons per year, accounting for 45 percent of China's total, and domestic sewage is 35 billion tons. The pollution is worsening the quality of the water and menacing wildlife, some of which, such as the white flag dolphin, are endangered species.

China's rampant water pollution creates an enormous strain on human health as well. Some estimates claim that nearly half of China's population (roughly 700 million) is drinking water that is severely contaminated. Moreover, the country is faced with a double dilemma in that what fresh, clean water it does have it cannot get to and distribute in any efficient manner. Since 1980, China has enacted laws and regulations for environmental protection. But despite many new rules, the problem continues to be difficult because of strong resistance. The courts have not been very helpful. In most cases penalties are too low to stop violations. The World Bank has warned that China needs to take drastic steps to encourage conservation of resources and to hit industrial polluters with tough penalties. "Chinese companies have no incentive to improve pollution control, unless the expected cost of violation is raised substantially."

Decentralization also makes it particularly difficult to protect the environment. Local officials are often reluctant to stop economic progress in the name of pollution. Or the economic web may be complicated, as provincial and local authorities often have vested interests in local industries. In other cases, it is the People's Liberation Army that runs a polluting factory and the lines of who can regulate whom effectively are blurred.

China's National Environmental Protection Agency (NEPA), a ministry-level agency, seems to be taking a tougher line on mandatory enforcement. NEPA claims to have closed nearly 65,000 factories in 1996 for failing to stick to pollution control regulations. It's not clear how many of these were failing industries, or how quickly some factories were allowed to reopen. Most Western analysts feel the fines for polluting are set too low, allowing factories to factor in the fines and fees as an acceptable operating cost.

Cleaning up the environment is a big challenge for a country whose growth rate is averaging 9 percent per year, and whose population has just passed the 1.3 billion mark. But what happens next doesn't really ride on what Beijing announces as environmental priorities or targets. Without tougher laws and rigorous enforcement at all levels, it's hard to see much progress in cleaning up China's environmental problems. Unfortunately, decentralization seems to have stacked the odds against those at the local level who want cleaner air and water.

The Three Gorges Dam

Construction is now well underway on the Three Gorges (San Xia) Dam, the world's largest dam. When completed, the dam will be 610 feet high. The Three Gorges Dam, in the upper Yangzi River above Yichang, has been discussed since the 1950s. Controlling the catastrophic and deadly Yangzi floods was the main priority, though hydropower generation was also a strong card the party hoped to play. The parameters were so complex that some tens of thousands of planners were drawn into the process by the 1980s.

The high construction costs ($30 billion, by today's estimates) were not the only concern. Whether the dam would work, and hold tight, were among the topics debated by central, ministerial, provincial, and local officials. If the dam failed, major cities along the Yangzi would be in real trouble. By some estimates, over 300 million people would be directly in the floodwaters' path. Just building the dam means resettling over *1 million* Chinese, including 13 entire cities. And much publicity has been given to the loss of several significant archaeological finds along the Three Gorges, and the plight of an endangered river dolphin species.

The Three Gorges Dam proved controversial enough that the World Bank and the U.S. government have been happy to stay on the sidelines, and have not committed loans or credits. And the dam produced a number of Chinese environmentalists, the best known of whom is Dai Qing. She argues that the political motivations of mounting a huge project have overshadowed the serious problems that will arise during the construction, as well as the long-term social costs.

Hu Nu?

The NPC (National People's Congress) has long been seen as a rubber-stamp organization, but some recent instances suggest that delegates are not always quietly toeing the party line. One case that has stirred a great deal of emotions as of late is the highly controversial Three Gorges Dam project. Various delegates are in disagreement about the dam's usefulness and the government's right to go forward with building it. One member is reported to have become so impassioned that he repeatedly banged his shoe on the lectern for emphasis as he argued!

The Rule of Law

Ever since the reform and opening of 1978, China's central leadership has been playing a chicken-and-egg game with many aspects of Chinese society. New laws on investment, bankruptcy, worker protections, and so on were issued to ease the transition to a market economy. But these laws were also designed to make China's legal system transparent enough to make foreign investors feel comfortable investing in China. Thus, there's an element of "create the environment, and the investors will come" in these legal reforms.

Other laws pay close attention to international norms. Without a clear environmental policy, for example, China would have trouble pursuing World Bank or Asian Development Bank funds for development projects. And the whole question of whether China could join the World Trade Organization prompted changes to hundreds of Chinese laws and regulations relating to trade and investment. Without the WTO deadline, it's unlikely China would have taken many steps to protect intellectual property or patents. In a free-market economy, who cares if someone in Ghangzhou wants to make a few bucks selling bootleg videos of *Harry Potter*? Well, it's the United States and the European Union who care that their firms are losing revenue. The new Customs Law, which became effective in January 2001, was also issued to address the many shortcomings in the earlier 1987 law.

In theory, of course, many of the plethora of new laws should ultimately benefit Chinese citizens. And the leadership has enacted other pieces of legislation that make some outside observers believe there is a gradual transition underway to a system marked by the rule of law. Many of the new laws, in fact, do address individual rights directly. The 1995 Labor Law spells out in great detail how labor contracts are to be set up, and the procedures that must be followed before an employee can be fired. Ceilings are set for the maximum number of hours that companies can require their employees to work each week, and there are provisions outlined for guaranteeing workers the minimum wage.

How the law is implemented, though, is largely up to the local governments. And the legal system's provisions for addressing complaints are still being worked out. Yes, in theory, workers can take their employers to court. In practice, particularly in regions where there is little alternative employment, employers get away with violating the law.

Beijing's civil rights policies continue to be a major pressure point for the party-state. See Chapter 13 for background and perspectives on the conflict between central government control and democratic reforms. Chapter 16 looks at the government's suppression of Tibetan Buddhism, Falun Gong, and Christian religious organizations.

The Least You Need to Know

- ◆ Due to privatization, the "working poor" now comprise China's largest population segment.

- ◆ Rural poverty is a major problem for 270 million rural residents who live below the poverty line.

- ◆ Government decentralization encourages corruption and undermines Beijing's efforts to enforce environmental legislation.

- ◆ The Three Gorges Dam is a highly controversial project that could displace up to 300 million people.

Chapter 16

Strained Relations

In This Chapter

- Relations between the governments of mainland China and Taiwan continue to be strained.

- China's rule of Tibet is an international human rights issue.

- Taiwan watches Hong Kong's transition to Chinese rule for clues to its future.

- China tightens its grip on the Muslim population of the Xinjiang Uygur Autonomous Region.

- Harsh measures are used against members of the banned Falun Gong.

Every country has its own internal troubles, and China is no exception. What's different in China's case, perhaps, is the number of regions, both within and outside its borders, in which there are deep, unresolved tensions. In a regime that allows for great economic freedom, Beijing faces a constant battle to maintain a tight political hold on all of China—and fight for what it believes *should* be part of China.

Just off its eastern seaboard, the "other China," or Taiwan, is the source of a major unresolved conflict. The PRC's view has long been that Taiwan is an errant province of the mainland that needs to be reunited—a view certainly not shared by everyone on Taiwan. Hong Kong, long a vibrant

British colony, may be the first test case of the long-term plans for the "peaceful reunification" of Taiwan. On June 30, 1997, the British turned Hong Kong over to Beijing. The Hong Kong Special Administrative Region (SAR) is now operating in uncharted waters.

Even within the mainland's 30 provinces and autonomous regions, it is clear that Beijing does not have anywhere near the level of control it wants to have. In the new China, economic reforms have proven a harsh test for the central leadership's political control. What happens in Guangdong Province or Hainan Island or any number of thriving local economies is often far from Beijing's watchful eyes. Deals are made, goods are smuggled, and taxes evaded—and these practices are so widespread that authorities in Beijing are largely powerless to crack down.

Far more worrisome to the Chinese leadership, no doubt, is what goes on in some of the poorer outer regions of China. Here the problem is not free-wheeling entrepreneurs playing fast and loose with central-level rules and regulations. Instead, there is a very real problem of insurrection among many of China's minority peoples. Tibet and Xinjiang have the CCP leaders worried, and for good reason.

Taiwan: The "Other China"

Taiwan, only 190 miles off the coast of Fujian Province, has been a headache for communist China since 1949. Under Japanese control since the first Sino-Japanese war in 1895, Taiwan came back into Chinese hands after the defeat of Japan in 1945. A revolt in 1947 was quickly suppressed by the Chinese nationalist government, leaving the island's native population weakened and unable to stop a full takeover by Chiang Kaishek's Guomindang forces in 1949. Chiang had nowhere else to run, and needed a safe haven from the communist forces.

Hu Nu?
Taipei's National Palace Museum contains many of the finest Chinese art treasures, almost all derived from the Qing dynasty's treasury. As they retreated from the mainland in 1949, Chiang's forces carried with them this collection—over half a million pieces of art—which had been hidden from the Japanese in Nanjing.

The Guomindang soldiers—or KMT as the political party is still called in Taiwan today—composed of mainly Han Chinese, quite overwhelmed and outnumbered the local Taiwanese. They brought with them their customs and language. Chiang Kaishek brought along the KMT's iron-fisted and corrupt ways as well. The KMT continued to say that Nanjing was the Republic of China's capital, with Taipei its "temporary" capital. Taiwan remained tightly under Chiang's control until his death in 1975. Chiang Chingguo, his son, then took over as president.

The U.S. government stood by its promise to support Chiang Kaishek and has given naval protection, military materiel, airplanes, and other assistance to Taiwan over the years. The presence of U.S. ships off the coast of Taiwan during particularly tense times in PRC-Taiwan relations, particularly in the 1950s, no doubt helped persuade Mao Zedong not to launch a military invasion.

But continued U.S. support can't alter Taiwan's strange reality: The Republic of China is no longer the "real" or official China, and is no longer recognized as an independent country by the vast majority of countries. Taiwan lost its seat in the United Nations in 1971 and remains a non-country in limbo. In the realm of economics, though, Taiwan holds its own. China's entry into the World Trade Organization was held up pending resolution of Taiwan's application for membership. A compromise was ironed out to allow China and Taiwan to join the WTO simultaneously—and as separate economies.

Politically, tensions, though they have certainly diffused in recent years, continue to flare between Taiwan and the mainland. The sabers rattle—and the world watches and waits to see if the United States and other superpowers will be dragged into the fray. In short, Taiwan's fate is anything but certain.

While it shares a common language and culture with much of the mainland, economically the two Chinas are worlds apart. A sort of economic miracle occurred in Taiwan, long before any party member dared propose economic reforms in China. In the 1950s, socioeconomic conditions on Taiwan were similar to those on the Chinese mainland. But by 1990, the per capita income of Taiwanese was $7,600 per year, 15 times higher than that of the PRC. Known as one of Asia's "Four Tigers," Taiwan prospered through rapid industrialization and by adopting an export-oriented policy.

> **Hu Nu?**
>
> General Douglas MacArthur wanted to use Taiwanese troops in the Korean War, but was restrained by President Truman. But MacArthur's unequivocal opposition to Chinese communism was one of the reasons Mao Zedong led China into the Korean War on the side of North Korea.

Rapid economic development in Taiwan has brought the emergence of a large middle class demanding political participation. In 1996, the island's first democratic elections were held. In March 2000, the Democratic Progressive Party's, or DPP, candidate was elected president, ending 50 years of KMT rule. The new president, Chen Shui-Bian, is seen as pro-independence. Until his term is up in 2004, some analysts believe, there is little chance of concrete breakthroughs in the impasse between China and Taiwan.

For many on both sides of the Taiwan Strait, reunification with the mainland has been a long time coming. "Peaceful reunification" has been the CCP's operative phrase, but it's anyone's guess how fast this is possible, or how the kinks are to be worked out. Officially, communist China has always counted Taiwan as China's twenty-third province.

In 1991, Taiwan issued a long-range plan for reunification with mainland China. Taiwan and Chinese leaders have since met several times for high-level discussions. Relations between the two Chinas took a step back in 1995, when China's military forces went on wartime maneuvers near Taiwan. That Taiwan was preparing for its first open elections at the time was probably no coincidence.

Since this last saber-rattling incident, Beijing's stance on Taiwan has become more conciliatory. During the March 2002 meeting of the National People's Congress, China's leaders seemed less agitated than before about the issue of Taiwan. In his opening speech, Premier Zhu Rongji repeated an offer made previously to resume negotiations with Taiwan for unification, without any of the usual threats. Nevertheless, during the recent official visit of Hu Jintao (presumed to become China's new leader after Jiang steps down) to the United States, Hu warned that increasing U.S.-Taiwan arms exchanges would undermine China-U.S. relations.

While China-Taiwan political dealings have been thorny for the past 50 years, economic ties have been quietly thriving through back-door means. Officially, the Taiwan government has prohibited investment projects in the mainland in excess of $50 million, and bans Taiwanese companies involved in defense and other strategic industries from making investments in China. Unofficially, these regulations are easily skirted by Taiwan's companies who create subsidiaries in Hong Kong or elsewhere, and then use them to route capital and technology via their subsidiary to the mainland. By the year 2000, nearly 75 percent of Taiwan firms had investments in China. The total amount of Taiwan monies committed to China's investment projects is somewhere between $50 billion and $100 billion. Many descendants of the KMT arrivals also funnel significant sums of money back to the mainland to build factories and schools in their "home" villages, especially in Fujian Province.

Trade across the Taiwan Strait, too, has been increasing rapidly. The official balance of trade, according to China's customs agency, shows China importing some $25 billion worth of Taiwan-made machinery, chemicals, metals, and other goods in the year 2000. Taiwan took in roughly $5 billion in PRC goods. Unofficially, the tally is probably much higher, as smuggled goods readily cross the Taiwan Strait in both directions.

Businesses on both sides of the Taiwan Strait would be happy if the political thorns could be put aside in favor of some very basic economic breakthroughs. Direct shipping and air links, for instance, would make business dealings infinitely easier. With no direct flights between Taiwan and the mainland, Taiwan's entrepreneurs have to travel via Tokyo or Hong Kong to reach their PRC investments.

President Chen has pledged not to declare Taiwan's independence, a move that would surely arouse Beijing's wrath and also be opposed by the United States and many of the people of Taiwan (though many in Taiwan are adamantly against joining the PRC under its current leadership). Since 1979, China has promised that Taiwan can continue its capitalist economic system, under the "one country, two systems" principle. In 1992, President Jiang Zemin reaffirmed this promise, noting that "After reunification, Taiwan ... will have its own administrative and legislative powers ... It may conclude commercial and cultural agreements with foreign countries ... It may keep its military forces ...."

Hong Kong

Everyone in Taiwan is eager to see how the "one country, two systems" promise will evolve in *Hong Kong*. Under British rule from 1842 to 1997, Hong Kong has long been a major trade and *entrepot* center of Asia. In terms of space, Hong Kong is a measly 1,092 square miles of islands and some territory on the mainland. In economic terms, though, it is a major global player.

What Hong Kong has is location, location, location. Few ports in the world come close to handling the amount of container traffic that goes through Hong Kong harbor. Much of China's trade has always come through Hong Kong, and much of the rest of Asia's goods also come through the port of Hong Kong. The new Chek Lap Kok Airport, built on land reclaimed from the sea on Lantau Island, also commands a huge share of Asia's growing air shipment traffic. Hong Kong is home to a wide variety of industries, though many of its factories have relocated across the border in Guangdong Province to take advantage of cheaper labor and operating costs on the mainland. Because of its proximity to China, it's no surprise that Hong Kong investors were quick to seek out opportunities on the mainland—and continue to be heavy investors in China ventures.

Language Lesson

Hong Kong means "fragrant harbor" in Cantonese. **Entrepot,** a French word, means "warehouse." Much of Hong Kong's prosperity comes from its bonded warehouses, which repackage and transship millions of tons of goods worldwide each year.

The 1984 Joint Declaration (signed by Britain and China) and the 1990 Basic Law of Hong Kong, which was ratified in Beijing in 1990, provide broad protections for Hong Kong's political and economic freedoms. In theory at least, Hong Kong should be able to enjoy a large degree of economic and political autonomy for 50 years beyond 1997, or until the year 2047.

> ### Han Help
>
> Just a short 40 miles from Hong Kong by hydrofoil ferry, the former Portuguese colony of Macao also reverted recently to Chinese rule. Once a busy port city, Macao's fortunes changed when the Pearl River silted up. Recently, Macao has been the region's Las Vegas, with casinos attracting many visitors from Hong Kong and other wealthy Asian cities. In December 1999, Macao became an administrative region of China. Its economy has long been tightly interwoven with the economy of Guangdong Province, so few in Macao objected to the handover. Macao is known for illegal gang activities, including money laundering. With other boiling pots on its front burner, Beijing may well turn a blind eye to these types of activities in Macao—at least for the time being.

Thus far, there have been few noticeable changes made in Hong Kong's economic system. Hong Kong is a member of the World Trade Organization, and continues to be rated as the world's "freest economy." One strong indicator of whether the transition to Chinese rule is going smoothly is in the mood of Hong Kong's business people. After the British agreed in 1984 to start preparations for the 1997 handover, many of Hong Kong's wealthiest entrepreneurs quickly sought residency elsewhere—in Canada, the United States, Australia, Singapore, and other places. But large numbers returned to Hong Kong even before the transition and continue to expand their business ventures in this lively entrepreneurial enclave.

On the political front there are reasons to be cautiously optimistic that the "one country, two systems" formula can work. The first Hong Kong SAR Chief Executive Tung Chee-Hwa was chosen by an election committee composed of business and professional leaders. Tung was reelected by the vast majority of the election committee in March 2002, and will serve a second five-year term. Seen by many in Hong Kong as a compromise candidate—someone Beijing could trust not to rock the boat—Tung has made it clear that business comes before politics. After 2007, the Basic Law permits direct election of the chief executive, though Beijing has made no statements promising that this will happen.

Hong Kong's Legislative Council (LegCo) includes both directly elected representatives and those from "functional constituencies," or different businesses. The third arm of government, the judiciary, is based on English common law. Freedom of the press and religious groups seem to be no problem, though it is interesting that Tung Chee-Hwa has begun to echo the Communist Party line on the Falun Gong, describing the group as an "evil cult."

For now, at least, Hong Kong's biggest challenges are economic in nature. How it weathers the current global downturn, for instance, is one area to watch. And, like other modern cities, Hong Kong has some serious air and water pollution issues to address. But if the first five years of Chinese rule are any indication, Hong Kong and Beijing seem to be moving in the right direction.

> **Hu Nu?**
>
> More than 90 percent of the Hong Kong population speak Cantonese, the Chinese dialect commonly spoken throughout southern China. English is the other official language in Hong Kong. After the 1984 declaration to return Hong Kong to Chinese rule, classes in Mandarin (Putonghua) were filled to capacity. Though the written language is essentially the same, the Mandarin and Cantonese words and intonation vary widely.

Tibet

Few places in the world can claim the rugged beauty of Tibet—or its muddled past and uncertain future. And few places have inspired such fierce outside condemnation of Beijing's heavy hand. To those in the Chinese Communist Party, past and present, there is no controversy: Tibet (known as Xizang or "western province" in Chinese) became part of China long ago, during the eighteenth century. In 1950, the People's Liberation Army invaded Tibet, intent on taking back what they believed to be a rightful part of China.

To many in the West, the Chinese invaded a peaceful, independent nation, destroying the peaceful lives of a devoutly religious people in their "Shangri-La" in the Himalayas. Large numbers of pro-Tibetan supporters have been quick to denounce the Chinese presence in Tibet, and blast the CCP's infringement on the human rights of Tibetans.

Tibet is a remote, geographically isolated land, about one third the size of the United States. The people of Tibet practice their own unique brand of Buddhism, and their spiritual leader is known as the *Dalai Lama*. The current Dalai Lama went into exile in India in 1959, and continues to lead his people spiritually though he cannot return to Tibet. His cause for a free Tibet has attracted much global attention, and he was awarded the Nobel Peace Prize in 1989. By being a gentle but outspoken reminder of his people's plight, the Dalai Lama is a continued embarrassment to Beijing.

Language Lesson

Dalai Lama means "All-Embracing Leader." Tibetan Buddhism is based on the four-teenth century Gelugpa sect of Buddhism, which believes that the soul of a deceased lama is reincarnated in a small boy, who is then trained to take his role. Traditionally, Tibet was a theoc-racy, its government run by monks.

Militarily, Tibet is important to China because of its long borders with India, Nepal, Bhutan, and Myanmar (Burma). Politically, Tibet has been a headache for the Communist Party since day one. When the Chinese communists occupied Tibet, the Tibetan leader, the Dalai Lama, refused to cooperate with the takeover. When he left for India in 1959, the Chinese attempted to appoint the Panchen Lama, the leader of another sect of Tibetan Buddhism, but the imposter was not recognized by the Tibetan peo-ple. China found itself in hot water with the United Nations, which passed several resolutions condemn-ing Chinese actions in Tibet.

The invasion of Tibet by the People's Liberation Army could have turned into a multinational war if it hadn't been for some pre-planning and negotiation on the part of the Chinese Premier Zhou Enlai. Zhou made sure that the military powers that might have been tempted to help Tibet defend itself—India and Great Britain—stayed out of the way.

For much of the 1960s, Tibet was in chaos. The PLA, and later the Red Guards, destroyed temple after temple. Tibet's religion was assailed, and the monasteries were emptied of monks, many of whom were slaughtered. The Chinese also resettled many Han Chinese in Tibet, and began to pursue mining and timber enterprises there. Tibet's first roads were built only a few decades ago, and life in the high moun-tains is tough, with little industry and a harsh climate for growing food. Though the Tibet Autonomous Region remains one of China's poorest provinces, the Chinese presence has meant increased living standards for many Tibetans. Nevertheless, Tibet's ancient cultural and religious traditions have been decimated by decades of oppressive Beijing rule, and are now in danger of extinction due to Han migration.

Hu Nu?

The only country to help Tibet in their war for independence against the Chinese was the United States. U.S. planes flew Tibetans to Colorado where they were trained in espionage and guerrilla warfare techniques. They were then returned to Tibet to fight against the Chinese occu-pation. The U.S. attempts to help the Tibetans were, in the long run, in vain.

For a brief time during the 1980s, Westerners were able to travel freely to Tibet. Travel restrictions were again put in place following violent clashes between Tibetans and Han Chinese in the capital city of Lhasa and other areas. Today, with no love lost between occupier and occupied, Chinese officials keep a very close watch on Tibetan religious and political activities.

Wise One Says

By the time Mao Zedong founded the People's Republic of China, in 1949, Tibet had figured into the nation's pre-eminent task: the reunification of the once-powerful mother-land... Tibetans see the influx of Han as yet another attempt to destroy their culture; Chinese see the issue as Deng Xiaoping did in 1987, when he said, "Tibet is sparsely populated. The two million Tibetans are not enough to handle the task of developing such a huge region. There is no harm in sending Han into Tibet..." An unbiased arbiter would find Tibetan arguments for independence more compelling than the Chinese version of history—but also, perhaps, would find that the Chinese have a stronger historical claim to Tibet than the United States does to much of the American West.

—Peter Hessler, *The Atlantic* (February 1999)

Xinjiang and Islam

Elsewhere in China's wild and woolly west, those nominally considered "Chinese" live in a world far from Beijing. The *Xinjiang* Uygur Autonomous Region is China's largest administrative region, accounting for nearly one sixth of the total land mass. Its 19 million people include Uygurs (8 million), Kazaks, Hui, and other minorities. And, like Tibet, Xinjiang experienced an inflow of Han Chinese, though the Han people are still in the minority there. This immigration has posed a problem as Han Chinese are migrating to Muslim areas at the rate of 200,000 a year. Outside of Xinjiang, in many places where Muslims once were a majority, they are now a minority.

Many of these minority peoples practice various versions of Islam, which was introduced to China by Saad ibn Abi Waqqas, one of the companions of the Prophet Muhammad. The Chinese emperor Yung-Wei found the teachings of Islam compatible with those of Confucius. The emperor even approved the establishment of China's first mosque at Changan (modern-day Xian), which still stands, 1,400 years after its construction. Today, there are an estimated 35 million Muslims in China, representing 19 distinct ethnic groups. The biggest of these groups is the Chinese Hui, who have settled in many of China's provinces and autonomous regions. They comprise over half of China's Muslim population. The largest of Turkic groups are the Uygurs, who are most populous in Xinjiang.

Language Lesson

Xinjiang means "New Frontier" in Chinese. The government has allowed the reinstatement of the Arabic alphabet for use with the Uygur language. There is, however, continued discrimination against the Uygurs by the immigrant Han Chinese (favored by the government) who have settled in Xinjiang.

Han Help

Since the death of Mao, the Chinese Communist Party has greatly liberalized its policies toward Islam and Muslims. There are now an estimated 28,000 mosques in the entire People's Republic of China, with 12,000 in the province of Xinjiang. Many of these mosques had to be rebuilt after the ravages of the Cultural Revolution. But the rise of Islamic fundamentalist groups outside of China has the Chinese leadership concerned about the spillover effect on China's Muslims, and police control over Muslim groups in China is on the rise. When Chinese Prime Minister Zhu Rongji visited Turkey in April 2002, he urged the Turkish government to stop supporting the activities of Muslim separatists in China—a charge the Turkish Prime Minister denied.

Strategically, Xinjiang is important to Beijing not only for its oil and gas reserves, but also because it borders on Mongolia, Russia, Kazakhstan, Kyrgyzstan, Afghanistan, Tajikistan, and Pakistan. Xinjiang is also home to China's nuclear weapons industry, and the site of weapons tests.

Since the 1950s, there have been periodic violent outbreaks between Uygurs and the communist authorities. Officially, on paper, ethnic minorities in China are entitled to retain their language and customs. But the strife continues in Xinjiang, and has grown more violent. Muslim fundamentalist movements in neighboring countries have encouraged Xinjiang separatists. In recent years, there have been bombing incidents in several Xinjiang cities. In Beijing, three bombings in 1997 brought the Muslim separatist movement into the Han Chinese heartland.

Regardless of whether the separatism shown in Xinjiang is a real threat to the unity of China, the Communist Party leadership is taking no chances. The CCP is not about to loosen its grip on the autonomous region, even if harsh repressive measures push even more Uygurs toward separatism. In a new development in repression, officials have taken a leaf from the Stalinist book of the old USSR and begun sending dissidents to mental hospitals for incarceration and "treatment."

In September 2000, Zhu Rongji vowed to maintain an "iron fist" in Xinjiang to preserve social stability. Resettlement of Han Chinese into Xinjiang—including some of the millions displaced by the construction of the Three Gorges Dam—will continue. But Beijing is aware that carrots may be as effective as sticks. The Western Big Development Project, announced in mid-1999, is slated to provide over $50 billion for agricultural and industrial developments in Xinjiang, including funds to build a natural gas pipeline all the way to Shanghai.

Religious Organizations

If you look at the map in Chapter 1 as you read this chapter, a pattern emerges: The areas along China's borders, those regions farthest from Beijing, are the areas where the "tight fist" of the CCP has trouble reaching. Scattered throughout China, and undergoing the same level of scrutiny, are many different religious organization.

Officially, freedom of religion is guaranteed by the Chinese constitution. There are five officially recognized religions: Buddhism, Daoism, Catholicism, Protestantism, and Islam. But to practice one of these recognized religions, a group has to register to start an approved venue for religious activities. Given the CCP's history of discriminating against religious organizations in the Cultural Revolution, many religious groups have been reluctant to register the names and addresses of their leaders and members. Other groups claim that they were denied the right to register.

By late 1997, according to official statistics, there were some 3,000 registered religious organizations in China, with 180 million "religious adherents." Some 8 percent of the Chinese population practice Buddhism and about 1.4 percent are Muslim. Less than one percent belong to the Catholic or Protestant churches. There are about 10,000 Daoist monks and nuns in China today.

In the new, open China, for the most part, there has been official tolerance for Buddhism and Daoism—up to a point. But it is no secret that Chinese police have closed many underground churches, temples, and mosques. Human rights monitoring groups outside of China have expressed concern about the periodic crackdowns on many of these religious groups.

Falun Gong

Much in the news of late is China's *Falun Gong* movement, though its leaders claim the group is neither religious nor political in nature. Started in the early 1990s by Li Hongzhi, Falun Gong is based on traditional deep breathing exercises and energy-building movements borrowed from both Buddhism and Daoism. The goal of these exercises is to promote better health and individual self-empowerment.

Language Lesson

Falun gong means "practice of the wheel of dharma."

This sounds innocent enough, so why is the Communist Party leadership cracking down so hard? According to some analysts, the answer may be simply that the leadership has serious concerns about any movement able to attract such a large following so quickly. Perhaps, too, the Falun Gong movement raises the specter of the Boxer Rebellion a hundred years ago—when a similarly fitness-oriented movement marked the beginning of the end of the Qing dynasty.

Whatever the reason, the government banned the Falun Gong in July 1999 and began arresting thousands of Falun Gong followers. Government officials who practiced Falun Gong were reportedly ordered to attend anti-Falun Gong study sessions and write criticisms of the group. A warrant was issued for the arrest of Li Hongzhi, who had left China for the United States.

Since the crackdown, there has been little sign that the momentum behind the Falun Gong is slowing. The CCP leadership labels the group an "evil cult," and the group has had their share of battles with Chinese law enforcement. The Falun Gong movement was hurt by an incident on the Chinese New Year in 2001 in which members of the group set themselves on fire in Tiananmen Square. A mother and her 12-year-old daughter died of their injuries.

Even though the group denied that they were behind the grotesque and fiery protest, the Chinese government used graphic footage of the incident to discredit Falun Gong. Leaders of the group have been put in jail and thousands of members have been sent away for "reeducation."

It has been estimated that 1,600 members of the group have died from police action or in prison. The government denies this, saying only a few have died—and those were from suicide or natural causes. The government says that the group has been responsible for far more deaths because of their policy of denying sick members medical treatment.

Hu Nu?

Two New Yorkers who went to China to protest the government crackdown on the Falun Gong group were sent back to the United States—and they had tales of police brutality when they arrived stateside. One man said that he was searched by Chinese police in the subway station beneath Tiananmen Square. When they found Falun Gong pamphlets on him, he was tackled to the ground and roughed up.

"They slammed my face onto the floor and took me to the police station," the man said. At the police station he saw an American woman emerging from her interrogation with a bloody nose and scrapes on her face. The pair considered themselves lucky that they were simply dragged onto an airplane and deported.

Although Chinese members of the Falun Gong have dwindled in recent months, Western members of the group continue to be a problem for the government. Falun Gong chapters are emerging at lightning speed around the world, and many of the foreign participants have been traveling to China in support of practitioners there. Dozens of foreign members were expelled from China during the early months of 2002 for organizing protests in Beijing. The group claims a membership of 70 million in China, and 30 million others worldwide.

Christians

In February 2002, a U.S. religious rights group published an internal Chinese government document that clearly showed official attempts to squash unauthorized religious organizations, including Catholic and Protestant churches. Unofficial Roman Catholic churches have been closed, for instance, and their Chinese bishops imprisoned for counterrevolutionary acts. According to unofficial estimates, there are as many as 30 million Christians in China.

The Committee for Investigation on Persecution of Religion in China, which is based in New York, said that the eight documents were smuggled out of the country by Chinese Christians working with sympathetic local police officers and a former Chinese intelligence official.

They revealed that China had placed "secret agents" within the underground churches and had used "forceful measures" to break up the banned Falun Gong. The Chinese Communist Party, the documents indicated, were going to expand their battle against Falun Gong to include all religions.

> **Wise One Says** _____
>
> "I've never seen anything like it in such quantity," said Robin Munro, a China specialist at the School of Oriental and African Studies in London who examined the Chinese government documents [those denouncing "unauthorized" religious organizations]. "These documents are from all around the country, all consistent, all quite draconian, and all expressing implacable hostility toward these groups and determination to eradicate them. The party sees these groups as a mortal threat, and it's really going into overdrive now."

One government document, written by Sun Jianxin, vice director of public security in Anhui Province, says, "Hostile organizations both in our country and abroad have shifted their focus to the inside of our country and have hastened their infiltration through various methods, such as via foundations or academic delegations, and all kinds of media. Hostile Western powers headed by the U.S. have hastened to carry out their strategies of Westernizing, splitting and weakening our country. [The Vatican] is still waiting for any opportunity to intervene in the internal affairs of Catholic churches in our country." He then said that even as Beijing and the Vatican were discussing diplomatic relations, his security forces "began to search, educate, convert, reconnoiter and control some key members of the underground Catholics. Find out the details about [Falun Gong] and tighten control on them. Make sure to keep them to their local areas and prevent them from connecting and gathering, or going to Beijing to stir up trouble. Put them in classes by force and use forceful measures if necessary."

The Least You Need to Know

- ◆ Taiwan long claimed to be the official government of China and now operates on a "one country, two systems" basis.

- ◆ The United States continues to arm Taiwan against potential threats from Beijing.

- ◆ Tibet was brutally annexed by China in 1950, and its leader, the Dalai Llama, was exiled.

- ◆ Many Chinese believe they have helped Tibetans by improving their standard of living.

- ◆ The popular Falun Gong movement was banned in 1999, but is still a source of worry for the government.

Part 5

The Outside World

In these pages we look at the state of China's relations with its Asian neighbors, and what they may look like in the future. We also give you a thumbnail sketch of China's transition from the closed and repressive society of the Mao era to the open society of today, with its new blends of traditional and international styles in art, music, and literature, and its fashion-conscious net-surfing youth.

The United States figures more prominently than ever in China's future. We look at some of the ongoing issues between the two countries—Taiwan and human rights—and the trade and investment relations that promise not just to benefit both countries' economies, but to lead to greater understanding and the exchange of ideas.

Chapter 17

Asian Neighbors

In This Chapter

- ◆ China maintains friendly relations with Russia, which sells China arms and has begun to invest in Chinese industry.

- ◆ China remains among the few countries with ties to North Korea, and South Korea is a major investor in Chinese business and industry.

- ◆ While diplomatic relations between Beijing and Tokyo are not the best, the Japanese are among the heaviest foreign investors in China.

- ◆ China's claims to the South China Sea, rich in oil and gas reserves, are contested by several other countries.

- ◆ APEC (Asian Pacific Economic Cooperation) works on developing an Asian free trade area similar to Europe's Common Market.

In the good old Cold War days, it was easy to know who was an enemy superpower, and who wasn't a threat. China, the Soviet Union, and the United States fit into a neat, if uneasy, triangle. By the late 1960s, for Mao Zedong, pretty much everyone outside of China was the enemy. But the emergence of new countries and new alliances—as well as new definitions of "superpower"—are changing China's relations with its neighbors.

Russia

Friend, enemy, friend again—it's hard to keep track. China's relations with the former Soviet Union tended to have more to do with security issues than with being communist brothers. The Soviet Union did help the Chinese Communist Party get going during the 1920s and '30s, but it also gave aid to the KMT (Guomindang), believing that Chiang Kaishek had a broader power base than Mao.

The Soviet Union wasn't much help in World War II, either. In 1941, the USSR and Japan signed a neutrality pact. After Hitler invaded the Soviet Union that year, China couldn't expect to get any more planes, pilots, or armaments from Big Brother Russia. After World War II, with Japan and Chiang Kaishek both out of the big picture, things changed.

Mao Zedong's first trip outside of China, ever, took place in 1949. Moscow was his destination, signaling a new era of closer connections between the communist giants. In the 1950s, China's Communist Party relied heavily on the Soviet model of agricultural and industrial reform. The five-year plans, for example, were right out of the Soviet handbook. And Soviet influences on the new Chinese state were visible everywhere—in military training, education, and propaganda techniques to architectural concepts. Soviet assistance was critical in building up China's naval, air, and land forces.

In the new post-World War II order, Mao realized that having the USSR (and its nuclear arsenal) as a buddy was a good thing. The real enemy was the United States, and Mao was happy to get Soviet help in developing China's own atomic arsenal. Soviet advisers agreed to help develop the uranium mines in western China.

Things were going along just fine until Stalin died. His successor, Nikita Kruschchev, rattled the communist world by questioning Stalin's actions and motivations. For China, this was the beginning of the end of a beautiful friendship. Mao made one last trip to Moscow in 1957, securing Kruschchev's help in designing an atomic bomb. Mao was pumped and ready to take on the capitalist world, but Kruschchev was sitting on the fence. Mao began to worry that Kruschchev was being far too lax about the uprising in Hungary—and far too eager to promote "peaceful coexistence" with the capitalist world. When Kruschchev met with President Eisenhower, and then the Soviets refused to provide China with blueprints for nuclear weapons, Mao felt betrayed and angry. China and the Soviet Union began to lob ideological criticisms back and forth, and the relationship soured altogether. By late 1960, Moscow had recalled all its technical experts working in the PRC.

Hu Nu?

If China had concerns about a strong Soviet Union on its doorstep, it soon learned that a fragmented Soviet Union and a host of new neighbors meant new security worries. China now finds itself sharing its border with Tajikistan, Kyrgyzstan, Kazakhstan, and Russia; and Beijing's security forces keep close tabs on cross-border separatist activities along the border zone. Economic ties and trade across the border are fine—anything that helps the poorer inner regions of China means that Beijing has to spend less money on jump-starting the economies of these ailing regions. To help solve the rural unemployment problem in northeast China, Chinese workers have even been "exported" to work across the border in Russia. Still, the cross-border flow of separatist ideas is a concern to Beijing.

The Chinese were worried about a strong Soviet Union, and were relieved to see the Soviets pull out of Afghanistan in the 1980s, but they soon had reason to be concerned about a dismantled USSR. The leadership had to be embarrassed when Gorbachev couldn't even be welcomed officially in 1989 because Tiananmen Square was filled with student protesters. Since the fall of the Soviet Union, China has had to worry about the spillover unrest from the former Soviet states into its own Xinjiang Uygur Autonomous Region and elsewhere along its border. (See Chapter 16 for more on this subject.) China knows full well it can't afford to have its own autonomous regions actually seek autonomy.

Today, Chinese-Russian relations are much improved: Russia is once again selling military equipment to China, including helicopters, fighter jets, submarines, destroyers, and cruise missiles. New Russian entrepreneurs are beginning to invest in China as well.

Wise One Says

In May 2002, following the announcement of Russia's new partnership with NATO, Chinese Defense Minister Chi Haotian met with Russian Defense Minister Sergei Ivanov and, according to the Associated Press, said "Partnership relations between Russia and China are very important for global stability, opposing hegemonism and constructing a multipolar world."

The Koreas

The Cold War in Asia quickly came to a head on the Korean peninsula in 1950. Carving up Korea after World War II was on Stalin's agenda. Korea had been occupied by the Japanese since 1910. At the very last stages of the war, just before the Japanese surrender, Stalin joined in the fight against the Japanese in Korea. The United States rushed to occupy the southern half of the peninsula, effectively splitting Korea at the 38th parallel. The United States was worried that Stalin would decide to occupy all of Korea.

Like China, Korea had some hefty war rebuilding to do, and it badly needed land reforms. By 1948, the Republic of Korea (the south) had been declared—with strong backing from the United States and the United Nations. In the north, Kim Il Sung's Democratic Republic of Korea (DPRK) had emerged. Both Moscow and Beijing supported the fledgling communist government.

By the summer of 1950, the North Korean troops were back home and ready for action. The North Koreans claimed that South Korean troops had launched a major assault in late June across the 38th parallel, and the war was officially on. The South Korean army was no match for the honed fighting force, and Seoul quickly fell to the North Koreans. By July, the United Nations and the United States were starting to rally their troops for a counteroffensive.

Stalin and the Soviet Union were pretty much out of the loop by now. One theory is that Stalin was hoping the whole Korean War mess would discredit both the United States and the United Nations. And Washington didn't want China to be dragged into the conflict. General Douglas MacArthur, leading the U.S. offensive, was told to keep U.S. troops away from the North Korean-Chinese border (he disobeyed the order). But Mao saw the presence of U.S. troops in the Korean conflict as proof that the United States was ready to roll back communism in North Korea. He sent Chinese troops to help the North Koreans, who had helped him just a few years earlier in his own war against Chiang Kaishek. Chinese troops suffered upward of a million casualties. After skirmishes back and forth, a ceasefire was signed in 1953. Ultimately, the stalemate was broken after the United States began to transfer atomic weapons to Okinawa for possible use in the Korean conflict. Both China and the Soviet Union/ Russia provided food aid to North Korea until 1990. North Korea, under a fading Kim Il Sung, became very xenophobic, and broke off relations with just about everyone, though China continued to send some limited military aid. After Kim died in 1994, he was succeeded by his son, Kim Jong Il, and in 1997, China, the United States, and the two Koreas sat down to discuss the future of the peninsula. By fits and starts, the process of reunification seems to be underway.

Nowadays, China and South Korea are raising pens together to sign new deals. Since 1978, South Koreans have been quietly investing in China, particularly in Shandong Province. Like other Asian "tigers," South Korea has been lured by cheaper labor on the mainland—and the prospect of a huge consumer market. South Korean investments include chemicals, automotive parts, electronics, insurance—you name it.

In 2001, South Korean firms signed 2,933 new China investment deals valued at $3.5 billion. South Korea is also pushing the creation of an Asian free trade zone that would replicate Europe's Common Market.

Nevertheless, China values its continuing relationship with North Korea. It is an advantage China has over countries that do not have diplomatic relations with North Korea's communist government. It has also put China in the middle of an ongoing problem: what to do with the tens of thousands of North Koreans who have fled there to escape famine and repression in their country. In May 2002, China came to diplomatic blows with Japan after Chinese guards entered the Japanese consulate in Shenyang and removed five North Koreans who had sought sanctuary there. A treaty between North Korea and China stipulates that China send North Korean asylum-seekers home.

> **Wise One Says**
>
> If you cannot sell things in China you will die; you will be swamped at home and in China by Chinese goods.
>
> —Kim Kycong-Won, Samsung Research Institute in South Korea (*Forbes Magazine*, April 30, 2002)

Keeping an Eye on Japan

China's old suspicions about many of its Asian neighbors tend to linger. The relationship with Japan had long been uneasy—and that was even before the Japanese began carving up parts of northeast China in the first part of the twentieth century (see Chapter 9 for details of the Japanese invasion). But once it became clear that post–World War II Japan was a technology leader, China came knocking at the door. China clearly needed Japanese technology, even before Deng Xiaoping announced his "Four Modernizations." In the early 1970s, China cut a deal with Nippon Steel to build a steel plant in Wuhan.

Japanese firms are among the heaviest foreign investors in China. New Japanese investment contracts signed in 2001 total around 3,000, valued at $5.3 billion. Cars, petrochemicals, chemicals, paper, consumer electronics, and many other types of products are currently being made in Sino-Japanese joint ventures.

But the political relations between Tokyo and Beijing have been rocky lately. Some within the Communist Party are leery that Japan is seeking to be a military power as well as an economic power. As evidence, they point to the 1996 U.S.-Japan Joint Declaration on Security and revised guidelines for U.S.-Japan defense cooperation, claiming that closer U.S.-Japanese ties are a threat to Asian stability.

In 2000, Japan made repeated complaints that the Chinese navy was entering Japanese waters. Japan's foreign minister warned the Chinese leadership in Beijing about the rising level of distrust between Japan and China. Chinese Premier Zhu Rongji agreed to help work out an advance notification system when China's navy goes on maneuvers near Japan. Others in the party leadership, taking a much harder line, have written in party newspapers about the growing concern that Japan is beefing up its coastal defenses and spy satellite capabilities—with China the main focus of Japan's "growing militarism."

Vietnam

After the Vietnam War was over for the United States, Vietnam didn't stop to take much of a breather. Once Vietnam invaded Cambodia in 1978, China stepped in and invaded Vietnam. Cambodia's Pol Pot was supported by Beijing, and China's leaders were not happy about all the Soviet military aid that was flowing into Vietnam. Chinese troops occupied the northern provinces of Vietnam for two months. By then, the Khmer Rouge in Cambodia had been toppled.

Conflicts along the land border have continued, but cross-border trade has flourished. A new agreement signed in 1999 paved the way for Vietnam to begin demarcating its land border, which should help with the border conflicts. Official two-way trade has grown rapidly, reaching $3 billion last year. Unofficial cross-border trade, some of it involving illegal drugs, is likely to be much higher. Trade links should continue to grow when the new Beijing-Hanoi rail service begins taking on freight as well as passengers.

Like the rest of the world, China has also lined up to invest in Vietnam. Some of its investment involves businesses in Yunnan Province, which shares a 806 mile border with Vietnam. Yunnan entrepreneurs have begun investing in ship building and other industries in Vietnam. Historically, there have been large numbers of ethnic Chinese living in Vietnam, particularly along the border.

At sea, though, the territorial issues are far from resolved. Beijing and Hanoi continue to have problems in the South China Sea, where several countries have long had competing claims.

The South China Sea

The South China Sea runs from Singapore to the Taiwan Strait, and includes several hundred small islands, most of them no more than a reef or a few rocks. The Paracel and Spratly Island chains have been disputed territory for the past 30 years. At stake are the offshore oil and gas reserves in the South China Sea and the strategic advantage of controlling a heavily traveled international sea lane. The Chinese and Vietnam navies came to blows over the Paracels and the Spratly Islands several times in the 1970s and 1980s.

Nobody cared much about the South China Sea until the first hints came of substantial oil and gas reserves. Several of the oil and gas fields being leased by various countries overlap, it turns out. And all of the parties seem to have a legitimate claim to the South China Sea, based on principles laid out in the Law of the Sea. China claims the entire South China Sea. Vietnam and Taiwan also claim that the Spratly Islands fall in their territorial waters, and Malaysia claims part of the continental shelf.

Hu Nu?

A Filipino lawyer visited the Spratly Islands in 1956 and claimed them for himself, laying the groundwork for the Philippines to declare the new land, named Kalayaan, a protectorate. At various times, the islands have been occupied by Philippine, Chinese, Vietnamese, and Taiwan troops. Oil and gas aren't the only profitable business near the Spratly Islands. There are also a lot of busy pirates in the South China Sea—nearly half of the world's reported piracy incidents take place there. Indonesia and Burma also claim part of the South China Sea, though not the islands.

At stake is an estimated 7.5 billion barrels of proven oil reserves, as well as natural gas reserves. Malaysia currently accounts for about half of the 1.3 million barrels per day being produced in the South China Sea. Gas production is also getting underway, though substantial investments are needed in the gas recovery infrastructure.

Singapore, Malaysia, Indonesia, and the Philippines

Like Vietnam, many of China's neighbors have significant populations of ethnic Chinese. Since 1978, China has given a warm welcome to these overseas Chinese, especially if they come with cash to invest. Economically, everyone has been getting along well. But there have been military conflicts with a number of surrounding nations over who has dibs on the South China Sea.

Singapore

Singapore, a tiny, modern, high-tech nation, can claim many achievements that China hopes to copy in its own high-tech centers, including the Pudong zone in Shanghai.

Singapore is a financial powerhouse in Asia, and many of the investment projects Singapore companies have signed in China deal with financial and banking services. In 2000, for example, the Singapore United Overseas Bank formed a joint venture in Beijing to invest in China's emerging technology companies. Other recent joint ventures have been announced in trade facilitation, food products, electrical wires and cables, and Internet technology, including one venture aimed at developing e-commerce in China.

The most recent investment statistics from China's Ministry of Foreign Trade and Economic Cooperation note that Singapore firms invested in over 600 China ventures for a total committed investment of nearly $2 billion in the year 2001.

Malaysia

Malaysia, too, has made a lot of investments in China. A quick glance at some recent deals shows a $28 million glass products joint venture in Sichuan Province, a number of fast food restaurants, and a new Malaysia-Canadian-Chinese joint venture to build the Hefei World Trade Center in Anhui Province.

Politically, though, Malaysia is not so comfortable with China's military moves. Malaysia has recently purchased frigates from the United Kingdom and the United States, as well as fighter jets from Russia—all because of the Spratly Islands dispute with China.

Indonesia

China has been clandestinely involved in Indonesian politics in the past, though it is no doubt eager to make sure that the growing unrest in Indonesia does not incite similar Muslim unrest in China.

In the mid-1960s, the Indonesian Communist Party (PKI) was growing in strength, aided by Chinese weapons and its alignment with President Sukarno. Sukarno was growing distrustful of the Western world and the United Nations, and pulled Indonesia out of the UN in January 1965. Indonesia then became allied with the communist and pro-communist governments of Cambodia, North Vietnam, China, and North Korea.

Armed with Chinese guns, the PKI waged a coup attempt in October 1965. It was brutally put down by the military under the leadership of General Suharno. After ousting Sukarno in 1967, Suharno was appointed president by the parliament. President Suharno normalized relations with China in the 1990s.

Much of the relationship between China and Indonesia today is in the realm of economic organizations, including the Asia-Pacific Economic Cooperation (APEC) forum, founded in 1989. There are also cooperative deals being struck, like a strategic alliance on fishing, and a new agreement to cooperate on ocean passenger and freight transport. But, like Malaysia, Indonesia is wary of China's claims in the South China Sea. Indonesia has been taking the lead in negotiating a mutual settlement on the issue.

The Philippines

And guess what? The Philippines also has a problem with China's claims to the South China Sea. In February 1995, China seized Mischief Reef, 70 miles within the Philippines' exclusive economic zone. Since then, the Philippines has initiated bilateral talks aimed at getting the Chinese off the reef, and out of its backyard.

Other than the ongoing scuffles in the South China Sea, China's relations with the Philippines revolve mainly around APEC and other Asian forums. China has also made a number of loans to the Philippines, including $100 million in 2000 for agricultural expansion projects. The two governments signed an agreement that year to expand cooperation in agriculture and fishing. Early in 2002, the Bank of China opened a branch in Manila.

India and Pakistan

If anything, the agreement signed with the former Soviet Republics reflects the experiences China has had with India. In the late 1950s, China and India disagreed about who owned some remote territories along their common border. When the Indian government sent security patrols into the area, the Chinese responded by attacking both Kashmir and Arunachal Pradesh. The Indian army was quickly overrun, and India turned to the United States for help. China then pulled a fast one: It withdrew its troops on its own after a month, but continued to occupy 15,000 square miles of Indian territory in Ladakh. The land was critical, as China was trying to build a strategic highway through it to link Tibet and Xinjiang. China continues to claim sovereignty over the entire 35,000 square miles of Arunachal Pradesh.

Relations between India and China were understandably rocky. It didn't help that India received a lot of military aid from the USSR. And it wasn't encouraging for India to see its archenemy, Pakistan, begin to get a lot of military assistance from China. India and Pakistan, fueled by their respective communist allies, began a nuclear arms race of their own.

It's a messy picture, but it worked to make an uneasy peace in the disputed area—at least for a while. China helped arm Pakistan to be a threat to India, thus making sure its own border with India wouldn't be threatened. And the Soviet Union used India to keep Chinese troops on alert on the Sino-Indian border, meaning less troops could be rallied to threaten the long Sino-Soviet border.

In 1996, the tensions finally got a little easier. China and India signed a "confidence-building" agreement. While the actual border has yet to be delineated, both sides agreed to refrain from any military activities or exercises near the border areas, including air reconnaissance missions. And China has stayed neutral in the more recent India-Pakistan clashes over Kashmir.

Han Help

The Reuters News Service (May 14, 2002) reported a Pakistani Foreign Ministry statement regarding Chinese foreign minister Tang Jiaxuan's talks with the foreign minister of Pakistan. It stated that "The two sides reiterated their shared resolve to expand and strengthen further the close and cooperative Pakistan-China relations" and "It was also agreed to institutionalize consultations between the (two) foreign ministries … in the areas of counterterrorism and arms control."

The latest twist in this twisted relationship was the recent revelation by India's defense minister that China is believed to be building a naval base on Myanmar's (formerly Burma) Coco Islands. China has been assisting Burma for several years. And China has taken a tough line on India's nuclear bomb program, urging the other four nuclear powers to refrain from legitimizing India's nuclear weapons.

Economically, though, China has been developing closer ties with both India and Pakistan. Chinese firms have been investing in consumer appliances in India, as well as software development ventures. And at least one Indian firm has signed up to be part of the Shanghai Pudong Software Park. China also signed a deal with Pakistan in April 2002, to develop two 300-megawatt coal-fired thermal power plants at a cost of $600 million.

Regional Trade

Politically, China has already proven itself as a major power in Asia. In the recent border conflicts between India and Pakistan, both sides seemed to listen to Beijing. Economically, China is a very large part of the Asian economic miracle. Unfortunately, it has also suffered its share of the "Asian flu," or economic downturn in Asia.

As a nation, China has been trying hard to achieve legitimacy. Booting Taiwan out of its UN seat was one big move, but China also needed to be a player on the regional scene. China is a member of the Asian Pacific Economic Cooperation (APEC), a group of 21 economies dedicated to promoting regional economic integration and global free trade among the countries that border the Pacific. APEC members have been meeting since 1992 to discuss trade matters. Many of the negotiations over China's accession to the World Trade Organization (WTO) took place within APEC.

Over the longer term, the APEC forum will lead to the development of an Asian free trade area. APEC is taking steps to standardize trade and investment regulations in its member countries, in tandem with the work being done on WTO compatibility.

If Asian trade and investment can keep up the fast pace of growth the region has enjoyed over the past 15 years, the twenty-first century may well turn out to be Asia's century. And China seems ready and waiting to play a main role in the region's economic clout.

The Least You Need to Know

◆ China buys arms and military equipment from Russia.

◆ South Korea invested $3.5 billion in China in 2001.

◆ Japan is one of the biggest investors in Chinese industry and business.

◆ Several countries are vying for control of the South China Sea's strategic maritime routes and gas and oil reserves.

◆ China and South Korea are leaders in APEC's initiative to develop an Asian free-trade zone.

Chapter 18

From Local to Global

In This Chapter

- ◆ China is going global, and the CCP doesn't seem to mind.

- ◆ Joint ventures with foreign magazine publishers take off.

- ◆ Television and radio broadcast just about anything but the Voice of America, if the government can help it.

- ◆ A great variety of books are available for the first time since the 1950s.

There have always been conquerors running amok in the world and endangering indigenous cultures. In the twenty-first century world of communications satellites, pirated Hollywood films and pop CDs—and of course, the World Wide Web—China, the most ancient of cultures, is as endangered as any other. Western—or American, or even global—popular culture is a powerful force. But once China opened to the world, how could it avoid being influenced by it? Many of the old folks are appalled by the changes they see all around them. But the government that nourished China's nationalist spirit and cultural respect doesn't seem to mind. The CCP leadership has been quite tolerant of the changes that are taking place in food, fashion, love, and lifestyle. It has been accepting of even the more bizarre cross-cultural products of China's artists and performers—as long as their work doesn't criticize the government.

Media Roundup

In the wake of Tiananmen Square and the market liberalizations under Deng Xiaoping, material wealth became a new goal for many. Now, along with the desire to be financially successful—though not necessarily as a worker for the state—there is a full-blown consumerism that demands popular culture information and entertainment. Long gone are the days of political lectures, and in are the times of rock music, late night radio talk shows, variety shows, sitcoms, karaoke bars, and Internet cafés. Media and entertainment are defining the lifestyles that Chinese lead today and therefore have become a powerful shaping factor on Chinese culture.

Media is one of China's newest frontiers where the hearts and minds of billions can be won and the ever-growing private business sector recognizes this great potential. As of the beginning of 2002, China's government set out discussing ways to allow private investment in Chinese media industries in the future. As of yet, however, these ideas are only in a discussion stage. State-owned enterprises (SOEs) remain the main investors in the media industry. Still, it is worth noting that even SOEs are increasingly becoming joint ventures between the private and foreign business sectors. In conjunction with SOEs, more foreign investors are finding ways to gain financial influence in the Chinese media market (see the following examples). Could this be the door which private sector investors use to enter into the media market? Many China experts are hopeful, but the government's ever-continuing commitment to controlling public information makes it unlikely to happen anytime soon.

Newspapers and Magazines

China had about 186 newspapers in 1978, before Deng Xiaoping launched the reform program. By 1995, there were about 2,200 papers. All told, China had some 28,000 publications in 1997, a general number that covers newspapers, magazines, and the multitudes of official reports at all levels of government. The government still maintains strict control over the publishing industry, which boasts an annual circulation of some 26 billion issues.

> **Wise One Says**
>
> Zhao Tingyang, a prominent contemporary Chinese philosopher, says, "Modern Chinese society is particularly difficult to understand because it is a remarkable amalgam, embracing a random melange of eras and lifestyles and producing an absurd but real China experience."

In a new twist, the Chinese Communist Party issued a consolidation order on CCP and government department newspapers, and forced papers with a daily circulation of less than 30,000 to close. There were an estimated 1,800 newspapers left in 2002, out of the more than 2,000 in existence.

Part of the reason is purely economic: The party doesn't want government funds used to prop up unprofitable ventures, and this means necessary consolidation and mergers in the state-controlled newspaper business. The consolidation may save China's government as much as $1 billion each year, as subsidies were needed to produce these papers—and pay for the mandatory subscriptions in the target audience of bureaucrats.

But the crackdown on newspapers is partly political, too. Some analysts feel the move is related to general tightening of the party line in preparation for the sixteenth Party Congress in the fall of 2002. Propaganda officials have been railing against tabloid publications that sensationalize sex and violence, for instance. Any publication seen as critical of the party, even if published within the party itself, was likely asked to shut down.

The People's Daily continues to be the main party newspaper, but the recent consolidation now means that it also includes *China Automotive News* and the ever-fascinating *Coal Information News*, for example. These publications are a holdover from an era when bragging about achievements in the coal and other industries was an important part of the Maoist propaganda machine. Now, they are probably of little interest to the general public, which would rather read about movies, pop stars, new restaurants, and other developments in Chinese society. Financial newspapers are a big hit, too, as China's would-be tycoons like to check the stock markets on a regular basis.

While newspapers remain off limits to foreign participation, there are more than 100 magazines now produced in China through ventures and other arrangements with foreign partners. *Elle China* has been a big hit, along with other fashion magazines aimed at the younger crowd. Financial magazines are also popular. Advertising rates in these magazines are rising steadily, making magazines a good investment for the foreign parties.

> **Hu Nu?**
>
> *The People's Daily (Renmin Ribao)*, the primary source of hefty discourse on the party line, just isn't what Chinese readers want to read. The paper's circulation has fallen from 6.2 million in 1979, to 2 million in 1999.

Radio and Television

Gone, for the most part, are the days when the evening's entertainment meant listening to "The East is Red" on the commune's loudspeaker. China now has more than 10,000 radio stations and 3,000 television stations. In the early 1990s, satellite dishes sprang up faster in southern China than mushrooms after a spring rain. No matter that the central government tried its best to ban the receivers, which can easily pick up the best and worst of Hong Kong television programming—as well as CNN and other foreign news broadcasts. China has seen an astounding increase in cable television subscribers.

Television, as is true everywhere, remains China's favorite form of media. It's easy to see why. When China first launched China Central Television in 1958, broadcasts consisted almost entirely of news about the Communist Party, followed by news about the Communist Party, followed by a discussion of how great the Communist Party was. Maybe there would be some scintillating images of tractors at work in the field—hardly the most exciting stuff.

Today's Chinese television features talk shows, music videos, and soap operas. Discovery Channel features are popular foreign shows, as is *Growing Pains* (an American sitcom) and Mickey Mouse cartoons. There are several foreign cable channels, including AOL-Time Warner's CET channel in Guangdong Province, and a new cable venture headed by Rupert Murdoch, who also runs the successful and popular Star TV channel in Hong Kong. Murdoch's China offering will feature no news broadcasts, but will concentrate on variety and game shows.

Hu Nu?

At century's end, worldwide information and popular culture were spreading throughout the entire country. Movies, television, and radio reached virtually every Chinese village. Popular culture, though an alternative to the official Party culture, was tolerated because its escapism not only reflected the Party's desire for an apolitical public, but also reflected the overwhelming desire of the population, after June 4th, to stay clear of politics.
—Fairbank and Goldman, *China: A New History* (1998)

In the very near future, the Chinese leadership may have a tough time controlling what gets broadcast in China. Once China joined the World Trade Organization, it agreed to allow increased imports of foreign-produced television programs. To compete with foreign media organizations, China recently merged its state film and TV enterprises, along with China National Radio and China Radio International. The new group has more than 20,000 employees and anticipated annual revenues of $2.5 billion.

Chinese radio stations broadcast everything from the party's agricultural forecasts to the Backstreet Boys. Anyone in China with a shortwave radio, a relatively modest purchase, can pick up a wide range of radio broadcasts. Chinese officials do try to jam broadcasts by the Voice of America and Radio Free Asia. Voice of America broadcasts to some 10 million listeners in China, who have long used the programming to practice their English. Radio Free Asia, founded in 1996, offers 15 hours a day of Chinese programming. Both stations use a network of transmitters around the world, and also broadcast in Tibetan and Uygur to these minority groups in China.

Han Help

The China Education and Research Network reports that the National People's Congress is drafting a new law to regulate the use of foreign words in China. (The French government tried in vain to do the same in the 1970s, by outlawing words like "hamburger" and "weekend" from the official language.)

The Chinese proposal would reportedly require television and radio broadcasts, as well as all publications, ads, and packaging to use *putonghua*, the official Mandarin Chinese language. Officials concede, though, that it will be difficult to keep words like "Internet," "WTO," and other common foreign borrowings entirely out of China's lexicon.

The Internet

Radio and television programs can also be accessed online in China. As of mid-2002, the number of Internet users in China was approximately 38 million. In recent years Internet use has expanded throughout China, linking all the large and medium-sized cities, and most provinces and regions, from Beijing to Zigong.

By most industry and government estimates, the Internet explosion has only just begun in China. And it's pretty amazing already to see the fast increase in Internet users in a country where only about 26 percent of homes have telephones. As more Chinese acquire computers and Internet access, China could have more Internet users than any other country. This could come as early as 2010, some industry projections say. Chinese industry statistics reveal that PRC surfers spend 8.3 hours on the Internet every week on average, and the period from 8 to 11 P.M. is prime surfing time.

Hu Nu?

China's attempt to control the flow of information within its borders met its match with the introduction to the world of the information superhighway. Despite numerous attempts to restrict the Internet sites that can be accessed in China, the technology has proven unblockable. Each time a censor from the government tries to block information on one site, another website opens up to provide a new access point. In the spring of 2002, without any great fanfare, the Chinese government abandoned its attempts to block many of these Internet sites. Some analysts are wondering if this is a low-key experiment on loosening central-level controls, or just a technical glitch.

But the digital divide in China is as visible as the Great Wall. Guangdong Internet users account for fully 10 percent of total Internet users in China, according to *China Daily*. Beijing and Shanghai each claim about another 10 percent of the total Internet users. Almost 40 percent of China's registered websites are located in Beijing—many of these are government websites. Out in the sticks, Internet users in Qinghai and Tibet account for a tiny 0.1 or 0.2 percent of total Internet users. The government of China has pledged to boost Internet availability in the poorer regions.

Books

According to a 1999 nationwide survey of reading habits conducted by the China Publishing Science Research Institute, books ranked fourth, after newspapers and magazines, among media used by respondents during their leisure time. New book publishers are regularly starting up in China, and some of the larger publishers are consolidating to form super-publishers. One such group, the China Publishing Group, formed in 2001, consists of 12 major Beijing-based publishing houses and distribution companies. One of the new conglomerate's first projects was to publish a dictionary for a language in Hunan Province that is used only by women.

According to "1999 Annual Report on the Reading and Book–Purchasing Habits of Chinese Adults," there has been a recent growth in Chinese readership, although a decrease in interest in "serious books." Like readers everywhere, Chinese people read for fun and often prefer "trash" to quality. Improved distribution systems, the report says, are the main reason for the upsurge in reading and book buying.

China's bookworms have access to a far greater variety of books than at any time during the past 50 years. Soviet novels were widely available in the 1950s, and then criticized during the Cultural Revolution, when anyone found reading anything other than *The Quotations of Chairman Mao* could be accused of being a reactionary.

> **Han Help** _____
>
> Li Ruihuan, a senior party leader, recently hailed the creation of an 1,800-volume supplement to a 3,600-volume Qing dynasty compilation. Li said the extra volumes will "benefit people for generations to come." The Qing dynasty compilation, known as the *Siku Quanshu*, delves deeply into Qing dynasty views of Chinese culture and education.

Today's readers can read all kinds of books, including large numbers of pirated and banned titles. The Beijing best-seller lists this spring listed a number of books devoted to stock investing, lottery tips, foreign markets, and other finance-related areas. Popular works of fiction include *Harvard Girl Liu Yiting*, about a Shanxi student who got into Harvard; *Poor Dad and Rich Dad*, an American book with worldwide distribution; and the runaway global success, the books about Harry Potter.

"Children's literature in China is too earnest. Things that inspire the imagination are too few. Bringing Harry Potter to China is a kind of breakthrough," said Ma Ainong, who is one of four translators working on the series.

What they can't read, at least not officially, are the works by many prominent Chinese writers of the past two decades. Many of China's best writers have left China for the West, where they have greater freedom of expression. The books of Nobel Prize winner Gao Xingjian, for instance, are banned by the CCP. But these books still make their way in from Hong Kong, or are read in pirated or online versions. Another popular banned book is *The Wrath of God—The Anti-Corruption Bureau in Action*. The book is a fictionalized account of the excesses of former Beijing Mayor Chen Xitong, who was implicated in one of China's most egregious corruption cases involving high party officials.

> **Wise One Says**
>
> Gao Xingjian, who left China for Paris in 1987, was the first Chinese writer to win the Nobel Prize. His novel *Soul Mountain* was described by the prize committee as "a novel of a pilgrimage made by the protagonist to himself and a journey along the reflective surface that divides fiction from life, imagination from memory. The discussion of the problem of knowledge increasingly takes the form of a rehearsal of freedom from goals and meaning."
>
> Gao is also the author of *One Man's Bible*, an account of his life as a political activist and victim during the Cultural Revolution.

Art in China

Today's artist in China enjoys more freedom than at any time since the communist takeover. But do not confuse that with the artistic freedom that we enjoy in the United States. It is still taboo to criticize the government or the Communist Party.

But once it would have been forbidden to create art that did not celebrate communism. Mao, of course, believed that art should exist only as a teaching tool, and all of Mao's teaching was on the same subject.

During the time of Mao's stranglehold on Chinese arts, those paintings that were created were predominantly large murals celebrating the worker as National hero, and Mao as a god. Now a variety of subjects may be addressed in ways recognizable as "hip" to the Western world.

In China it is once again okay to like art for art's sake. It is no longer essential, as it was in the days of Mao, that the artwork be created solely to serve the government. Of course, you could still get in trouble if you created art for the sole purpose of criticizing the government, but that's not the point. A wide variety of subjects are now available to Chinese artists.

Exhibits of Chinese and foreign artwork are available in museums and galleries in most of China's major cities, and the lives of China's top artists are celebrated in the Chinese media. For example, many Chinese artists and fans of art attended the recent Shaanxi International Peasant Painting Exhibition, an exhibition of paintings by artists from 13 countries and regions as well as Chinese farmers from 47 counties nationwide. The art was on display in Huxian County in northwest China's Shaanxi Province.

The Western influences on Chinese art now exist side by side with traditional Chinese art, which remains as disciplined and unchanging as ever. Tradition is just that, a prideful routine, always unchanging. That set-in-stone nature remains the same despite the new penchant for irony and surrealism among China's modern artists—who are, in some ways, the first modern artists China has ever had. Previous attempts to break from tradition, as we've seen, have been stifled by the restrictions of political dogma.

Music

During the Cultural Revolution in particular, Maoist songs of heroic model workers filled the airwaves, day and night. After 1978, Taiwan and Hong Kong singers crooning love ballads became extremely popular. These songs, China's version of "elevator music," continue to be popular, especially in the countryside.

One of the first signs that China was open to the outside world was the resumption of weekly jazz concerts in Shanghai's Peace Hotel in the early 1980s. Several of the musicians were original players in the hotel, and had been stashing away their Western instruments and music for nearly two decades. By the 1990s, China was welcoming large numbers of foreign musicians and touring companies. Puccini's opera *Turandot* even played in the Forbidden City in Beijing.

> **Hu Nu?**
>
> The new artistic freedom has opened up the world of classical music to China once again. During the time of Mao and the Gang of Four, music was used for propaganda purposes only. Now Beijing and Shanghai both have their own philharmonic orchestra. Most of the "long-hair" music in China is Western, but there is a growing fan base for traditional Chinese opera as well.

What's new and hip among young, trendy Chinese is changing as fast as their hairstyles. It's significant to note that Cui Jian, the "godfather of Chinese rock," and other rock bands are important expressions of popular culture—and popular dissatisfaction. Cui Jian, for instance, writes songs like "Nothing to My Name," a lament that China's youth is adrift in the new China. What filled the musical void, according to one music critic, was …

a sickly-sweet Westernized ballad style currently popular in Taiwan and Hong Kong. To this day—with the exception of the rock music of Cui Jen and his recent influences—these escapist love songs can be heard on every bus, taxi and streetcar throughout the major cities, and well into the countryside.

But this is not to say that China's current youth isn't keeping up with the "in" trends in music—they are catching up fast! In the big cities like Beijing, Shanghai, Hangzhou, and even the smaller urban centers, discotheques pump techno-music and other flavors of rock music late into the evenings. China's homegrown music scene includes punk, rap, and grunge bands—pretty much every kind of music can be heard somewhere if you know where to look.

Hu Nu?

One of mainland China's hottest music "scenesters" is the young female pop singer, Wang Fei. Her style is unique and affecting, but like many budding Chinese musical artists, she's found inspiration from Western and Japanese artists as well. Many Chinese (and Taiwanese) pop singers pepper their albums with several remakes of Western hits as well as their own original tracks.

Chinese music of all sorts can be downloaded off the Internet. And Chinese listeners can download Western pop songs just as easily. China's own contribution to global music may be new "fusion" music blending the traditional sounds of ancient Chinese instruments like the *er hu*, *pipa*, and *yang chen* with Western synthesizers, drums, and guitars.

Foreign Film Distribution

Movies in China, too, have come a long way from the staid party propaganda films about model workers heroically doing their very best to boost production. *Spiderman* opened in China the same week it opened in the United States.

And when Hong Kong returned to Chinese rule, China inherited Hong Kong's thriving film industry. The "Hollywood of China," Hong Kong has more than 30 film companies churning out action pictures—mostly kung fu movies. Any action flick with Jackie Chan and Beijing martial artist Jet Li is a big hit on the mainland.

Hu Nu?
When foreign films were first shown in China in 1994, *The Fugitive*, *The Lion King*, *Speed*, *Forrest Gump*, *True Lies*, and several Jackie Chan movies were huge hits. The 10 imported films snared 70 percent of the movie market in China that year, leaving Chinese officials very concerned about foreign domination of the movie sector.
Hollywood, in turn, has had serious complaints about bootleg videos and DVDs in China. U.S. movie lobbyists have been pushing Beijing hard to beef up its intellectual property protection laws and enforcement methods. A pirated version of *Harry Potter and the Sorcerer's Stone* was widely available weeks before the film opened in China.

Joining the WTO means that China will have to do a better job on the piracy front. Beijing will also have to let more foreign films be shown in China, a move that could put its own film industry at risk.

The best of China's film directors, though, have already shown they can hold their own at various international film festivals. As in other areas of the arts in China, filmmakers are constantly pushing the political envelope. The "Fifth Generation" filmmakers from the China Film Academy are blazing new trails with their films. Chen Kaige's *Yellow Earth* and *The King of Children*, Zhang Junzhao's *One and Eight*, Tian Zhuangzhuang's *The Horse Thief*, Zhang Yimou's *Red Sorghum*, and Woo Ziniu's *Evening Bell* have won critical acclaim. The spectacular cinematography and imagery convey, in many cases, quiet criticism of the Maoist era, modern corruption, and other common themes.

Han Help

It would be wrong of Westerners to think that Chinese filmmakers are working in a vacuum. Even though they have a precarious relationship with the Chinese government (and its view of their movies' content), such Chinese directors as Zhang Yimou, for example, have been favorites at various Western movie festivals and at the box office for years. Zhang's *Red Sorghum* (1987), *Raise the Red Lantern* (1991), and *To Live* (1994) are but a few of his films that have won critical acclaim in the West.

Fashion

Fashion, as is true in the rest of the world, is for the young in China. Long gone are the days when every man and woman in China wore the drab and practical Mao jacket. In Shanghai, Beijing, Guangzhou, Shenzhen, Dalian, and Chengdu, the young and trendy sport the latest Hong Kong fashions. Shanghai, long the most cosmopolitan of China's cities, is doing its best to nurture a Chinese fashion industry before global competition heats up under the WTO. Shanghai holds an annual fashion show, attracting a number of foreign fashion designers such as Celine, Fendi, Lagerfeld, and Loewe. Shanghai and other Chinese designers also showcase their own designs. It's not quite Paris or Milan, but it's getting there.

Han Help _____

China's fashion industry is helping to spawn a modeling industry. The ultimate example of capitalist decadence, the beauty pageant, is also becoming a fixture in modern China. Miss Universe 2002, recently crowned in Puerto Rico, is Ling Zhuo, a Shanghai model.

For those who can afford it, it is very important among China's youth to *ganshimao*—that is, keep in style. The trend these days among China's young people is to dye their hair. Henna tints are popular, and many young people have reddish highlights or blond tints. Slick outfits are a must for men, and trendy wear is equally important for China's young urban women.

Any new look that pops up in a big U.S. movie tends to make an impression on young Chinese audiences. Hollywood's fashion effect is really global.

According to one Chinese fashion maven: "In modern Chinese society, men are frequently seen at social occasions wearing the dignified and refined traditional Chinese long gown. Women often wear the *qi pao*, a modified form of a traditional Qing dynasty fashion, on formal occasions. There are endless variations of height, length, width, and ornamentation in the collar, sleeves, skirt length, and basic cut of this elegant and very feminine Oriental fashion."

Hu Nu?
Many affluent Chinese women are having cosmetic surgery (*meirongshoushu*) done on themselves. But they're not middle-aged women who are hoping to look younger, as is the case with most patients for cosmetic surgery in the United States. These women are having their eyes made round, their noses made long and pointy. In other words, they're being operated on to look more Western.

The classy look for the young male white-collar worker these days is a gray jacket and suit pants, with a white shirt and metallic silk tie. White socks are in. You know, gym socks. And all guys carry a little leather bag for their beeper, mobile phone, cash, and cigarettes.

And tradition is not forgotten. Traditional design elements such as guardian deities, lions, and masks of Chinese opera characters are often used in modern fashions.

Clothes-makers have also taken the silk-making techniques of the old days and built upon them to create a modern textile industry, where traditional elements and modern chic often go hand in hand.

Food

If you think you know what the Chinese eat because you have dinner regularly at Chinese restaurants in the United States, well you couldn't be more wrong. People who've eaten in China and then return to the United States inevitably find the American version lacking.

The difference is that, in China, a greater effort is made to distinguish the flavors. If you eat *kung pao*, a chicken dish in which much of the flavor comes from chili peppers, in the United States you'll usually find that the chili flavor is dominant. In China, however, the food is cooked in layers so that a variety of flavors are allowed to come through. But don't expect boneless chicken in China, where it's more common to find cooks that use the whole bird, from head to toe, in their cooking. And though fish is a perennial favorite, few Chinese would expect it to be filleted before eating. Try using chopsticks to eat fish with the bones still intact—if you can, you have taken your mastery of chopsticks to the next level!

Anyone spending much time in China, or just among the Chinese anywhere, should notice the importance of food in everyday culture. A great deal of attention is given to its preparation and quality. Thousands of years of this kind of attention has contributed to one of the richest food cultures in the world. It's hard not to be taken aback by the sheer number of dishes in traditional Chinese cuisine. The regional difference in China's languages and local culture has certainly contributed greatly to this wonderful diversity of cooking.

> ### Hu Nu?
>
> Been to an open market lately? In China and even Taiwan, many people still prefer to buy vegetables, fruits, and meats at daily markets operated in the open air instead of sprawling supermarkets. Night markets are also popular (and, of course, operate only at night). Food vendors of every kind can be found at night markets and do a very brisk business. Health standards are a greater concern today, however, and thus vendors are, in theory, required to register their food stands so they can be monitored.

In China's larger cities, particularly those that are more cosmopolitan, foreign restaurants are thriving. Beijing has its Hard Rock Cafe, TGIF, and a vibrant nightlife that includes the Nashville Bar, Metro Cafe, the Jazz-Ya, and pizza at Restaurant Adria.

There's also the Internet Café, and the Rollerworld Pub, where waiters scoot around on rollerskates. Thai food is popular, but so is regional Chinese fare. Wine bars, karaoke bars—you name it, Beijing's got it.

Lifestyles

If you're thinking that China's cities are turning into lively, action-packed metropolises, you're right. Taxis and private cars hog the roadways where there was once only the jingling of a thousand bicycle bells at rush hour.

The bikes are still there, but are now forced to share the road with China's growing number of drivers. China's newest "little emperors" are to be found sitting on the back of a bicycle, while their mothers struggle to pedal with the flow of traffic. Well spoiled and well fed, these youngsters often outweigh their mothers, but still get ferried about on the back of a parental bicycle. Traffic is rather erratic and anarchical—don't expect to see many drivers following common rules of the road in China. It's just: pedal to the floor and go for it.

Pagers and cell phones add to the general cacophony of the city streets, which are already filled with noise from the honking drivers and the rumbling trucks and bulldozers. It's no wonder that China's environmental legislation includes "noise pollution" as a serious problem. To the average Chinese, the decibel levels are as serious as the poor air quality from so many vehicles and factory smokestacks, not to mention the coal briquettes commonly burned in many cities for cooking and heating.

Han Help

During the Chinese New Year celebrations in 2002, trendy Beijing mobile phone users sent a record 100 million text messages to each other.

"Generation Yellow"

The up-and-coming urban residents, the ones who like all the high-tech bells and whistles, are known as "Generation Yellow." They're the 18- to 35-year-olds who comprise nearly 80 percent of Internet users, and use the Internet to surf for news that is not carried on state-run Chinese television.

Families used to arrange marriages through traditional matchmakers. Now Gen Yellows meet their future mates—sometimes from the other side of the world—on the Internet.

According to the BBC (February 15, 1999), "The results of China's first-ever sex survey shows a surprising openness on sexual matters—a taboo subject for decades after the communist revolution. The survey shows that more than half of China's urban youth were comfortable with the idea of pre-marital sex, while one-third approved of extramarital relationships. A total of 6,500 young people, aged between 14 and 28, were questioned by a Communist Party organization, and the results were published in the official media."

Chinese naming practices traditionally work to shape the personality and fate of the name bearer. Long gone, however, are the days when parents gave their children such names as *Jianguo* ("build the country") or *Jiangun* ("build the army"). Both of these names were popular soon after the establishment of the People's Republic of China in 1949 and were so given to celebrate China's push toward progress. During the Cultural Revolution, *Hong* ("red" or "revolutionary") became very popular. Many babies were named *Yonghong* ("forever red") or *Chaoyang* ("toward the sun"). By the 1980s, *Zhifu* ("getting rich") and *Xinghua* ("rejuvenate China") were common names.

 Wise One Says

By incorporating the flexibility of Chinese naming conventions with stimulus from Western popular culture, the younger generation of urban Chinese is expanding the base of ready-made English names like David and Amy. English names used among young Chinese today can be inspired from sports, culture or simply the dictionary, ranging from Magic Johnson and Manchester United to Skywalker and Medusa or Fish and Power.

—Jennifer S. Lee, *The New York Times* (February 12, 2001)

There's an admiration for Western gizmos and products, but not the same overwhelming desire to emulate the United States that there once was. China's Generation Yellow are the people likely to hang out at Starbucks or catch a quick meal at McDonald's, but they're also likely to be very critical of U.S. foreign policy and economic hegemony. And this generation is mighty proud—proud to be Chinese, proud of their country's economic growth, and proud to be the site of the 2008 Olympics.

The Gay Lifestyle

Pride doesn't come quite so easily or openly to one group in China—homosexuals. But modernization has come to them, in part. No longer is it essential for gays to stay completely secretive about their lifestyle, though most choose to do so because of the social stigma attached to being a homosexual.

Unlike in other parts of the world, most gay men in China are also married and have children. They feel—despite their sexual orientation—as if that is their duty. More than an interesting social phenomenon, this overlap between hetero and homosexual activity has made control of HIV and AIDS more challenging.

Wise One Says

"In China there is a very strong tradition that to be a man you must get married and have a child, so I did," explained Mr. Wu, who refused to give his full name. "We also respect and obey our parents' wishes, so I did it for them, too."... The simplest solution for those who can afford it is to lead two lives—homosexual in the city, heterosexual in the hometown—since there is a long tradition of Chinese businessmen moving to big cities to work, leaving wives and children as well as parents behind ... Shenzhen, a city of transients and traders ... is the perfect safe haven for an estimated 150,000 gay men who live here.

—Elisabeth Rosenthal, *The New York Times* (April 12, 2002)

AIDS

China first acknowledged that it had an AIDS problem during August 2001, by which time the problem had grown into a serious crisis. Before that, the Chinese government played ostrich and hoped that, if only they kept looking the other way, the problem would disappear.

Current estimates by the Chinese government claim there are 850,000 people in China who test positive for the HIV virus—but there are those who say those estimates are wildly optimistic. The most pessimistic estimate is that there are up to 1.5 million people already infected. Officially, the Ministry of Health had recorded only 30,736 people with the HIV virus by the end of 2001. There have been a number of reports that reusing needles is the primary source of HIV infection in China. Infection rates are reportedly high in Yunnan Province, where there are rising numbers of drug addicts. And officials in Beijing also noted that many farmers in rural Henan Province were exposed to the virus when they sold their blood.

The United Nations has predicted that by 2010 China might have as many as 10 million people with HIV. Other groups have predicted 20 million.

The Chinese government announced in 2001 a plan to stem the tide of HIV. The object of the plan is to keep the growth rate of new cases to less than 10 percent annually. The rate had been closer to 30 percent in recent years.

Han Help

The Chinese government prohibited the importation of blood and blood products in 1988, in hopes of preventing AIDS from entering the country. But the move was at least three years too late, as the first HIV infection was reported in China in 1985—but up until 1988, most cases had been limited to foreigners living in coastal areas.

There you have it. From movies to makeup, and books to nightclubs, China today is undergoing an endless cultural assault from the outside world. Hong Kong, U.S., and European influences are seen everywhere, even in the most remote outposts. And, as is the case, China will find new and creative ways to shape these influences into something distinctly their own. It's an exciting time to be in the artistic world in China, but also a nerve-racking time. At the back of every Chinese artist's mind, there's likely to be some thought that this period of artistic freedom may be a limited run. To those on the outside, though, it seems like the artistic cat is well out of the bag. The next century of China's history may well see the best and worst of foreign culture being absorbed into China's own rich cultural experience.

The Least You Need to Know

♦ Global popular culture can be seen in all China's media.

♦ Artists and musicians are free to experiment with nontraditional approaches.

♦ Young urban men and women are on the cutting edge of fashion.

♦ "Generation Yellow" is a term used for China's young adult crowd that is adopting Western fashion styles and technology, but is carving out its own uniquely Chinese lifestyle.

♦ Alternative lifestyles are also being accepted, though slowly. Most that live alternative lifestyles must go to large urban centers to do so more comfortably.

Chapter 19

China and the United States

In This Chapter

- ◆ China and the United States become allies against Japan during World War II, but they fight on different sides in the Korean War.

- ◆ President Nixon's visit to Beijing in 1972 ends 22 years of ruptured U.S.-China relations.

- ◆ American military aid to Taiwan and China's human rights violations continue to be problems in the China-U.S. relationship.

- ◆ The United States engages in increased trade and makes major investments in China.

Several experts agree that both the East and the West are on a potential collision course. Although no one can be sure who those members of East and West may be, or in fact, if this is even an accurate prediction. One can be fairly certain, though, that China and the United States represent the most likely actors in such a scenario.

There is no reason to see the United States' dealings with China in a shadow of doom and gloom, however. It's clear that both countries would benefit greatly from mutual cooperation and understanding. The gap that stands between the United States and China has existed for decades and has been bridged at times of open communication (for example, Nixon's visit with Mao) and widened at other times during hard-line crackdowns or isolation-ist policy (for example, the Tiananmen Square massacre or Cultural Revolution).

The United States is certainly at a new crossroads with China. Again, China is chang-ing its approach to the outside world, but it's difficult to say how this will play out in China and how it might affect its political system. Understanding this question will be a key for the United States to have better relations with China in the future.

Looking Back

Americans have long felt a close relationship with China, a connection that dates back long before President Nixon made his 1972 trip to Beijing. The history of modern China is interlaced with that of the United States. Modern education, particularly for women, was brought to China by American Protestant missionaries. By the 1920s, there were over 4,000 students enrolled at foreign universities in China, accounting for about 10 percent of all university students in the country at the time. And there were over 3,000 American missionaries working in China during the 1920s, along with increasing numbers of YMCA and YWCA branches and members throughout China.

The anti-foreign sentiment of the Boxer Rebellion at the turn of the twentieth century (see Chapter 3) was in part a reflection of the imperial government's resentment of foreigners—Christian missionaries in particular. The Boxers laid siege to Beijing's diplomatic quarter, and rampaged through China, killing Christian missionaries and thousands of Chinese Christians. When an interna-tional suppression force brought the Boxers under control, the United States was the only participating nation that took no profit from the reparations assessed against the Qing government for its—at a minimum—acquiescence in the Boxer Rebellion. Instead, the American reparations were used to establish scholarships for Chinese students at American educational institutions. Later, in 1924, the U.S. Congress voted to earmark the remaining $12.5 million in Chinese reparations for the devel-opment of new educational institutions in China.

> **Hu Nu?**
>
> Dr. Sun Yatsen, the father of the Republic of China, was educated in Hawaii at American schools and colleges. Many of the lead-ers of the Revolution of 1911 that he led—and of the Chinese communist revolution—were influ-enced by Western ideas.

But on U.S. soil, immigration policies in the early part of the twentieth century were anything but friendly to Chinese citizens. The 1882 Chinese Exclusion Act, which effectively shut down Chinese emigration to the United States for awhile, was backed by U.S. labor unions and others who feared the loss of mining, construction, fishing, and agricultural jobs to new Chinese immigrants. Never mind that Chinese workers had made great contributions to the United States—and great sacrifices—mining for gold and building the cross-country railway line.

World War II

China had suffered a devastating defeat in the Sino-Japanese War of 1894–1895. When the Japanese launched a full–scale attack against China in 1937, the United States sympathized with Chiang Kaishek's Nanjing government; it sent aid, and a volunteer air group (The Flying Tigers) to fight the Japanese aggressors. These American pilots shot down many Japanese planes and helped build Chinese morale. When the Burma Road was cut off from China, American aircraft flew in supplies over the Himalaya Mountains.

After Japan's attack on the U.S. military base at Pearl Harbor, American troops were sent to China. During its war with Japan, the United States became a major player in Chinese affairs, embarking in late 1941 on a program of massive military and financial aid to the troubled nationalist government.

In January 1943, the United States and Great Britain revised their treaties with China, ending 100 years of unequal treaty relations.

Also in 1943, a new agreement was signed between the United States and China for the stationing of American troops in China for the common war effort against Japan. In December 1943, the Chinese Exclusion Acts and subsequent laws enacted by the United States Congress to restrict Chinese immigration into the United States were repealed.

The U.S. wartime policy was at first designed to help China become a strong ally and a stabilizing force in postwar East Asia. The United States tried to get the competing nationalists and communists to get along for the duration of the war so as to put up a better struggle against the Japanese, but these efforts were largely unsuccessful.

After the War

China was named a member of the "Big Four" nations prosecuting the war against the Axis powers. With the global war over, the United States continued to support Chiang Kaishek's Nanjing government, which was made a member of the United Nations and its five-member permanent Security Council. At the same time, the United States continued trying to arrange a negotiated peace between Chiang's Guomindang (KMT) forces and Mao's People's Liberation Army, who were fighting a civil war for control of China.

> ### Han Help
>
> The United Nations, the post-World War II peace-keeping body, knew that it could not recognize both the governments of mainland China and Taiwan, since both claimed to be the one and only government of China. The communists were irked when the UN chose to recognize Chiang's government instead of their own. Taiwan retained the China UN seat until 1972 when President Nixon, seeking Beijing aid in extricating the United States from the Vietnam War, adopted a "one China" policy and the UN seat passed to Beijing.

After the communists conquered mainland China, the KMT government retreated to Taiwan but remained the "China" represented in the United Nations. Afterward Chiang Kaishek vowed to return in force to conquer China; and the communists, in turn, ranted about attacking and conquering KMT forces on Taiwan. The U.S. Navy announced that it would use the U.S. Seventh Fleet to patrol the Taiwan Strait and prevent any attacks by the KMT on the Chinese mainland or by the communists on Taiwan. "One China" became, and continues to be, U.S. policy, but the fact was that the United States strongly backed Chiang Kaishek's government, and Mao Zedong deeply resented it.

What the communist Chinese didn't know was that the United States was starting to regret its decision to push the UN to recognize Taiwan instead of the mainland. The more the United States learned about Chiang Kaishek's government, the less it liked. Chiang Kaishek had always had strong connections with the Chinese mob, and a lot of the corruption that exists in Taiwan today was brought over by Chiang and some of his henchmen.

By the end of the 1940s, many facts had come to light indicating that Chiang's regime had fallen through its own ineptitude and corruption. The United States, in fact, gave indications that it was about to abandon Taiwan and recognize communist China as the true China. Mao's China was of great strategic and economic importance to the United States; it was a huge potential market. More important, after tense relations with the Soviet Union turned into the Cold War, China became a potential counter-weight to the Soviet threat. But then everything changed.

Korea

In 1950, war broke out between communist North Korea and the U.S.-backed South. Chinese troops soon joined the Soviets in helping the North Koreans, and the United States and its allies were in an undeclared war against the threat of a worldwide communist revolution.

The United States turned its attention to Japan—even in its debilitated state, the obvious counterweight to the combined Chinese-Soviet bloc. Japan became the beneficiary of American aid and trade. It was a major turning point in world history. For U.S.-China relations, it was the beginning of a state of hostility that would last for the next 22 years.

U.S.-China Detente

During the 1960s, ideological differences plagued relations between China and the Soviet Union. By the end of the decade, there was a clear Sino-Soviet split.

In 1972, President Richard Nixon, guided by Secretary of State Henry Kissinger's *realpolitik* approach to diplomacy, made a historic visit to China. This opened a new era in U.S.-China relations, dubbed "Ping-Pong diplomacy" at first, as the first official exchange between the two sides involved a table tennis competition.

The Sino-Soviet break had set the stage for a new equilibrium between China, the United States, and the Soviet Union. The advantages to China were that it could obtain help from the United States in the form of recognition of its government, membership in the United Nations, an ally against threats from the Soviet Union, and a major trade partner. The United States also sought a trade relationship with China and a counterweight to the Soviets.

Language Lesson

U.S. foreign policy in the post-World War II era recognized the very real threat that another world war could erupt at any time and destabilize the global balance of power. **Realpolitik,** or political realism, holds that politics should be dictated not by moral beliefs, but by reality—however harsh. Thus, though the United States and China were at opposite ends of the political spectrum, Henry Kissinger convinced President Nixon that forging better ties with China was in U.S. national interest. In the end, the United States would benefit from a more stable and peaceful world order that included China.

In the negotiations that followed, Taiwan was the major remaining obstacle to a new era in U.S.-China relations. It was resolved in the Shanghai Communiqué, signed in 1972, when the United States acknowledged that Taiwan was a part of China, and agreed to withdraw its troops.

Han Help

In the Shanghai Communiqué, the United States declared that it "acknowledges that all Chinese on either side of the Taiwan Strait maintain there is but one China and that Taiwan is a part of China. The United States government does not challenge that position. It reaffirms its interest in a peaceful settlement of the Taiwan question by the Chinese themselves. With this prospect in mind it affirms the ultimate objective of the withdrawal of all U.S. forces and military installations from Taiwan. In the meanwhile, it will progressively reduce its forces and military installations on Taiwan as the tension in the area diminishes."

The U.S.-China detente also precipitated a new era of rapprochement between China and Japan. China was fast learning the realpolitik ropes.

Taiwan Troubles

The "One China" concept of 1949 did not designate who would lead the country—Chiang or Mao. The Shanghai Communiqué of 1972 avowed that Taiwan was part of "China"; it did not specify "The People's Republic of China." This anomaly in U.S. diplomacy has dogged U.S.-China relations into the twenty-first century.

♦ In 1979, the United States signed the Taiwan Relations Act, supporting peaceful reunification of Taiwan with the mainland as well as committing itself to the defense of Taiwan in case of Chinese aggression.

♦ In June 1995, Taiwan's President Lee Teng-hui visited Cornell University (his alma mater) and made a speech in which he referred to Taiwan as "The Republic of China on Taiwan," challenging the "One China" formulation. The PRC immediately began testing nuclear-capable missiles, and during the following year, conducted a series of similar tests, landing one missile a mere 35 miles from the Taiwan coast.

♦ In December 1995, the United States sent the USS *Nimitz* and six other ships to the Taiwan Strait between Taiwan and China to monitor the PRC's exercises. Beijing and Washington exchanged some harsh words and the ships left the area soon afterward.

♦ In 1996, Chinese President Jiang Zemin made a state visit to the United States, and President Clinton visited China in 1998.

♦ In 2001, China downed a U.S. spy plane, and again conducted missile tests near Taiwan.

In the spring of 2002, PRC Vice President Hu Jintao, who is expected to replace Jiang Zemin as president of the PRC and chairman of the CCP, made an official visit to Washington. He expressed his government's concern over increased military exchanges between Washington and Taipei, and said to a group of business executives and China policy specialists that "If any trouble occurs on the Taiwan question, it would be difficult for China-U.S. relations to move forward." He also was critical of President Bush's reference to Taiwan as "The Republic of Taiwan." China considers Taiwan one of its provinces.

Nuclear Weapons Proliferation

One of the goals of the United States in engaging China in international organizations such as the United Nations was to help lessen the threat of global nuclear war. China, after all, was a member of the Nuclear Club, which meant it had a special responsibility to keep nuclear weapons from proliferating any further. The United States has long been concerned that China has been sharing nuclear weapons technology with Pakistan and other nations.

In the early 1980s, there were multiple reports that Pakistan was buying weapons-grade enriched uranium from China. Other reports warned that Pakistan had also gotten a bomb design from China. By the end of the decade, Pakistan reportedly had developed several small nuclear devices. By 1996, Pakistan also had bought a nuclear-capable M-11 missile from China, along with 5,000 ring magnets, which are used in nuclear warheads.

The rumors proved quite real: In May 1998, Pakistan detonated five nuclear devices. India, feeling the threat of the Pakistan nuclear weapons program, had conducted its own nuclear tests 17 days earlier.

Han Help

In the late 1990s, the United States discovered that China was also planning to sell uranium-enrichment material to Iran, though China had promised not to do so at an official U.S.-China summit in October 1997.

Human Rights

U.S. foreign policy toward China, particularly in recent years, is no longer cut and dried realpolitik. The American public, in particular, felt dismayed and betrayed by the 1989 Chinese crackdown in Tiananmen Square (covered in detail in Chapter 13). In a peculiar way, the U.S. thinking seemed to be "How could they do that to their own people? And they were coming along so well in embracing capitalism and other

Western ideals." In other words, the affinity America as a nation seems to have for China left many Americans bewildered and hurt—and even more concerned about human rights in China.

For much of the past two decades, U.S. foreign policy toward China has tried to balance concerns about China's human rights with the belief that "engagement" with China is the best way to bring about the democratic reforms in China that ultimately will improve the human rights situation.

Even before Tiananmen, China's human rights record was shaky, at least to many Americans. China's strict birth control policies, for example, prompted the Reagan administration to withhold U.S. assistance from the U.S. Agency for International Development (AID).

Amnesty International, the international human rights monitoring organization, has cited numerous cases of Chinese citizens being imprisoned without trials, periodic mass campaigns against crime that end in public executions, persecution of religious leaders in Tibet and other places in China, and other abuses of human rights. Political prisoners, in particular, often face long and harsh sentences for their political views. More recently, there have been allegations that China actually sells the organs of executed prisoners to hospitals in China and other Asian countries, where there is a lucrative black market for kidney and other organ transplants.

U.S.-China Relations After 1989

In the aftermath of the Tiananmen Square crackdown, the U.S. government had to make some policy shifts. The message to China had to be loud and clear that China's reprisals were too harsh. In the immediate months after Tiananmen, the U.S. government suspended the activities of many programs in China, including financing by the U.S. Export-Import Bank and the Overseas Private Investment Corporation. The U.S. government also led a movement within the World Bank to suspend, at least temporarily, all China loans and credits. Only those loans devoted to "basic human needs," for projects helping the poorest regions and peoples of China, could go forward. And the United States granted some 40,000 Chinese students studying at U.S. colleges the right to remain indefinitely in the United States.

Most-Favored-Nation Status

The U.S. Congress found it had a powerful tool to censure China's actions.

The Jackson-Vanik amendment to the U.S. Trade Act of 1974 required the United States to treat trade with communist countries in a special way. This law required the

U.S. president to issue an annual waiver, declaring that the Chinese had made progress on human rights. Congress, if it disagreed, could vote to overturn China's *Most-Favored-Nation (MFN) status.* If Congress did not disagree, the United States would grant China another year of MFN status.

Language Lesson

Most-Favored-Nation status meant that the United States and China would give each other the lowest possible tariffs on their exchanges of goods and services. MFN status, despite what it sounds like, doesn't mean any "favored" trade treatment, but simply normal trade relations. Odd as it sounds, the United States in the 1990s automatically gave MFN status to a number of countries with which it had terrible relations—these countries just didn't happen to be communist.

So, playing its MFN card, Congress began to make greater demands that China clean up its human rights record. In response to the ever-growing list of complaints of China's human rights violations, congressional amendments to deny China MFN status began to be proposed every year. This had the business community up in arms; the loss of MFN would be a catastrophe for U.S. companies trading or investing in China. Every year, for many years, the president would issue his MFN for China waiver and the congressional vote would come close to overriding it.

Permanent Normal Trade Relations

Finally, in May 2000, President Clinton was able to get Congress to agree to pass legislation to secure Permanent Normal Trade Relations (PNTR) for China. His argument was that it was better to engage China in the commercial arena, letting U.S. companies continue to transfer Western ideas—and leave it to the appropriate bilateral and multilateral forums to discuss the political issues. Some of the strongest support for PNTR came from Tiananmen dissidents, who are now living in the United States.

One of the main reasons to move ahead with PNTR was to end the year-to-year scrutiny and censure of Chinese human rights, which was not helping U.S.-China relations much. And the laws of the new World Trade Organization, coupled with the convoluted U.S. trade laws, meant that the United States really had to confer MFN status—permanently—on China.

The new PNTR legislation does contain a provision to create a special commission to monitor human rights in China, giving the U.S. government some continued leverage over human rights issues. And the United States has other laws on its books to address certain aspects of human rights. For instance, prisons in China tend to be working factories, and prisoners work while being "reformed." Prisons in China reportedly make everything from socks to consumer electronics, and at least some of their products are destined for export. Prison labor imports into the United States have been a violation of U.S. Customs law since 1890. In reality, though, it is often extremely difficult to figure out which prison-made products are actually destined for the United States.

Is U.S. Policy Effective?

Few in Congress, let alone the nation, ever agree on U.S. foreign policy moves. And the past decade, in particular, shows just how complicated U.S.-China relations are. There are sometimes small but significant breakthroughs that can be linked to U.S. actions. In 1998, China released Wang Dan, one of the student leaders on Tiananmen Square nearly a decade earlier, and allowed him to leave China for medical treatment in the United States.

But other news from China suggests that the United States, or any foreign government, really has very little say in China's internal affairs. In 2001, news began to trickle out that a massive anti-crime drive was under way in China, and the number of executions was rising rapidly. The "Strike Hard" campaign has reportedly executed over 2,000 Chinese accused of embezzlement, tax fraud, drug trafficking, and other crimes. Millions of people have reportedly attended public executions that have been held throughout China. Tens of thousands have been sent away for "re-education through labor" without charge or trial. In a worrisome development, many Uygur and Tibetan dissidents have reportedly been executed.

China Questions U.S. Human Rights

In March 2002, China, tired of continual criticism of its human rights record by the United States, looked to turn the tables by issuing the results of its own lengthy and detailed report accusing the United States of a long list of abuses. Ted Anthony of the Associated Press summarized the highlights (March 11, 2002):

> The United States is "wantonly infringing upon human rights of other countries" with military and political actions.

> American mass media are "inundated with violent content," which in turn encourages more violence. "A culture beautifying violence has made young people believe that the gun can 'solve all problems,'" the report says.

> Racism and discrimination continue unabated.

> Police brutality, torture and forced confession "are common," and death row is full of "misjudged or wronged" inmates. Prisons are overcrowded and inhumane.

Americans living in poverty are "the forgotten 'third world' within this super-power," and the gap between rich and poor is growing.

Violence against women and sexual abuse of children are common. It cited sexual molestations of children by American clergy, calling that "the greatest scandal in the United States following the Enron case."

Trade and Investment Relations

The political scuffles often skirt around the economic reality that China and the United States have grown increasingly important to each other as trading partners. U.S. trade with China rose rapidly after the two countries established formal diplomatic relations in January 1979. A bilateral trade agreement followed later that year, and the two countries began according each other MFN benefits beginning in 1980. Total trade (exports plus imports) between China and the United States tallied $4.8 billion in 1980; by 2001 it had risen to $128.6 billion.

As China's industrial base expands, its types of exports expand as well. China is now a major world exporter of everything from chicken feet to motorcycles. Increasingly, the consumer products sold in the United States, Europe, and other countries have a "Made in China" label. Overall, China exported some $266.2 billion worth of goods last year, and imported $243.6 billion. Not bad for a country that once tried to shut itself off from the outside world.

The United States is not happy about importing more goods from China than it sells there. Other trade-related beefs include ...

Han Help _____

The U.S.-China trade relationship, like overall Sino-U.S. relations, has its ups and downs. One growing concern is the trade imbalance: China exports far more to the United States than it imports. This means that the $128.6 billion in two-way trade broke down into $109.4 billion worth of Chinese goods ending up on the U.S. market, but only $19.2 billion worth of U.S. goods went to China.

- ◆ **Protectionism.** Does China use artificial barriers to protect its infant industries from outside competition? Some in Congress believe this is the case. U.S. trade officials have been negotiating point by point to get Chinese trade officials to be more clear about their import laws and regulations. (With China's accession to the World Trade Organization (WTO), many of these barriers will have to come down anyway.)

- ◆ **Transshipments.** The United States maintains quotas on textiles that can be imported from each country. China, a major textile and apparel producer, has been found to be "transshipping" its textile goods via a third country to evade the U.S. quotas. Thus China is actually able to sell the United States more textile products in a given year than it is legally entitled to do. At stake is the competitiveness of America's remaining textile mills and garment factories.

- ◆ **Intellectual Property Rights.** U.S. movie studios, record companies, and computer software firms have all had problems with piracy in China. And look-alike products and packaging are common, with many products made to simulate a popular foreign brand of snack food or medicine, for example. Blockbuster movies that have just opened in U.S. theaters can be available on bootleg video within a day of the premiere. Copies have been sold in China and elsewhere in Asia, and some have even made it back to the United States to be sold by street vendors. Microsoft and other software developers also reported untold lost earnings because intellectual property was a relatively unknown concept in China, and the legal regime offered few protections against infringement.

Many U.S. firms have worked with the Chinese ministries and other organizations to develop both the laws and the enforcement mechanisms to clean up China's record on intellectual property. U.S. companies and trade officials are confident that China's accession to the WTO will help solve many of the enforcement problems, as China will be bound to abide by multilateral intellectual property rights enforcement procedures.

U.S. Investment in China

Many types of U.S. companies have also played a strong role in U.S.-China relations. The American business community looked on eagerly as the two countries' political leaders made their first cautious steps toward closer ties. In 1973, the U.S.-China Business Council opened its doors to help American companies enter into trade and investment deals with China. On its early rosters were some 700 companies looking to strike it rich in China.

Hu Nu?

For many U.S. multinational companies, there was a powerful double lure: set up a plant in China to tap into China's cheap labor market; and then sell the output to a domestic market of one billion consumers. If you sold sneakers, you looked at the China market as a place to sell two billion shoes.

According to Kimberly Silver at the U.S.-China Business Council, 80 percent of the first foreign companies to invest in China in the 1980s were profitable after 10 years. Coca-Cola Co., Foxboro, Hewlett-Packard Co., McCormick & Co., Fluor Daniel, and Babcock & Wilcox were among the pioneering U.S. ventures in China. Their initial joint ventures involved everything from spices to engineering and construction services.

The good news is that many of these companies are still going strong, and starting to invest in second and third ventures in the PRC. By 1997, U.S. and other foreign firms had invested $223 billion in China. U.S. foreign direct investment in China between 1990 and 2001 accounted for 32,937 contracts, or about 9 percent of the total foreign investment contracts signed during that period. And these U.S. investors committed $64.2 billion in new China investments.

The bad news is that no foreign company can really say that it found the investment process in China an easy one. And there are plenty of foreign investors with sour deals, and no profits. Some deals quickly ran aground because the Chinese partner didn't turn out to have the promised connections, or *guanxi*. Or worse—they found out they had picked a state-owned enterprise with 100,000 surplus workers that the new venture was expected to take care of. Other deals went nowhere because the foreign investor found out, after wasting a lot of time and money, that the proposed scope of business was really off limits to foreign investment in the first place. And some unlucky investors were even led astray by local and provincial officials with shady plans to circumvent national-level investment approval regulations.

Even if a venture got up and running, there were new minefields every year for foreign investors in China. One common problem was "poaching" of trained employees. The foreign partner would invest considerable resources to train its top Chinese employees to become managers, only to find these employees would jump ship to work at another company.

Language Lesson

Guanxi is the personal connection you have with another human being(s). The idea is that the more connections you have to people, the more you will be able to accomplish with their help.

Other problems revolved around sudden changes in China's laws that had unexpected consequences for foreign investors. U.S. investors, for example, found it really hard to exchange their *renminbi*—the unit of currency used in mainland China—for foreign exchange when the Chinese leadership waged an urgent crackdown on illegal currency conversion by corrupt officials. With nobody able to exchange for hard currency, U.S. and other foreign investors were temporarily unable to buy machinery and inputs they needed for their China ventures.

Many of the problems encountered had to do with unclear and overlapping rules and jurisdictions. At the beginning, there were no published lists of what the Chinese leadership really wanted in foreign investment. This information, like many other types of data in China, was considered *neibu*, or for internal use only. It was only in recent years that the Catalogue Guiding Foreign Investment in Industry was released, finally spelling out in which sectors foreign investment would be "encouraged," "permitted," "discouraged," or "prohibited." So companies trying to set up retail ventures early on, for example, would have been left spinning their wheels.

Even with the more transparent rules that began to emerge in the late 1990s, there are many restrictions on foreign investment in China. Officially, central-level approval is still required for projects over $30 million and investments in "discouraged" sectors. Smaller projects can be approved at the local level. And, according to experts, "Equity and geographic restrictions still exist in many sectors, particularly services; what the PRC terms 'pillar industries' like aviation, autos, and chemicals; and in sensitive areas like publishing."

Three Ways to Invest in China

U.S. companies have three main investment choices in China. Often, the first step is opening a representative office (*daibiaochu*), which allows the company to engage in only limited activities. No sales are permitted, for example, but the office can undertake some of the market research and early groundwork for establishing a China venture. Once the foreign company is sure it is ready to commit substantial funds in a China venture, it will pick one of the following investment structures:

- **Equity joint ventures (*hezi qiye*).** These are the most common form of foreign investment. By June 2000, foreign companies had signed 201,848 EJV contracts. The foreign and Chinese partners decide how much equity each partner will put into the joint venture. The partners share control over management decisions.

- **Contractual joint ventures.** Contractual joint ventures or cooperative JVs (*hezuo qiye*) differ slightly because the partners can operate as separate legal entities. This investment form has proven popular in property development and build-operate-transfer projects.

- **Wholly foreign-owned enterprises (*waizi duzi qiye*).** These were the choice for 100,624 contracts signed by June 2000. In the wholly foreign-owned venture, foreign investors get to make all the decisions about personnel, marketing strategies, and other key areas. They don't need to worry that a Chinese partner might steal its industrial secrets. The downside is that these ventures don't have a Chinese partner with the *guanxi*, or connections, and may need to develop a market for their products.

Han Help

Wholly foreign-owned enterprises, WFOEs for short, now account for half of the new contracts signed in China between 1997 and 1999. Between 1979 and June 2000, foreign firms signed 100,624 WFOE contracts.

Some of the upsurge in the popularity of the WFOE model is due to the anticipated changes in laws for China's WTO entry. Just as it will require China to liberalize its trade regime, the WTO will require changes to China's foreign investment regulations. Once China accedes to the WTO, WFOEs in China will no longer be required to export most of their products.

Mixing Business and Politics

The stakes are high for U.S. companies in the Chinese market. Not surprisingly, the U.S. business community has made sure that the American government listens to its views. U.S. companies don't want to lose out to European, Japanese, and other foreign competitors in China. And they certainly don't want the U.S. government to do anything that would jeopardize the substantial sums of U.S. money already invested in China.

During the Clinton administration, the U.S. government worked closely with the business community. By declaring PNTR for China and helping to work out the remaining obstacles to China's joining the WTO, the U.S. government has become a strong proponent of U.S. business in China. At the core of this initiative is the belief that American companies are a quiet force working for liberalization in China. By operating in China, U.S. companies help develop an awareness there of the importance of certain freedoms and obligations.

Other important reforms such as industrial safety and environmental controls are strictly enforced in U.S. ventures in China. In both the short and long terms, the U.S. business community believes their presence will help China on the road to greater individual freedom.

The Least You Need to Know

- Many of modern China's leaders and intellectuals were exposed to Western ideas through Protestant missionaries and American schools.

- The United States and China were allies in World War II, but the Korean War suspended their relations for 22 years.

- President Nixon opened the door to relations with China in 1972.

- U.S. support of Taiwan, the "other China," and criticism of China's human rights record remain major sticking points.

- The U.S. business community and the government are committed to increasing U.S. trade with China and investments in Chinese industry and business.

Part 6 China's Future: Place Your Bets

Here you can learn all about the major changes that are scheduled to take place in the leadership of the PRC and what the new government will be dealing with: the lagging privatization of state-run industries that run in the red, the changing role of the People's Liberation Army, growing unemployment, continuing government corruption, and potential problems with other countries.

We end with a look at the global economic picture and where China stands in it: prospects for foreign investment and trade, requirements for World Trade Organization membership, international relations, and China's potential as a military threat. We also look at Chinese society and how the conflict between an economically open society and a government that represses dissent will play out.

Li Peng

Zhu Rongji

To Be Continued

20

Running the Store

In This Chapter

◆ The coming change in China's leadership takes shape.

◆ What we know about the "big three" and other leaders who are likely to have roles in the new regime.

◆ The challenges, old and new, the new leadership is going to face.

As this book goes to press, China's leadership appears to be preparing for a huge reshuffling—not for the first time, but in a different way. We've come to expect abrupt changes in the Chinese Communist Party line-ups, but this time there's far more information about the process and about the new faces waiting in the wings. Even so, China-watchers around the world know enough to expect some surprises. There may be a schedule for the smooth transition of power to the next generation of CCP leaders, but that doesn't mean things will go according to plan.

The State of the Party-State

The word "China" is often accompanied by "reform," "liberalization," and "modernization." All these terms reflect the wide variety of ongoing changes in China. It's easy to believe that Mao Zedong would roll over in his grave if he could see China today. But don't think for a moment that

China is on the brink of becoming a democratic nation, or that some monumental liberalization within the Chinese Communist Party's power structure is about to take place. China is, and remains, an odd hybrid "socialist market economy," with continuing economic reforms encompassing both widespread changes and small tinkerings. But it is also a one-party, Marxist-Leninist state led by the Chinese Communist Party. For those who live in countries where democratic principles rule, it can be hard to look at the ongoing transitions in so many facets of Chinese society without thinking that China is well on the road to democracy. This may be so, but it is likely to take a very long march. Yes, China has many dissidents both inside and outside the country calling for "democracy." But at this point, the party is not about to relinquish its power—or whatever power it has left. To do so would mean risking it all—destroying China's economic progress and global status alike if the worst-case scenario came to be. For China's leadership and for many of its citizens, that worst-case scenario would mean political disintegration and chaos.

Nonetheless, many political scientists might say that democracy is inevitable in a rapidly changing society. Open the floodgates in some areas and people will expect further change in others. And some analysts point to the recent experiments with village elections as a concrete step toward greater democracy.

Since 1987, more and more villages have been able to elect their local leaders, who in turn now have somewhat greater responsibilities to raise funds for roads, schools, and health services. In theory, the CCP candidate is no longer automatically elected, as was true in the past. In practice, the CCP seems to be using these elections to boost its ranks, as the newly elected village committee members are often tapped to join the CCP! And for now, the higher levels of representative government, the Township People's Congress and the National People's Congress, have nomination procedures that remain tightly controlled by the party.

The New Leadership

We don't have a crystal ball, so we can't tell you what lies ahead for China. But we can tell you about some of the new faces in the top CCP line-up, and how they got to a position of power. These are the faces to watch in the sixteenth Party Congress, reportedly scheduled to be held in late 2002.

Most Americans can easily identify photographs of Mao Zedong and Deng Xiaoping. That is hardly surprising, given that both had exceedingly long reigns of power. The current leaders, including Jiang Zemin and Zhu Rongji, are less well recognized, but at least Americans tend to know their names. As a nation, though, America knows little about the up and rising "Fourth Generation" of Chinese leaders and how they got to the top ranks of the Chinese Communist Party.

Han Help

The "Fourth Generation" of CCP leadership refers to the latest group of leaders, most of whom were not even born when Mao was leading the PLA on its Long March. The First Generation refers to Mao Zedong and his closest allies from the early days of the CCP—those who helped form the new China in the 1950s and 1960s. Deng Xiaoping and other reformist cadres make up the Second Generation, remembered for his monumental policy shift in opening China up to the outside world. And the Third Generation, the group now starting to step down from power, includes both reformists like Zhu Rongji and Li Ruihan, as well as the Soviet-trained and generally more hard-line Li Peng.

The first and obvious question is why are so many current leaders now stepping down? The answer lies in the 1982 Chinese constitution, which sets a mandatory retirement age of 70 for the country's leadership. This rule was apparently invoked, and thus fortified, to bump Qiao Shi out of his National People's Congress chairman position at the fifteenth Party Congress. It wouldn't look too good if Qiao's ousters didn't play by the same rules. Jiang Zemin, born in 1926, is now 76. (He squeaked in under the wire to be reelected to his current five-year term.) Li Peng, born in 1928, is now 74. Zhu Rongji was also born in 1928.

The incoming leaders don't have any Long March party credentials to wave around. For most of them, the Cultural Revolution is the only revolution they've known. And all of them can be considered technocrats; many are engineers, trained at Qinghua or other top universities. Yes, they have strong party connections and have been through the party ranks, which means serving the CCP in the provinces. But they also have strong backgrounds in the sciences, and in economics and banking, all of which are emerging as important new credentials for China's leaders. And they have been groomed to be comfortable representing their country abroad, something Mao Zedong never was. Hu Jintao, for instance, was sent to meet with U.S. government and business leaders in the spring of 2002.

Hu, Wen, and Li are the "big three" to keep an eye on.

Hu Jintao

The hottest young star, perhaps, is Hu Jintao. Born in Jixi, Anhui Province, in 1942, Hu Jintao is widely acknowledged as the man most likely to lead China for the next few years. If the succession plan moves ahead as scheduled, Hu will be named president of the PRC and chairman of the CCP (the two jobs Jiang Zemin now holds) at the sixteenth Party Congress in late 2002.

A graduate of Qinghua University, Hu joined the CCP in 1964 while studying engineering. During the Cultural Revolution, Hu was a "sent-down youth" dispatched to live in one of China's poorest regions, Guizhou.

Hu is somewhat of a boy wonder in Chinese political circles. Working his way into a close-knit group of old party hacks, he became the youngest provincial party secretary in modern Chinese history. In 1992, he became the youngest man ever tapped to join the Politburo Standing Committee. He was named vice president of the PRC at the fifteenth Party Congress in 1998. He reportedly was hand picked by Deng Xiaoping to be the core of the Fourth Generation leadership, and has been under Jiang Zemin's tutelage for much of the past decade.

Hu has worn many CCP hats, including vice chairman of the Central Military Commission. These are all signs that he is being groomed to take over the party leadership. For the last six years, he has headed Beijing's Communist Party School, a sort of elite ideological training program for the top leadership. But he paid his party dues for many years, working his way up through the ranks of the Ministry of Water Conservancy and Power until the early 1980s. He then worked for the Communist Youth League, Young Pioneers, and All-China Youth Federation. At the time, his party mentor appears to have been Hu Yaobang (no relation), who was working hard with Deng Xiaoping to push through major economic reforms.

His next postings took him far away from Beijing, which was probably a good thing, as Hu Yaobang soon found himself out of favor. Hu Jintao was appointed party secretary of Tibet and Guizhou Province from 1985 to 1992. In 1988, Hu had the tough job of stopping the Tibetan separatists in their tracks.

Wen Jiabao

Vice Premier Wen Jiabao is known to have close personal ties to Hu Jintao and several ministers in the State Council. Wen was born in 1942 in Tianjin and studied geology in Beijing. He spent some time as a geologist in Ganusu Province, and reportedly met Hu then. Wen was a protégé of both Hu Yaobang and Zhao Ziyang, but seems to have flown low enough under the radar to escape any problems. (Both Hu Yaobang and Zhao Ziyang were ousted in the 1980s. Hu's death in 1989 helped spark the Tiananmen demonstrations and Zhao remains under house arrest for sympathizing with the student protestors.)

Currently one of the four vice premiers under Zhu Rongji, Wen seems a good candidate to be named premier, taking over Zhu's position. Wen is known to be a little more diplomatic than Zhu, who has a quick temper. He may be a good choice to guide the overall progress on implementing the changes China needs to make to join the WTO.

Li Ruihuan

Born in 1934 in Tianjin, Li Ruihuan came from a peasant family. He was a carpenter by trade, and joined the CCP in 1959. Despite his humble background, he was persecuted during the Cultural Revolution. Once "rehabilitated," Li rose though the ranks to become mayor of Tianjin. He joined the inner circle of party leaders in 1989, when he became a member of the Politburo Standing Committee and a member of the Central Committee's Secretariat in 1989.

Reportedly, he has hinted several times that he wishes to retire, even though he is under the 70-year threshold. Some analysts say he will be urged to stay on, and will be given Li Peng's post as chairman of the National People's Congress. One scenario is that the new version of the Jiang-Zhu-Li triumvirate will have Hu Jintao, Wen Jiabao, and Li Ruihuan working together.

If so, Li will be one of the more liberal-minded party members at the top leadership levels. Reportedly, Li has worked to make sure non-party personnel also get included within the ranks of provincial and municipal governments. He is also believed to be more tolerant of the Falun Gong.

The Shanghai Clique

Much has been written about the "Shanghai Clique," or the steady stream of top leaders coming out of the Shanghai CCP ranks. The Shanghai leadership pipeline has produced two of China's top three current leaders. Jiang Zemin served as mayor of Shanghai from 1985 to 1987. Jiang proved to be an efficient leader, and got kudos for attracting a lot of foreign investment into the city. Jiang also built up his own set of Shanghai connections, including his successor as mayor, Zhu Rongji. But Jiang and Zhu are not particularly close to each other ideologically, especially on the topic of how fast and how far China's economic reforms should proceed.

Zhu developed a reputation for being a no-nonsense manager with a keen sense of business priorities. As Shanghai's mayor from 1987 to 1991, Zhu forged close ties with many foreign business leaders. They appreciated his "one-stop chop" approach to streamlining the local bureaucratic approvals needed by foreign investors (a "chop" is the Chinese practice of stamping one's name for the approval of official documents). As premier, Zhu has never been shy about taking on tough but necessary reforms to the economy, including painful choices like shutting down failing state enterprises. Zhu also managed the nearly unthinkable by proposing huge cuts in the national bureaucracy, including slicing out a dozen ministries and cutting some four million civil service jobs.

It's only natural to look at the current mayor, Chen Liangyu, and others in the wings, to see if they will be tapped to move up to the major leagues in Beijing. And former Shanghai vice party secretaries Meng Jianzhu and Chen Zhili are also thought to be rising stars, as both enjoy Jiang Zemin's support. But in a surprise move recently, the previous mayor, Xu Kuangdi, seemed to have been shunted off to a minor role, perhaps ending his political aspirations.

In the sixteenth Party Congress, some insiders say to look to Zeng Qinghong and Wu Bangguo to be Jiang Zemin's Shanghai connections on the all-powerful Politburo Standing Committee.

Other Prominent Leaders

Some of the other people to watch are the following:

- **Huang Ju.** Born in 1937 in Zhejiang Province, Huang has been a member of the Politburo since 1994. He has close ties to both Jiang Zemin and Zhu Rongji, and worked with both in Shanghai. He became mayor of Shanghai in 1991, and has served as Shanghai party secretary since 1994. He is a contender for the Politburo Standing Committee.

- **Jia Qinglin.** Jia Qinglin joined the party in 1959, and worked his way up through the Fujian Province party ranks. He became mayor of Beijing in 1997. A member of the National People's Congress, he has also served on the fourteenth and fifteenth Central Committees. He is 65.

- **Li Changchun.** Born in 1944 in Dalian, Liaoning Province, Li is an electrical engineer. He currently wears quite a few hats and logs a lot of miles in addition to sitting on the Politburo. He is a vice premier under Zhu Rongji, in the State Council, and also party secretary in Guangdong Province. He is also believed to hold several military posts in the Guangdong Military District. He had some previous military experience as secretary of the CPC Committee of the Henan Provincial Military Area Command in 1992. It's likely he'll be named to the Politburo Standing Committee.

- **Li Lanqing.** Like Li Ruihuan, Li Lanqing is getting close to retirement age. Aged 68 and a close associate of Jiang Zemin, Li Lanqing joined the Politburo Standing Committee in 1997. Naming him for another five years would be a good move, perhaps, as he would likely be a stabilizing influence between potentially competing factions. Jiang Zemin is reportedly pushing hard to keep Li at the top CCP level.

◆ **Li Tieying.** Li Tieying, age 65, has served on the Politburo since 1988. He served in the Shenyang and Liaoning party ranks, rising to Liaoning Province party secretary in 1983. He became a state councilor in 1998, and was recently appointed president of the Chinese Academy of Social Sciences.

◆ **Luo Gan.** If Jiang is pushing for Li Lanqing, Li Peng is pushing for Luo Gan. Born in 1935, Luo joined the CCP Politburo in 1997. Insiders say that if Luo gets promoted to the Politburo Standing Committee in October 2002, it's a sure sign that Li Peng is still pulling some punches behind the scenes.

Luo has a long and distinguished career record as a steel engineer, industry researcher, and provincial governor and party secretary (he served in Henan Province). He was also head of the All-China Federation of Trade Unions, and labor minister.

◆ **Wei Jianxing.** Wei Jianxing, age 66, has been the point man on party corruption since 1992. Reportedly, Wei's Central Discipline Inspection has taken disciplinary action against more than 660,000 party members. Wei took over as Beijing party chief when Chen Xitong was booted out for corruption in 1995. He is a mechanical engineer by training, but also studied business management in the Soviet Union. Wei is likely to be asked to sit on the Politburo again.

◆ **Wu Bangguo.** Born in 1941 in Anhui Province, Wu has lots of CCP connections through both Qinghua University and the Shanghai CCP. He studied radio electronics at Qinghua. He joined the Politburo in 1992, after working with Jiang and Zhu in Shanghai. He is a vice premier, and is thought to be closer to Jiang than Zhu. He will probably stay on the Politburo, and has an outside chance of being named as premier.

◆ **Wu Guanzheng.** Wu Guanzheng, 63, is another technocrat. He studied thermal engineering at Qinghua University and taught there before being sent to work on power plants in Wuhan. He rose up through the Jiangxi Provincial party ranks to be named governor of Jiangxi in 1993. He joined the Politburo in 1997, and is likely to stay on in that capacity. He is also a deputy to the National People's Congress.

◆ **Wu Yi.** Wu Yi, the lone woman at the top party ranks, is a petroleum engineer turned trade negotiator. She was born in 1938 in Wuhan, Hubei Province, and served as deputy manager of the Beijing Yanshan Petrochemical Corporation during the 1980s. She then served as vice mayor of Beijing before moving on to the Ministry of Foreign Economic Relations and Trade.

She's a familiar face to U.S. businesses, and has a reputation for talking tough in some heated Sino-U.S. trade negotiations during the 1990s. Wu has long had close ties with Zhu Rongji. She was named an alternate to the Politburo in 1987, and is expected to be named to the new Politburo Standing Committee in 2002.

♦ **Zeng Qinghong.** Another of Jiang Zemin's allies, Zeng served as Shanghai CCP vice-chief. Zeng also accompanied Jiang to the United States in 1997 as his chief of staff. Head of the CCP's Organization Department, Zeng is seen by some as destined for the Politburo Standing Committee. He currently serves as Politburo alternate. Zeng is 62 and a former rocket scientist.

Some Hong Kong papers have identified Zeng as Jiang's "hatchet man," and worse names: the "head eunuch" of the *Zhongnanhai* leadership compound. Zeng could even emerge as a rival for Hu Jintao, though both apparently enjoy support from Jiang Zemin at the moment. If Jiang has enough power, he will succeed in getting Zeng named to the Politburo Standing Committee.

Hu Nu?

Zeng is a member of China's elite group of "princelings," the sons and daughters of top leaders. His late father, Zeng Shan, a Red Army veteran, was vice mayor of Shanghai in 1949. His mother, Deng Liujin, ran an orphanage for children of "revolutionary martyrs" and counted current Parliament chief Li Peng among her charges.

—John Ruwitch, Reuters (April, 28, 2002)

Language Lesson

Zhongnanhai—meaning "central and south seas"—is a government domestic compound located near Beijing's Forbidden City. Originially built between the tenth and thirteenth centuries, it serves as a home for many of China's top Communist Party officials. More recently, the government's leaders were given a surprise when 10,000 Falun Gong members staged a peaceful demonstration outside the compound gates on April 25, 1999. Many believe that this demonstration precipitated the government's subsequent harsh crackdown against Falun Gong practitioners.

Behind the Scenes

In the past, it was common for China's leaders to step down and yield control over day-to-day operations. Deng Xiaoping, after all, had not officially been in charge of China for many years. But it was very clear that he was making a lot of the decisions from behind the scenes, almost up to his death in 1997.

While the CCP leadership controls the party, and thus the state, they don't operate in a vacuum. And the new leadership, lacking a lot of direct experience actually ruling the country, is likely to be pushed and pulled by others within China, particularly the "Third Generation" of retiring leaders. Some of the leadership changes and behind–the-scenes power plays will likely be made in secret when the CPC leaders meet each summer at the Beidaihe beach resort to talk about personnel issues.

It's hard to imagine that Jiang Zemin, Zhu Rongji, and even Li Peng will be out of the picture completely. Some reports even say that Jiang Zemin and Li Peng are look-ing to have the Politburo formalize the role of party elder, by requiring their input on important decisions. Other reports claim that Jiang is not ready or willing to step down in late 2002, which would put the succession plan in disarray and quite possibly open new instabilities within the party leadership.

Whether the structure is formalized or not, Jiang, Zhu, and Li will likely be guiding the new leaders, whether they want the help or not. If the succession plan goes ahead as scheduled, Hu Jintao and his colleagues may be subjected to a lot of advice and outright arm-twisting. Most analysts see Hu Jintao as following in Jiang's footsteps when it comes to maintaining stability. But Hu is likely to get an earful from the retiring "Economic Czar," Zhu Rongji, about the need to push ahead with painful economic reforms. The old guard may be gone, but don't expect them to be sitting in their deck chairs, enjoying retired life. And any ideological struggles behind the scenes may tie the new leadership's hands, at least until they solidify their positions and priorities.

The Role of the PLA

The new leaders will have to forge their own ties with the People's Liberation Army. A decade ago, Jiang Zemin had few dealings with the military. But he and other CCP top guns could see plainly what happened in the Soviet Union in 1991 when the mili-tary did not stand by the government. The fear of a similar disintegration happening in China prompted Jiang to work hard to gain control over the military. By the late 1990s, Jiang was even in a position to begin the slow and painful process of getting the PLA to divest itself of its commercial dealings (no small feat).

According to Andrew Scobel, an expert in China's military structure, "There seems to be an unwritten pact that the PLA supports the CCP, and in exchange the CCP gives the PLA autonomy over military affairs and appropriate levels of funding and guidance."

Hu Jintao doesn't appear to have any formal military training. But he did get some experience working with the PLA in Tibet, where he was assigned as party secretary. Hu was in charge of a large-scale crackdown on Tibetan dissidents, and had to work with the PLA to get the job done.

New and Continuing Challenges

Like the Soviet Union in its waning years, China has two types of leaders. Zhu Rongji and his followers, taking a more macroeconomic approach, would argue that tough economic reforms have to be made if China is to grow stronger. Jiang Zemin and his followers are more cautious and feel the need to focus on stability first. So far, the two camps have managed to navigate a tricky course over the 1990s.

But China, like most of the world, is still in dangerous economic waters. The global recession has been an equal-opportunity damper, and China had barely begun to recover from the Asian recession in the late 1990s. The challenge for the new CCP leaders will be to figure out how to chart their own course.

Unemployment, corruption, agricultural shortages, environmental problems, migrant workers—all of these social stresses will continue to plague the party leadership. And the banking, currency, regulatory, and trade reforms that will be needed as part of the WTO accession package will all add some new problems to worry about. Yes, the WTO does offer some degree of protection for infant industries. But the terms are not indefinite, and don't extend to every industry or sector of the Chinese economy.

Over the long term, the WTO helps China by opening up many more markets worldwide to Chinese products. But the WTO also opens up China to greater foreign competition, and there may be some harsh lessons learned. Someone is going to feel the pain of global competition, and it may just turn out to be the inefficient state enterprises, or the agricultural sector.

The Fourth Generation of Chinese leaders will have to show they can tackle these types of increasingly complex economic and governmental problems.

Growing Unemployment

According to the Associated Press (April 29, 2002), the state-run *China Daily* newspaper quoted Deputy Labor Minister Wang Dongjin as saying, soaring joblessness "could well undermine social stability." An otherwise upbeat report, issued by the Chinese cabinet's Information Office, acknowledged that "structural unemployment will become more serious for a long time to come." "An excessive labor supply coupled with pressures caused by obsolete job skills has resulted in a grim employment situation," Wang had said at a seminar. China's true unemployment situation is even worse, because official figures count only those formally registered as jobless. They ignore tens of millions of out-of-work farmers and furloughed employees who are still counted on their companies' books.

Authorities in China's northeast, a center for heavy industry that has suffered massive job cuts, have faced recent protests by tens of thousands of laid-off factory and oilfield workers in the cities of Daqing and Liaoyang. State companies have cut tens of millions of jobs in an attempt to become profitable. Millions more are expected to lose their jobs as a result of China's new membership in the World Trade Organization. China has promised to open its markets to foreign competition, exposing farms and companies to competition by cheaper, higher-quality imports and more efficient rivals.

Wise One Says

In "Blue-Collar Blues" (*The Atlantic,* February 2000), Trevor Corson, managing editor of Harvard University's *Transitions* Magazine wrote:

> The growing "free" market in China is mostly about well-connected entrepreneurs speculating with public funds, pocketing the profits, and assigning the losses to the state.

Government Corruption

Government corruption continues to be a major concern. New regulations get formulated, and new crackdowns are announced. The age limits are reportedly being observed, not just at the very top levels of the CCP. Provincial party secretaries and ministers are also being pushed toward retirement, ostensibly to clean up corruption and nepotism.

Corruption seems to exist at virtually every level within the party and state operations. One particularly worrisome development is the rising number of protests at the local level against corrupt bureaucrats.

Local officials have been found guilty of extortion, after having been caught stealing the tax receipts they basically beat out of residents. Provincial authorities, far from Beijing, find it easy to put their hands in the cookie jar. The problem is likely to worsen as Beijing tries to shift more development funds to the interior.

In Beijing, Mayor Chen Xitong and some 45 city bureaucrats were arrested and implicated in a $37 million bribery and embezzlement scheme. Until his arrest, Chen was a rising star in the CCP, and had already been named to several top posts. Chen's son Chen Xiaotong was convicted for misappropriating $24 million in state assets. Vice Mayor Wang Baosen shot and killed himself after the investigation was opened.

Pressure Points Outside of China

The new core leaders will also have to find their stride internationally. They have one strong card in their hand: China's resurgent nationalism. Patriotic feelings are running high in China these days, and the party can use this to deflect attention from some of the internal imbalances.

When the United States accidentally bombed the Chinese Embassy in Belgrade in 1999, there were widespread protests in China. For once, the CCP could breathe easy, as the protestors were ardently pro-China, and just as ardently anti-American. And the deep pride in being selected to host the 2008 Olympics is evident everywhere in Beijing. To China, the Olympics are a symbol of being a full-blown international player.

Joining the WTO has been accomplished, so at least the new leaders won't have that complex and seemingly unending task before them. But there will no doubt be areas of disagreement as the accession process moves forward. And the leadership will have to sell some tough new regulations and policies to the Chinese population. If the economy isn't doing particularly well a few years from now, or if there is massive unrest from too many laid-off workers, the long-term appeal of the WTO may not be so appealing.

Perhaps the biggest threats are those events that would precipitate change in the balance of power in Asia—on all sides. What happens in Taiwan always has the potential to rock the boat on the mainland. The next elections in Taiwan, or any signs that the Taiwan leadership is hinting that it's moving away from the "one country, two systems" model, and some more gunboats could be heading for the Taiwan Strait.

The failure to reach some sort of mutually acceptable conclusion to the Spratley Islands claims may also be a pressure point. With significant oil and gas finds at stake, the parties involved simply can't continue to overlap with the territorial claims of the other countries. Any further incidents in the South China Sea would surely test a new Chinese leadership with little track record in foreign affairs.

And the fate of the Korean Peninsula is a huge wild card. If reunification of North and South Korea is just around the corner (a scenario that might have seemed more likely two or three years ago), what would China's reaction be? Having a weak and hungry—but ideologically simpatico—neighbor to the east is one thing. But having a reunified and resurging Korea as its new neighbor would be a whole new ballgame. Seen from China's perspective, preserving the status quo on the Korean Peninsula might suit the leadership just fine.

Relations with the United States

Several analysts suggest that U.S.-China relations may go through a fairly low-key period while the leadership gets itself sorted out. The road to the WTO has been a long one, but there will likely be new trade disagreements to be ironed out. The WTO provides the blueprint, but China still has to build the trade and investment regimes.

One interesting new wrinkle in the Sino-U.S. bilateral relationship is the global war on terrorism. China was waging its own battle against Muslim insurgents, even before the September 11 attacks in the United States. One of China's moves was to sign a pact against "terrorism, separatism, and extremism" with six Central Asian countries. Since September 11, Jiang Zemin has made several trips to Arab nations.

Is China taking these steps to establish itself as a global player in the war against terrorism? Perhaps the motivations are on several levels. China certainly wants to keep a tight lid on cross-border flows of Muslim unrest. And China has been a major supplier of arms to the Arab world. Don't forget, too, that China has reportedly been helping Pakistan develop nuclear weapons. An unstable Pakistan would not be welcome news in Beijing.

The Least You Need to Know

- China's leader, Jiang Zemin, and other aging, top party leaders are reportedly scheduled to step down next year.

- The changes in leadership are likely to be voted on at the sixteenth Party Congress in late 2002.

- The man most likely to replace Jiang Zemin is Hu Jintao.

- China's leaders will face many challenges, including growing unemployment and corruption.

Chapter 21

The Globalization Game

In This Chapter

- ◆ China becomes a powerful global player.
- ◆ China's entry into the World Trade Organization is a major victory, but has its downside.
- ◆ The United States pressures less and maneuvers more on human rights issues.
- ◆ China-watchers differ on China's future course.

The year 2001 was a watershed year for China. On December 11, 2001, China formally joined the World Trade Organization after a decade of negotiations. In July, the International Olympic Committee approved China's bid to host the twenty-ninth Olympic Summer Games in 2008. In October, Jiang Zemin welcomed leaders from the 20 other Pacific Rim "member economies" to Shanghai for the annual meeting of the Asia Pacific Economic Cooperation group (APEC).

It would be easy to say that these are just agreements and meetings, nothing out of the ordinary in the busy schedule of any country's international dealings. But for China, these events signaled something more important: Barely two decades after emerging from virtual seclusion, China was front and center on the world stage. For the CCP leadership, these developments showed the world—and all of China, too—that the People's Republic of China is a global player.

What else remains to cement China's status as a powerful economic force, a massive global trader, and a regional and global military presence? China is already a member of the United Nations, the World Bank Group, and perhaps thousands of other international organizations devoted to everything from library management to scientific cooperation.

Membership in the highly exclusive G-7, or Group of Seven industrialized nations, might be the remaining step. Russia, after all, has been included as number 8 in many of the group's meetings. Adding China would be the ultimate closure on the Cold War era: Chinese and Russian leaders cooperating with their former enemies to forge a more stable and secure world order. And acceding to the "G-9," as it may have to be renamed, would reflect a remarkable shift in how the industrialized world views and engages with China. Only a short decade ago, after the events on Tiananmen Square, the G-7 was quick to censure China's actions and suspend many relationships with the PRC government.

Ready or Not

Membership has its perks and privileges, to be sure. For China, the quest for legitimization seems nearly complete. But there are also a host of new responsibilities to bear. In Beijing, city officials now face the almost impossible task of getting the municipality ready for its Olympic debut.

Funds already earmarked for Olympics-related work include $5.4 billion to relocate factories, increase the greenbelt around the city, and convert thousands of buses and taxis to natural gas—all to improve the city's poor air quality. Add $10.8 billion for roads and light rail projects, $1.8 billion for utilities and digital cabling, $208 million for restoring historic buildings, and considerable sums for property development, including a massive Olympic Park, and the costs really start to add up.

Wise One Says

The PRC government has reportedly drawn up a budget of RMB180 billion ($21.7 billion) for 142 Olympics-related improvement projects in Beijing. Of this, some $14 billion will come from the PRC government and the remaining $8 billion will come from domestic and overseas private-sector investment.

—Andrew Ness, *The China Business Review* (March–April 2002)

The Global Economic Picture

This "can-do" attitude toward the Olympics can be seen in other arenas as well. China has pushed hard to join the World Trade Organization and has made considerable concessions in the process. And there are further painful economic reforms to be made over the next decade. In his remarks at the Shanghai APEC meeting in October 2001, PRC President Jiang Zemin urged continued collaboration on economic issues. The APEC meeting, moreover, committed APEC members to continue working toward the 1994 Bogor goals. These targets call for APEC members to reduce trade tariffs to zero by 2010 for developed nations and 2020 for developing ones.

Hu Nu?

The United States does $700 billion in business with the 20 other APEC members, which is about two thirds of total U.S. trade. In 1999, APEC's 21 members had a combined GDP of more than $18 trillion, and accounted for almost 44 percent of global trade. APEC member economies include: Australia, Brunei, Canada, Chile, China, Hong Kong, Indonesia, Japan, South Korea, Malaysia, Mexico, New Zealand, Papua New Guinea, Peru, Philippines, Russia, Singapore, Chinese Taipei, Thailand, the United States, and Vietnam.

Globalization, some of the lower-income Asian countries have argued, inherently benefits the wealthier nations. Wouldn't China, too, stand to lose in the globalization game? APEC tariff concessions or WTO accession reforms mean short-term hardships for China, as well as a number of uncertainties. How will China stack up in the global order 5, 10, and 20 years from now? The stakes are high, particularly for the Chinese government. On the one hand, WTO accession has helped fortify the economic reforms undertaken by Jiang Zemin and Zhu Rongji. Having the WTO banner to wave around gives the Chinese government a powerful PR tool. The message is that "together, we can work toward something really great." Many of these reforms, like reducing subsidies given to unprofitable state enterprises, will put millions more out of work. The Chinese leadership knows that these reforms are necessary for China's long-term economic health, as well as for WTO accession.

On the other hand, there is a chance that the WTO wheeling and dealing could actually cost the Chinese leadership more than it had bargained for. When Jiang Zemin offered a number of deep concessions to Bill Clinton in 1999, Clinton refused them. Upon returning to China, Jiang lost face, and many of the CCP conservatives had some serious ammunition to let loose against the WTO, and against Jiang's leadership capabilities.

And there are deeper undercurrents of ideology and power to be considered. According to Robert A. Kapp, president of the U.S.-China Business Council:

> The paradox at the heart of China's WTO implementation is that it requires the far-reaching exercise of behavior-changing power by China's central government to create a WTO-compatible socioeconomic order in which the role of central power is itself sharply curtailed. Huge issues of ideology and policy await resolution in this country with 60 million Communist Party members and more than a million towns and villages.
>
> —*The China Business Review*, January–February 2002

So Jiang Zemin and Zhu Rongji took a gamble on the WTO, and seem to have won, at least for now. How the next generation of leaders, most likely led by Hu Jintao and Wen Jiabao (see Chapter 20), carries out the next rounds of economic reforms remains to be seen. Stability will be the key economic goal now, not 7 percent growth.

The WTO: Who Wins, Who Loses?

The Clinton administration argued that bringing China into the WTO would help the United States make up some of its huge bilateral trade imbalance. Clinton argued, also, that bringing China into the WTO would give the world a strong multilateral forum to challenge China on trade grievances. Opening up China's trade and investment regime to global market forces would also strengthen those within China who support the rule of law. Clinton's policy of engagement with China ultimately holds that commercial and economic ties with the outside world will strengthen the forces for democracy within China.

For China, the choice to pursue WTO accession seems an obvious one. Already a global trade powerhouse, China stands to gain from the expanded exports that seem possible. Decreased trade barriers around the world, thanks to the WTO, mean more export opportunities. It's quite likely Jiang Zemin, Zhu Rongji, and other Chinese leaders saw the writing on the wall. Be part of the WTO, or be left behind as the rest of the world lowers its trade barriers and welcomes an unprecedented increase in global exchanges of goods and services.

If nothing else, figuring out China's WTO accession protocol has kept lawyers and politicians busy on both sides of the Pacific for the better part of a decade. The rules are both sweepingly broad and painstakingly specific. Here are some of the main winners and losers in a WTO-ready China.

Chinese Enterprises

For Chinese companies, joining the WTO could be a good thing—or not—depending on what business you're in and the connections you might have. The pros and cons of WTO accession also change with the time frame. Over the longer term, it's easier to see the benefits.

Under the WTO, China has to reduce its non-tariff import barriers. Thus, many types of imported vehicles, machinery, electronics, medical technology, and a long list of other items will be easier to obtain. And many of the existing quotas, like those for auto parts, will gradually be reduced. Many of these changes are already in progress. If your venture needs these items to expand production, you're in luck—your investment costs should be lower.

If you are looking to get into the lucrative import-export business, the chances of succeeding now are better than ever. Until just recently, China allowed only state-owned trading companies to engage in the import and export trade. Under the WTO, it should become much easier for domestic Chinese enterprises to set up trading companies.

But if your business relies on heavy state subsidies, watch out. Controls on the prices of 128 different categories of goods and services were eliminated in 2001. China had to promise not to use price controls to protect its industries. And if your business would be sunk without government protection, you may be in even worse shape. As part of the WTO process, China has promised to wean its state-owned enterprises, and let more and more of these hulking, inefficient beasts fend for themselves.

The Workforce

Unfortunately for millions of Chinese who are employed, or underemployed, by these hulking, inefficient beasts, the WTO process means you may lose your job. State enterprises employ about 75 million workers in China, and up to a third of these workers are considered "surplus" or "unproductive" labor. The worst effects will likely be felt in China's cities, where many of the state enterprises are located.

All these layoffs will put added pressure on local officials, as most state-owned enterprises are owned or controlled by municipalities. Laying off that many people without inviting massive public protests will not be easy. According to some news reports, many of China's mayors now have to deal with organized protest marches. Unemployed industrial workers are leading the protests, which often center on unpaid benefits. These problems are likely to get worse, and put new pressure on the government at all levels to provide some sort of safety net.

Han Help

Labor Minister Li Boyong cautioned that state-owned enterprises are likely to lay off an estimated 8 to 10 million workers over the next few years. In 1997, 12 million workers were furloughed (*xiagang*). In Shenyang, the heart of China's heavy industry in Liaoning Province, an estimated 14 percent of state-owned enterprise workers are already on furlough. The furlough rate is twice as high in Fujian Province.

Down on the Farm

For the 350 million Chinese who work in agriculture, the WTO is also a mixed bag. Ultimately, China should be able to compete with the rest of Asia in exporting agricultural products. But this will take some time and quite a few changes. Very few of China's agricultural enterprises would meet the WTO's current standards for quality control, labeling, or pesticide content, for example.

And, like other aspects of the WTO, there will likely be different benefits depending on the region in China. In the prosperous regions, particularly where local investors are also interested in investing in food processing facilities, it's very possible that the local fruits and vegetables could start to be exported for a tidy profit. But once again, the poorer regions of China stand to lose out. In the mountainous interior, for instance, it's hard to imagine crops being grown for export—and easier to see where cheaper imports of foodstuffs would undermine the locals' livelihood.

Wise One Says

Economic regionalism has grown to the point of threatening overall economic reform... This new regionalism—the "New Warlordism," as some have called it—has led to extraordinary competition among China's regions, provinces, and local governments to attract foreign investment and keep existing industries afloat by providing all manner of foreign investment tax breaks ... with severe effects [due to decrease in tax revenues] particularly on institutions concerned with social welfare.

—James V. Feinerman; James M. Morita Professor of Asian Legal Studies at Georgetown University Law Center

Rural unrest is already enough of a headache for the central leadership. In January 2000, Zhu Rongji announced the Great Western Development Strategy (*Xibu Da Kaifa*) to shift substantial portions of foreign loans and central government resource allocations to beef up industries and infrastructure in rural areas. The funds were specifically targeted for Gansu, Guizhou, Qinghai, Shaanxi, Sichuan, and Yunnan Provinces, three autonomous regions (Ningxia, Tibet, and Xinjiang), and one province-level municipality (Chongqing).

If this pans out for Beijing, the program would have an added bonus. Part of this strategy is designed to give minority peoples in these areas greater economic opportunities, and fewer reasons to instigate revolts against the Han Chinese government. That would ease another great pressure on the central leadership.

Foreign Investors

Billions of dollars in foreign investment flow into China each year. Some of this money is well disguised Chinese funds, funneled out to Hong Kong or the Virgin Islands to come back to China. "Round-tripping" is one way Chinese investors tap into the tax holidays and other perks offered to foreign investors.

But much of the funds, especially in the past five years, have been invested in large joint-venture or wholly foreign-owned enterprises in China across a broad spectrum of enterprises. And foreign investors have had to fight many battles to get their projects approved. Just finding out which sectors were completely off-limits to foreign investors was not easy, at least until recently. Foreign investors are probably the one group that stands to gain the most from China's WTO accession.

Under the WTO, China will have to change many laws and internal, or *neibu*, regulations. Foreign investors are particularly interested in those related to market access, which would allow foreigners to invest in a much broader range of industry sectors. China is now circulating drafts of new legislation on foreign investment in banking, transportation, hospitals, cinemas, construction, engineering, and many other areas. Yes, even railway transportation is on the list—historically, allowing foreign participation in China's railways was a bad call on the Qing government's part (see Chapter 3).

Intellectual property rights (IPR) legislation should also be strengthened under the WTO. In recent years, China has made great progress toward making its copyright, patent, and other related laws compatible with international norms. Enforcing the law is not always so easy. Foreign firms will be looking to the WTO to help enforce court decisions or arbitration awards. In the past, a foreign firm with an IPR beef could take the Chinese party to court and win the case, only to find later that the Chinese court had no jurisdiction over the matter, and could not enforce the settlement award.

Playing by the Rules

Eager as China is to reap the economic benefits of the WTO, and bask in the glow of being an Olympic host, there are other responsibilities that come with being a global player. China will now have to step up to the plate and show that it's a player, again and again.

It's far too early to say that China is definitely living up to its WTO agreements. It is encouraging to note the huge numbers of new and amended laws China has put through to implement the agreements, and the seminars on the WTO that are being sponsored throughout China by the United Nations and governments of many countries, including the United States. Saving face is important, so it's likely that China will live up to its end of the WTO deal—or at least use the many different conflict-resolution arenas under the WTO to air its grievances.

Other analysts point to China's past record in other international organizations as being generally very positive. As a member of the United Nations, China is expected to participate in UN peace-keeping operations.

> **Hu Nu?**
>
> In 1990, China began to assign military observers to UN peace-keeping operations. Since then, 437 Chinese observers have joined in six UN operations in Africa, the Middle East, and Southeast Asia.

According to Margaret Pearson, associate professor of government politics at the University of Maryland:

> China's likely behavior in the WTO is also predictable based on its record in other international economic organizations, particularly the World Bank and International Monetary Fund (IMF). Here, the record is unambiguous ... Since joining the bank in 1980, China has acquired long-term funding, technical assistance, and strategic advice on reforming its economy. The bank has become China's largest single source of long-term foreign capital, and China became the bank's largest client in 1993. As of June 1999, the bank had committed a total of $32.5 billion to China.

> World Bank officials often cite China as a model member. The quality of the bank's project portfolio in China is one of its best. According to bank officials, China projects are well implemented, within budget, and on time, and China has grown from a quiet presence to a mature partner. Over time, the Chinese officials and economists posted to the bank have gained confidence as well as knowledge, and have become more able to contribute to the bank's daily operations.

China's profile has been lower in the IMF. The PRC has borrowed minimally and repaid immediately. More important, China has been an active recipient of IMF advice, particularly in the steps it has taken toward currency convertibility.

—*The China Business Review* (January–February 2000)

Is China a Military Threat?

Economically, China is strong and growing stronger. And China seems willing enough to abide by international economic norms. Militarily, though, many analysts might have questions about China's long-term military goals. In a world where strength and power are measured increasingly in terms of exports and GDP, why does China seem to be spending a lot of money on its military?

Today, the People's Liberation Army has about 2.5 million members, headed by the chairman of China's Central Military Commission (currently Jiang Zemin). In 2001, Finance Minister Xiang Huaicheng revealed that China would spend more than $17 billion on defense this year, an increase of almost 18 percent. Last year China increased its military spending by nearly 13 percent. This has raised some eyebrows among Western military analysts.

A substantial portion of these funds, though not all, will likely go toward beefing up military salaries. This seems to be the compromise Jiang Zemin made when he began the military divestment program in 1998. Until that time, the PLA was freely allowed to pursue business opportunities, and did so, investing in everything from hotels to ice cream production to local taxis. Jiang thought it a wise move to make the PLA a professional fighting force, not an entrepreneurial power as it has been, so he promised to help the PLA cover more of its operating costs if they would divest. To date, an unknown number of PLA enterprises have been sold off.

But China clearly has its eye on being a strong regional presence. According to some reports, China has plans to buy several aircraft carriers over the next 15 years, along with newer ships equipped with the latest anti-ship missiles, surface-to-air missiles, and anti-submarine capabilities. New fighter aircraft are being developed, along with nuclear attack submarines and land-based mobile intercontinental ballistic missiles.

It's hard to imagine that there is some overall regional or global attack plan here. After all, China is so intent on abiding by international rules and regulations in so many arenas. There's a current saying in China, "*fuguo qiangbing*," which means "rich country and strong army." The resurgence in Chinese nationalism and patriotism cuts along both economic and military lines.

But it's also hard to ignore the very real possibility that some sudden new instability within the Asian region could put China's army on the move. A new belligerent voice from Taiwan, perhaps, or a reunified Korea right at China's back door, might well alter the scope of China's military strategy. And any such developments would affect other nations, both inside and outside Asia.

China–U.S. Relations

For the United States and China, these are uncertain times, but then the same could be said of the U.S.-China relationship ever since the normalization of relations more than two decades ago. The United States will likely continue to make its yearly arms sales to Taiwan, which will provoke some criticisms from Beijing. And the United States will continue to push and prod on trade and investment liberalizations. It now has a bigger stick—the WTO—to use.

In granting China Permanent Normal Trade Relations (PNTR), the United States has given up one of its other sticks for the carrot of the WTO. The one unsettled issue, to the U.S. government, is human rights in China. Human rights are not a part of the WTO, and are covered in unenforceable United Nations resolutions.

Many conservatives in the United States worry that the United States no longer has much leverage to influence the course of human rights in China. Chinese conservatives, as well as many others both inside and outside China, would argue that the United States never had this leverage in the first place, nor the right to interfere in China's domestic affairs.

U.S. companies with investment deals in China would counter that the presence of Western businesses, and the ideas they bring into the Chinese workplace, are as powerful a diplomatic tool as any other. Western management principles, for example, espouse open, fair promotions based on performance. This runs counter to Chinese practices, where personal loyalties and connections tend to dictate who gets promoted. In the long run, Western companies would argue that these subtle changes in the workplace help open the Chinese population to new ideas, and new thoughts of a more open and democratic society.

China's Future

Strong economic growth will be the linchpin in China's future. Currently, the world's sixth-largest economy in terms of GDP, China could conceivably become the world's largest economy by 2040.

There are considerable potholes and dangers along the way, though. Economic disintegration would mean chaos and rising opportunities for corruption, and weaken the central government's ability to rule. And a weaker China, ultimately, is a more dangerous China to the outside world.

For now, the stage seems set for continued international collaboration in China's economy. Perhaps, too, there will continue to be quiet inroads into the nagging question of China's human rights policy. The Western world has long been fascinated with China, and never so much as during the past two decades of "reform and opening."

For other facets of the vast and fascinating nation that is the People's Republic of China, the questions and variables are never-ending. Over the short term, will the Fourth Generation of leaders, with Hu Jintao thought likely to be at the forefront, be able to chart a stable course? The Third Generation has done an admirable job of making tough economic decisions, but the signs of social unrest are everywhere, and growing. Keeping a strong central hand in it all will be the leadership's biggest task.

China's long march has taken many twists and turns. The coming months, years, and decades will no doubt provide their share of surprises. With the colossal shift from a nonmarket economy to one dictated by market forces, China seems to be getting its economic house in order, step by step. Or make that one step forward and two steps back, at times. It's yet to be seen whether other social and political changes necessary for the nation's health will follow.

There's a Chinese proverb that goes like this:

> May you live in interesting times.

The Least You Need to Know

- In 2001, China became a member of the World Trade Organization and won its bid to host the 2008 Olympics.

- China is now the world's sixth largest economy in terms of gross domestic product, and the fastest-growing economy in the world.

- The United States hopes to promote democratic values and human rights in China through long-term trade and investment relationships.

- In the short term, the unemployed and workers in state-run industries are least likely to benefit from China's global economy.

- Whether China can remain politically stable through its economic transition is anybody's guess.

Glossary

bianzi   A queue, or long braid of hair, that the Qing dynasty required men to have.

boddhisattva   In Buddhism, an individual who has achieved enlightenment and vowed to stay in a cycle of birth, death, and rebirth until all sentient beings have achieved enlightenment.

Cantonese   The Chinese dialect that is spoken by 50 million people in the area of Ghangzhou (Canton).

Chung   A Confucianist principle that includes loyalty to the state.

Dalai Lama   "All-Embracing Leader." In traditional Tibetan Buddhism, the Dalai Lama is the religious leader as well as the leader of the state.

Daoism   "The Way" or a nature-oriented philosophy that began in China in the sixth century and contrasted sharply with Confucianism in that it did not concern itself with social or political concepts.

Falun Gong   "Practice of the Wheel of Dharma" or a sect, founded in China in the 1990s, that practices *qigong*, or focusing breathing exercises. The Chinese government has banned it and jailed—some say also executed—many of its followers.

Generation Yellow   China's younger generation of 18- to 35-year-olds. Their parents are known as Generation Red.

Guomindang   Also Kuomintang (KMT), it is the Nationalist People's Party that was founded by Dr. Sun Yatsen and established the Republic of China in 1912 to replace the Qing dynasty.

Hakka   A Northern Chinese people who migrated to the south centuries ago, they have retained their distinct dialect and many of their cultural traditions, and can be found throughout China.

Han   The name of the dynasty during which Chinese culture was formed, it also is the word for Chinese people who speak the Putonghua language (better known in the rest of the world as Mandarin), and increasingly for racially non-Chinese whose language is Putonghua.

hsiao   Confucian principle of love within the family: love of parents for their children and of children for their parents.

hua jiao   Chinese who live outside of China, also expatriates.

Inner Asia   The vast sweep of land from Manchuria, through Mongolia and Turkestan, and south to Tibet; its peoples have been part of China's culture since the Qing dynasty.

jen   The word for benevolence and humaneness toward others, it is the highest Confucian virtue.

KMT   Acronym for Kuomintang, as Guomindang was spelled in the romanization system that preceded pinyin. Today this acronym is most recognized as the Guomindang political party in Taiwan. *See* Guomindang for definition.

li   The word for "proper conduct," it is a Confucian principle of social behavior that includes ritual, propriety, etiquette, and other practices.

loess   A mixture of sand and clay with a yellowish color that is carried by the Yellow River.

Mandarin   *See* Putonghua.

most-favored-nation status   A term used in international trade relations to designate the *absence of barriers* to trade with another country, rather than the granting of any special favors.

pinyin   The version of romanization of the Chinese written language that is favored by Beijing and used most widely today, as it is in this book.

proletariat   In Russia, the term meant the urban industrial working class who constituted the major segment of the population. China was an agrarian society, so it was the rural peasants who, in Mao Zedong's adaptation, were the proletariat.

Putonghua Literally "common speech," it is the term adopted by the People's Republic of China to refer to the standard Chinese language (formerly known as Mandarin).

Quanguo Renmin Daibia Dahui National People's Legislative Congress.

queue A long braid of hair that had to be worn by Chinese men during the Qing dynasty. (*See also* bianzi.)

realpolitik "Political realism." A belief that politics should be dictated by reality, however harsh, rather than by morality.

romanization An alphabetic scheme for the Chinese language using Latin letters, it was created by Chinese and Russian scholars in the early 1930s. (*See also* pinyin.)

San Min Zhu Yi Dr. Sun Yatsen's "Three Principles of the People," nationalism, democracy, and the livelihood of the people.

sheng Province.

shi Municipality.

soviet The Russian word for a communist governing council.

Taoism *See* Daoism.

wuwei A go-with-the-flow approach to life that is a major aspect of Daoism.

xin Honesty and trustworthiness

xinao Brainwashing.

Xinjiang "New Frontier," the name of a huge autonomous region in northwest China that has a majority population of Muslim ethnic groups.

yi Righteousness.

Zhongguo In Chinese, "central land." The ancient Chinese name for China.

Zhongguo Gongchandang The Chinese Communist Party.

zizhiqu Autonomous region.

Appendix B

Further Reading

Books

Associated Press. *China: From the Long March to Tiananmen Square*, New York: Henry Holt & Company, 1990.

Banister, Judith. *China's Changing Population*. Stanford: Stanford University Press, 1987.

Baum, Richard. *Burying Mao: Chinese Politics in the Age of Deng Xiaoping*. Princeton: Princeton University Press, 1994.

Becker, Jasper. *Hungry Ghosts: China's Secret Famine*. London: John Murray, 1996.

Bell, Oliver. *The Two Chinas*. New York: Scholastic Magazines, Inc., 1967.

Brook, Timothy. *Quelling the People: The Military Suppression of the Beijing Democracy Movement*. Stanford: Stanford University Press, 1998.

Ching, Julia. *Chinese Religions*. New York: Macmillan, 1993.

Davin, Delia. *Mao Zedong*, Stroud: Sutton Publishing, 1997.

Davis, Deborah, and Steven Harrell. *Chinese Families in the Post-Mao Era*. Berkeley: University of California Press, 1993.

DeFrancis, John. *The Chinese Language: Fact and Fantasy*. Honolulu: University of Hawaii Press, 1990.

Dittmer, Lowell, and Samuel S. Kim, eds. *China's Quest for National Identity*. Ithaca: Cornell University Press, 1993.

Dreyer, Edward L. *China at War, 1901–1949*. London: Longman, 1995.

Evans, Richard. *Deng Xiaoping and the Making of Modern China*. London: Hamish Hamilton, 1993.

Fairbank, John King, and Merle Goldman. *China: A New History*. Cambridge, Massachusetts: The Belknap Press of Harvard University Press, 1998.

Garraty, John A. and Peter Gay, eds. *The Columbia History of the World*. New York: Harper & Row, 1972.

Garver, John W. *Foreign Relations of the People's Republic of China*. Berkeley: University of California Press, 1992.

Goldman, Merle. *Sowing the Seeds of Democracy in China: Political Reform in the Deng Xiaoping Era*. Cambridge, Massachusetts: Harvard University Press, 1994.

Goodman, David S.G. *Deng Xiaoping and the Chinese Revolution: A Political Biography*. London: Routledge, 1994.

Hook, Brian, ed. *The Cambridge Encyclopedia of China*. Cambridge, Massachusetts: Cambridge University Press, 1991.

Hoyt, Edwin P. *The Day the Chinese Attacked*. New York: Paragon House, 1990.

Lattimore, Owen. *The Situation in Asia*. Boston: Little, Brown and Company, 1949.

Mackerras, Colin. *China's Minority Cultures: Identities and Integration Since 1912*. New York: St. Martin's Press, 1995.

———. *The Rise of the Chinese Republic: From the Last Emperor to Deng Xiaoping*. New York: McGraw Hill, 1989.

Mackerras, Colin, Donald H. McMillan, and Andrew Watson. *Dictionary of the Politics of the People's Republic of China*. London: Routledge, 1998.

Mann, James. *About Face: A History of America's Curious Troubled Relationship With China from Nixon to Clinton*. New York: Alfred A. Knopf, 1999.

Martin, Christopher. *The Boxer Rebellion*. London: Abelard-Schuman, 1968.

Nathan, Andrew J., and Robert J. Ross. *The Great Wall and the Empty Fortress: China's Search for Security*. New York: W.W. Norton, 1997.

Naughton, Barry. *Growing Out of the Plan: Chinese Economic Reform, 1978–1993*. Cambridge, Massachusetts: Cambridge University Press, 1995.

Needham, Joseph, and Colin A. Roman. *Shorter Science and Civilisation in China: An Abridgement of Joseph Needham's Original Text*. Cambridge, England: Cambridge University Press, 1978.

O'Neill, Hugh B. *Companion to Chinese History*. Oxford: Facts on File, 1987.

Poston, Dudley L., and David Yaukey, eds. *The Population of Modern China*. New York: Plenum Press, 1992.

Salisbury, Harrison E. *The New Emperors: Mao and Deng, a Dual Biography*. London: HarperCollins, 1992.

Schell, Orville. *Mandate of Heaven: A New Generation of Entrepreneurs, Dissidents, Bohemians and Technocrats Lays Claim to China's Future*. New York: Simon and Schuster, 1994.

Spence, Jonathan D. *The Gate of Heavenly Peace: The Chinese and Their Revolution*. London: Faber and Faber, 1982.

Starr, John Bryan. *Understanding China*. New York: Hill and Wang, 2001.

———. *The Search for Modern China*. New York: Norton, 1990.

Stevenson, Jay. *The Complete Idiot's Guide to Eastern Philosophy*. Indianapolis: Alpha Books, 2000.

Wilson, Dick. *China the Big Tiger: A Nation Awakes.* London: Abacus, 1997.

Zhang, Xinxin, ed. *Chinese Lives: An Oral History of Contemporary China.* London: Macmillan, 1987.

Journals

Eckstein, Alexander, "Economic Growth and Change in China: A Twenty-Year Perspective," *The China Quarterly* (April–June, 1973): 54.

Fitzgerald, C.P., "Tension on the Sino-Soviet Border," *Foreign Affairs* (July 1967): 683–93.

Gittings, John, "The Great-Power Triangle and Chinese Foreign Policy," *The China Quarterly* (July–September 1969): 39, 41–54.

Schwartz, Benjamin I., "On the 'Originality' of Mao," *Foreign Affairs* (October 1955): 74.

Zagoria, Donald S., "Mao's Role in the Sino-Soviet Conflict," *Pacific Affairs* (Summer 1974): 139–53.

Appendix C

Chronology

c. 2000–1500 B.C.E.   Xia Kingdom

1700–1027 B.C.E.   Shang Kingdom

1027–771 B.C.E.   Western Zhou dynasty

770–221 B.C.E.   Eastern Zhou dynasty

551–479 B.C.E.   Life of Confucius

475–221 B.C.E.   Warring States period

372–289 B.C.E.   Life of Mencius

221–206 B.C.E.   Qin dynasty

221 B.C.E.–1912 C.E.   Qin Empire

206 B.C.E.–9 C.E.   Former Han dynasty

25–220 C.E.   Later Han dynasty

221–618   Period of the "Six Dynasties"

618–906   Tang dynasty

960–1279   Song dynasty

1162–1227   Life of Genghis Khan

1206   Genghis proclaimed "Ruler of Rulers"

1215   Mongols break through the Great Wall

1215–1294   Life of Kublai Khan

1254   Marco Polo born

1279–1368   Yuan (Mongol) dynasty

1368–1644   Ming dynasty

1514   Portuguese reach China by sea

1582   First Jesuit missionary in China

1644–1911   Qing (Manchu) dynasty

1839–42   Opium War, era of disunity

1851–64   Taiping Rebellion

1861   Empress Dowager Cixi assumes regency of Qing dynasty

1887   Chiang Kaishek born

1893   Mao Zedong born

1898   100 Days of Reform

1894   First Sino-Japanese War

1900   Boxer Rebellion

1905   Sun Yatsen begins Republican Revolution

1906   Pu Yi born

1908   Pu Yi chosen to succeed Emperor Guangxu

Death of Emperor Guangxu

Death of Empress Dowager Cixi

Succession of Pu Yi as emperor

1911   Guangzhou (Canton) Rebellion

October 10, 1911   Republican Revolution successful

January 1, 1912   Republic of China established at Nanjing

1912   Emperor Pu Yi abdicates

Yuan Shikai becomes president of Chinese Republic

1913   Yuan dissolves parliament

1914   Sun Yatsen founds Revolutionary Party of China

1916   Death of Yuan Shikai

1918   Li Dazhao forms the New Tide Society

1920   Chen Duxiu founds Marxist Study Society and Socialist Youth Corps

1921   Birth of Chinese Communist Party

1923   Sun Yatsen sets up regime in Canton

1925   Death of Sun Yatsen

1926   Chiang Kaishek's Northern Expedition

1927   Li Dazhao executed by warlord Chang Tsolin

Chiang establishes new capital in Nanjing

1931   Japan invades Manchuria

1934   Start of the Long March

1935   Japanese control five northern provinces

Students riot in Beijing

1936   Chiang Kaishek kidnapped and released

1937   Second Sino-Japanese War starts at Marco Polo Bridge

Rape of Nanjing

1945   Japanese defeated, ending World War II

1947–49   Civil War between Communists and Nationalists

1949   Communist-controlled People's Republic of China founded

Defeated Nationalist government flees to Taiwan

1950–53   Korean War

1951   Beginning of mass campaigns and thought reform

1953   Mao Zedong's first Five-Year Plan

1953–57   Transition to socialism

1954   Constitution adopted

1956   The Hundred Flowers movement

1958–60   The Great Leap Forward

1959   China crushes Tibet and the Dalai Lama flees

1960   Famine takes as many as 20 million lives

1961–65   Period of recovery

1963   Sino-Soviet split

1964   China explodes first atom bomb

1965   United States aids South Vietnam, China aids North

1966–76   The Great Proletarian Cultural Revolution

1968   China explodes first hydrogen bomb

1971   PRC gets UN seat formerly occupied by Taiwan government

1972   U.S. President Richard M. Nixon visits China

1975   Death of Chiang Kaishek

1976   Death of Mao Zedong and Zhou Enlai

Deng Xiaoping becomes China's leader

1977   Deng's Four Modernizations begin

1978   Open Door policy

1979   Democracy Wall Movement

1981   Sentencing of the Gang of Four

1980–88   Deng's Era of Reforms begins

1982   Chinese population surpasses one billion

1984   Coastal cities opened for foreign investment and trade

1989   Tiananmen Square Democracy Movement ends in massacre

1990   Deng retires but remains in control

Jiang Zemin succeeds Deng

1991   Premier Zhu Rongji makes the new economy a reality

1994   Work begins on Three Gorges Dam

1997   Hong Kong returned to China

Death of Deng Xiaoping

Jiang Zemin visits the United States

1999   China gains entry to the World Trade Organization

2000   Jiang Zemin announces "Three Representatives" initiative to widen the Party's base

2001   U.S. spy plane downed over Chinese waters

Index

A

Agrarian Reform Law, 132
agricultural collectivization, Mao Zedong, 133
agriculture
   current trends, 9
   modernization, 193-194
   reforms in, 157
AIDS problem, 261-262
air pollution, problems with, 214-215
Alexander the Great, 23
Anglo-American Open Door Doctrine, 44
Anglo–Chinese War, The, 38-39
Anthony, Ted, 272
anti-Americanism, growth of, 173
APEC (Asian Pacific Economic Cooperation), 244, 297
Arigh Beki, 31
arts, 110
   Bronze Age, 110-111
   Buddhist Era, 111-112
   evolution of, 253-254
   flower-and-bird paintings, 113
   Ming dynasty, 114
   Qing dynasty, 114-115
   Song dynasties, 113-114
   Tang dynasty, 112-113
   Yuan dynasty, 114
Asian Pacific Economic Cooperation (APEC), 244, 297
autonomous regions (local government), 99

B

baihua (vernacular speech), 60
Bamboo Annals, The, 108
banking reforms, 206
Beijing, 10
   weakening of, 159
Bernstein, Richard, 178
bianzi, 48
birth control
   Chinese policies, 156
   female infanticide, 195
   modern trends, 195
"Blue-Collar Blues," 291
Bo Juyi, 112
bodhisattvas, 112
Bolshevik Revolution (Russia), 61-62
Book of Tao, The, 24
book sales, growth in, 252
bordering nations, 8
Borodin, Mikhail, 64
Bortei, wife of Genghis Khan, 29
Boxer Rebellion, 43-44, 264
   "Open Door Policy," 44
   Treaty of Beijing, 44
Bronze Age, artistic developments during, 110-111
Buddhism, 76-77
   bodhisattvas, 112
   Chan, 77
   Hinayana, 76
   Mahayana, 76
   Pure Land, 77
   Theraveda, 76
   Tibetan, 16, 77
   Zen, 77

Buddhist Era, artistic developments during, 111-112
Bush, George H. W., 179
Bynner, Witter, 27

C

calligraphy, development of, 114
Cantonese Chinese, 79
Cao Xueqin, 115
CCP (Chinese Communist Party), 61-63, 98, 124
   day-to-day operations, 288-289
   formation of, 62
   leaders, 124-125
   Mao Zedong, 67-68
   mass campaigns, 138-139
   new leadership, 282-283
   power of, 131
   purging of, 147
   Shanghai Clique, 285-286
Central Cultural Revolution Group, 148
central government, current system, 98-99
Central People's Government Council, establishment of, 130
Chai Ling, 181
Chan Buddhism, 77
Chan, Jackie, 255-256
characters, Chinese, 81-83
Chen Duxiu, 61-62
Chen Kaige, 256
Chen Xitong, 253, 291
Chen Yun, 130
Chen Zhili, 286
Cheng Dequan, 51
Chi Haotian, 237
Chiang Chingguo, 220
Chiang Kaishek, 14, 34, 64-65, 95, 120-121, 125-126, 134-135, 167, 220-221
   communists, purge of, 66
   decline in popularity, 128

   early life, 65
   emergence of, 64-65
   Japan, view of, 120
   kidnapping of, 121
   military training, 65
   Taiwan, escape to, 128-129
   warlords, defeat of, 65-66
China National Committee on Care for Children (CNCCC), 201
China Publishing Group, formation of, 252
China: A New History, 104
Chinese civil war, 128-129
Chinese Communist Party. *See* CCP
Chinese language, 77-83
   characters, 81-83
   dialects, 78-79
   homonyms, 79-81
Chinese People Suing Officials, 194
Chong (Confucian value), 24
Chongqing, 12
Christian missionaries
   rise of, 39
   treatment of, 231-232
chung yung, 94
city government, 99
civil service placement tests, improving social status, 89
civil war (China), 128-129
Cixi, the Empress Dowager, 41, 43, 45
   Boxer Rebellion, The, 44
   death of, 45
classes, growing disparities in, 207
clerical script (Chinese characters), 82
Clinton administration, 277
CNCCC (China National Committee on Care for Children), 201
colleges, modern system, 96
Commission on Science, Industry and Technology for National Defense, 171
Common Man, The, 43
commoners, old social order, 89-90

communes, 144
compasses, 107
compradors, 60
compulsory education, 95-96
Confucianism, 86-89, 104
    resurgence in, 100-101
Confucius, 23, 86
    Socrates, compared, 86
contractual joint ventures, 276
corruption
    government corruption, 210-212, 291
    modern developments in, 159
Corson, Trevor, 177, 291
cuisine, 258-259
Cultural Revolution, 146-150
cursive script (Chinese script), 83

D

Dalai Lama, 225-226
Daodejing, 24
Daoism, 74-76
Darwin, Charles, 40
decentralization policy, Deng Xiaoping, 158
Democracy Wall movement, 177
democraticization policy, Deng Xiaoping, 158
demographics
    current, 9-10
    minority groups, 15
    minority nationalities, 13
    regions
        eastern, 10-11
        northern, 17-19
        southern, 13
        western, 15-17
        Yangzi River Valley, 12-13
        Yellow River Valley, 11
Deng Pufang, 151
Deng Xiaoping, 124, 140-141, 150-155, 166-169, 180, 204, 227
    assumption of power, 150, 155
    death of, 166

decentralization policy, 158
democratization policy, 158
depoliticization policy, 158
"Four Modernizations" policy, 156-158
market economy, commitment to, 156
persecution of, 151
retirement of, 163, 166
second assumption of power, 151
socialism, views on, 156
tax cuts, 159
Tiananmen Square demonstrations, 159-163
Deng Xiaoping, 248
depoliticization policy, Deng Xiaoping, 158
Derrida, Jacques, 173
dialects, Chinese, 78-79
dissidents
    Falun Gong, 184
    Tiananmen Square, 181-184
Documents of Han, 107
"Double-Ten Day," 50
Dream of the Red Chamber, 115
drug abuse, modern problems with, 159
dynasties
    Han dynasty, 4, 25-26, 73
    Manchu dynasty, 5
    Ming dynasty, 7, 33-34
        artistic developments during, 114
    Qin dynasty, 4-5, 24
    Qing (Manchu) dynasty, 7, 17, 34, 47-48
        artistic developments during, 114-115
        end of, 50-51
        fall of, 21
    Shang dynasty, 22
    Shu dynasty, 26
    Song dynasties, artistic developments during, 27-28, 113-114
    Tang dynasty, 5, 26-27
        artistic developments during, 112-113
    Wei dynasty, 26
    Wu dynasty, 26

Yuan dynasty, 18, 31-32
    artistic developments during, 114
Zhou dynasty, 4, 7, 22-24
    accomplishments of, 23
    Confucius, 23
    Great Wall, 23
    Laozi, 24
    Mencius, 23

E

eastern region, demographics, 10-11
economic future, China, 304-305
economic reforms, Zhu Rongji, 170
educational system
    access to, 197
    compulsory education, 95-96
    current system, 95
    higher education, 96
    imperial China, 94-95
Einhorn, Bruce, 193
Einstein, Albert, 60
Engels, Friedrich, 48
entertainment industry, growth of, 248-253
environmental problems, 213-214
    air pollution, 214-215
    Three Gorges Dam, 216
    water pollution, 215-216
equity joint ventures (hezi qiye), 276
eunuchs (huan quan), 50
Evening Bell, 256
Evolution and Ethics, 40
examination system, improving social status,
 89
executive branch (central government), 98

F

Fairbank, John King, 104, 107
Falun Gong movement, 184, 229-231

families
    new social order, 92-94
    old social order, 90-92
farming
    modernization, 193-194
    reforms in, 157
    poverty, growth in, 208-210
fashion, evolution of, 256-258
Feinerman, James V., 300
female infanticide, 159, 195
females
    prostitution, 196
    role of, 194-197
    suicide rates, 195
"Fifth Generation" films, 256
fireworks, invention of, 27
first "Five-Year Plan," Mao Zedong, 133
flower-and-bird paintings, 113
food, 258-259
Forbidden City, 176
foreign film distribution, 255-256
foreign investors, growth of, 301
foreign policy, Mao Zedong, 134-135
Formosa. *See* Taiwan
"Four Modernizations" policy, Deng
  Xiaoping, 156-158
"Fourth Generation," 190
freedom, restrictions on, 160

G

Gang of Four, 147-150, 153
    backlash against, 151
    creation of, 147
    demise of, 154
    Jiang Qing, 154
    Zhang Chunqiao, 154
Gao Gang, 140
Gao Xingjian, 115, 253
Gemingdang, founding of, 56
"Generation Red," 198

"Generation Yellow," 198, 259-260
Genghis Khan, 18, 28-30
gentry, old social order, 89-90
geography
    arable land, 6
    bordering nations, 8
    current, 8
    early China, 3-4
    first expansion, 4
    isolational aspects, 6
    Junggar Pendi basin, 9
    Mongolian Steppe, 8
    mountain ranges, 8
    North China plain, 8
    Takla Makan desert, 9
Giddens, Anthony, 173
Gifford, Rob, 177, 179
Gittings, John, 292
globalization, 297-298
Goldman, Merle, 104
Gorbachev, Mikhail, glasnost policy, 166
government corruption, 210-212
    growth of, 291
Grand Canal, construction of, 7
grass script (Chinese characters), 83
"Great Administrative Areas," establishment
    of, 130
Great Britain, Opium War, 38-39
Great Hall of the People, 175
Great Leap Forward campaign, Mao
    Zedong, 143-145
Great Proletarian Cultural Revolution,
    146-150
Great Wall
    construction of, 7
        Zhou dynasty, 23
        Qin Shihuang, 25
Great Western Development Strategy (Xibu
    Da Kaifa), 300
Guan Hanqing, 113
Guangxu, 41-46, 49

guanxi, 275
Guanyin, the Buddhist Goddess of Mercy,
    112
gunpowder, invention of, 106
Guomindang, formation of, 53

H

Habermas, Jurgen, 173
Haike, Jin, 200
Hainan, geography and demographics, 14
Hakka Chinese, 39, 79
Han Dynasty, 4, 25-26, 73
Harvard Girl Liu Yiting, 252
He Dongchang, 162
Hessler, Peter, 227
Hinayana Buddhism, 76
homonyms, Chinese, 79-81
homosexuals, treatment of, 260
Hong Kong, relations with, 223-225
Hong Xiuquan, 39
Household Responsibility System, Mao
    Zedong, 157
Hu Jintao, 98, 167-169, 222, 283-284
Hu Shi, 60
Hu Yaobang, 158-160, 166, 177-179
    death of, 161
Hua Guofeng, 151-153, 158, 205
    assumption of power, 151
Hua Mu-Lan, 26
Huang Di, 109
Huang Ju, 286
Hui minority, 15
human rights, and relations with United
    States, 269-270
Hundred Days of Reform, 43
Hundred Flowers campaign, Mao Zedong,
    141-142
Huxley, T. H., 40

I

Ibsen, Henrik, 60
Ikuhiko Hata, 122
Incident at Marco Polo Bridge, 122
income
    growing disparities in, 207
    modern disparities in, 197
India, relations with, 243-244
individual liberties, restrictions on, 160
Indonesia, relations with, 242
industrial development under Mao Zedong,
    133-134
Injustice to Tou O, 113
Inner Mongolian Autonomous Region of
    People's Republic of China, 18
intellectual property rights, 274
    infringements, 217
intellectuals, 198-200
Internet
    growth in usage, 251-252
    increased usage in, 199
inventions, 115-116
    gunpowder, 106
    mariner's compass, 106
    paper, 104-105
    printing, 105-106
investment relations, United States, 273-277

J

Jamuga, 29
Japan
    attack on Pearl Harbor, 126
    China, invasion of, 122
    relations with, 239-240
    threat from, 119-120
Jefferson, Thomas, 67
Jet Li, 255
Jia Qinglin, 286
Jiang Mianheng, 167
Jiang Qing, 146-147, 150-154

    suicide of, 154
Jiang Zemin, 166-173, 191, 285-286,
    295-298
    assumption of power, 163
    "Cultural Revolution," 190-191
    early life, 167
    "New Generation," 190
    Three Representatives initiative, 172
Journey to the West and The Golden Lotus, The,
    114
judicial branch (central government), 99
Junggar Pendi basin, 9
Junzi (Confucianism), 87

K

Kan Chinese, 79
Kang Yuwei, 42-43
Kaplan, Robert, 179
Kapp, Robert A., 298
Kissenger, Henry, 267-268
KMT (Kuomintang), 53
Kong Fuzi. *See* Confucius, 23
Kong Qiu, 86
Kongfuzi, 86
Korea, relations with, 237-239
Korean War
    Chinese role in, 135
    United States, relations with, 266-267
Kublai Khan, 6, 18, 30-32
    Grand Canal, construction of, 7
Kuomintang (KMT), 53
Kycong-Won, Kim, 239

L

land reform, Mao Zedong, 132
Langfitt, Frank, 184
language, Chinese, 77-83
    characters, 81-83
    dialects, 78-79
    homonyms, 79-81

Lao Tzu. *See* Laozi
Laozi, 24
Lattimore, Owen, 44, 51
legal reforms, 205-206
legislative branch (central government), 99
Li (Confucian value), 24, 87
Li Boyong, 300
Li Changchun, 286
Li Dazhao, 61-62
Li Lanqing, 286
Li Lu, 181
Li Peng, 160, 162, 166, 182
Li Po, 27, 112
Li Ruihuan, 252, 285
Li Shizhen, 109
Li Tieying, 287
Li Yuanhong, 51
Li, Jet, 255
lifestyles, 259
Lin Biao, 124-125, 128, 140, 146, 149
    disappearance of, 149
Lion King, The, 256
literacy rate in Communist China, 97
literature, 110
    evolution of, 252-253
    poetry, Tang dynasty, 112
    thirteenth century, developments in, 113
"Little Red Book, The," 125, 148
Liu Hui, 108
Liu Shaoqi, 125, 130, 145
local government, current system, 99-100
Long March, The, 68-69
Lunde, David, 112
Luo Gan, 287

M

Ma Ainong, 252
Macao, Portuguese relinquishment of, 100
MacArthur, Douglas, 221
magazines, evolution of, 248-249
Mahayana Buddhism, 76
Malaysia, relations with, 242
Man (Manchu) minority, 15
Manchu dynasty. *See* Qing dynasty
Manchuria, 17
Mandarin Chinese, 79
Mandarin dialect, 5
Mao Zedong, 61, 67-68, 120, 125-126,
    129-130, 147, 155, 176, 189-191, 221, 227,
    281
    agricultural collectivization, 133
    assumption of power, 129
    birth control, stance on, 156
    CCP, rise to power, 67
    constitutional structure, 130
    death of, 151
    early life, 67
    early policies, 123
    education, views on, 95
    first "Five Year Plan," 133
    foreign policy, 134-135
    Great Leap Forward campaign, 143-145
    Great Proletarian Cultural Revolution,
      146-150
    Household Responsibility System, 157
    Hundred Flowers campaign, 141-142
    industrial development, 133-134
    Korean War, 135
    land reform, 132
    landlords, disdain for, 130
    Long March, The, 68-69
    "Mao Zedong Thought," 129
    mass campaigns, 138-139
    "New Democracy," 131
    People's Republic of China, creation of,
      69
    political positions held, 131
    second "Five Year Plan," 142-146
    thought reform initiatives, 139-140
    Three Three Three System, 123-124

U.S.S.R., early relationship with, 134
United States, disdain for, 135
Yan'an era, campaigns, 123
"Mao Zedong Thought," 129
mariner's compass, invention of, 106
market economy
    Deng Xiaoping, commitment to, 156
    ramifications of, 204-205
Marx, Karl, 43, 48, 62
Marxist Study Society, foundation of, 61
mass line, 147
Materia Medica, 109
May Fourth Movement, 61-62
media, growth of, 248-253
medicine, traditional Chinese medicine,
    108-110
Meiling Soong, 65
Mencius, 23
Meng Jianzhu, 286
Mengzi. *See* Mencius
Metger, Thomas, 107
Miao minority, 15
middle class, growth of, 191-192
migrant workers, growth of, 207-208
military, possible threat of, 303
military factories, 171
Mills, J. S., 40
Min Chinese, 79
Ming dynasty, 33-34
    artistic developments during, 114
    Great Wall, construction of, 7
minority groups, 15
minority nationalities, 13
Mongke, 31
Mongolia, geography and demographics,
    18-19
Mongolian Steppe, 8
Morita, James M., 300
most-favored nation status, granting of,
    United States, 270-271
motion pictures, foreign film distribution,
    255-256

mou, 132
mountain ranges, 8
Mu Suixin, 210
Muhammad, 26
Mulan, 26
Munro, Robin, 231
music, evolution of, 254-255
Muslims, treatment of, 227-228

N

National Environment Protection Agency
    (NEPA), 215-216
National Palace Museum (Taipai), 220
National People's Congress, first meeting of,
    130
natural resources, 9
Nature of Herbal Healing, The, 110
NEPA (National Environment Protection
    Agency), 215-216
nepotism, 167
Ness, Andrew, 296
"New Democracy," Mao Zedong, 131
"New Generation," 190
New Tide Society, 61
newspapers, evolution of, 248-249
NGO (nongovernmental) sector, social
    responsibility, 200-202
Ningxia, geography and demographics, 17
Nixon, Richard M., 264
    visit to China, 150, 267-268
nongovernmental (NGO) sector, social
    responsibility, 200-202
North China plain, 8
North Korea, relations with, 237-239
northern region, demographics, 17-19
NPC (National People's Congress), 217
nuclear weapon proliferation, United States,
    relations with, 269

O

offshore China, demographics, 14
Olympic Summer Games in 2008, attainment of, 295
On Contradiction, 189
On Liberty, 40
One Man's Bible, 253
one-child family planning restrictions, 195
one-child policy, 195
"Open Door Policy," 44
Opium War, 38-39
Our Beliefs, 75

P

Pakistan, relations with, 243-244
Pan Ku, 107
Pan Piao, 107
paper, invention of, 104-105
parties, current system, 97-98
patent laws, infringments, 217
Pearson, Margaret, 302
Peng Dehuai, 140, 146
Peng Ming, 200
Peng Zhen, 146
people's communes, organization of, 143
People's Republic of China, creation of, 69
People's Supreme Court, establishment of, 130
Permanent Normal Trade Relations (PNTR), 304
    granting of, 271-272
Philippines, relations with, 243
philosophical influences, 74
    Buddhism, 76-77
    Confucianism, 86-89, 104
        resurgence in, 100-101
    Daoism, 74-76
pinyin romanization system, 80
piracy, 274
    problems with, 217

PLA (People's Liberation Army)
    corruption of, 172
    current role of, 289
    evolution of, 170
    possible threat of, 303
    governmental relationship to, 170-172
PNTR (Permanent Normal Trade Relations), 304
    granting of, 271-272
poetry, Tang dynasty, 112
Pol Pot, 240
Politburo Standing Committee, establishment of, 130
political parties, current system, 97-98
Polo, Maffeo, 32
Polo, Marco, 6
    visit to China, 32-33
Polo, Nicolo, 32
population
    current statistics, 8
    demographics, 9-10
        eastern region, 10-11
        northern region, 17-19
        southern region, 13
        western region, 15-17
        Yangzi River Valley, 12-13
        Yellow River Valley, 11
PRC, 213
printing, invention of, 105-106
private enterprise, modern developments in, 158
Procurator-General's Office, establishment of, 130
proletarian movement, 147
prostitution
    growth of, 196
    modern problems with, 159, 196
protectionism, 273
Pu Yi, 45-46, 49, 51, 53
Pure Land Buddhism, 77

Q

Qin dynasty, 4-5
Qin Empire, 24
Qin Shihuang, 25
Qing (Manchu) dynasty, 17, 34, 47-48
    artistic developments during, 114-115
    end of, 50-51
    fall of, 21
    Great Wall, construction of, 7
Qinghai, geography and demographics, 16
queues, 48
Quotations of Chairman Mao, The, 125, 148, 252

R

radio, evolution of, 249-250
Rao Shushi, 140
"Rape of Nanjing, The," 122
realpolitik, 267
record keeping, development of, 107-108
Records of the Historian (Shiji), 107
Red Army, growth of, 126
"Red Detachment of Women, The," 150
Red Flag Commune of Zhengzhou, 144
Red Guards, formation of, 148
Red Star Over China, 68
regional imbalances, modern problems with, 159
regional trade, 244-245
Reischauer, Edwin, 107
religion
    Buddhism, 76-77
    Daoism, 74-76
religious organizations, 229
    treatment of, 229-232
Ren (Confucian value), 24, 87
Ren Zhi, 194
Republic of China, founding of, 52-54
restaurants, 258-259

Rongji, Zhu, 167
rural poverty, growth in, 208-210
Russell, Bertrand, 60
Russia
    Bolshevik Revolution, 61-62
    relations with, 236-237
Russian Revolution of 1905, 48

S

San Min Zhu Yi (Three Principles of the People), 62-63
Science and Civilization in China, 108
Scobel, Andrew, 289
Seal script (Chinese characters), 82
Search for Modern China, The, 38, 98
second "Five Year Plan," 142-146
SEZs (special economic zones)
    establishment of, 157
    corruption, 210
Shang dynasty, 22
Shangdu (Xanadu), 32
Shanghai Clique, 285-286
Shanghai Stock Exchange, reopening of, 169
Shen Mingming, 192
Shen Nong, 109
Shen Zhou, 114
Shenyang, corruption in, 210
Shiang Chinese, 79
Shu dynasty, 26
Siku Quanshu, 252
Silk Road, 5
Silver, Kimberly, 274
Sima Qian, 107
Sima Tan, 107
Singapore, relations with, 241-242
Sino-Japanese War, 42
Sino-Tibetan language, 4
Situation in Asia, The, 44
Snow, Edgar, 68
social stratification issues, 159
Socialist Youth Corps, formation of, 61

socialized cooperatives (farms), 133

Socrates and Confucius compared, 86

Song dynasties, artistic developments during, 113-114

Song dynasty, 27-28

Song Jiaoren, 54

"Song of Pure Happiness," 27

Soong, Charles, 65

Sorghaghtani Beki, 31

Soul Mountain, 253

South China Sea
  claims on, 240-243
  oil reserves, 241

South Korea, relations with, 237-239

southern region, demographics, 13

soviets, 66

special administrative regions (local government), 99

special economic zones (SEZs), establishment of, 157

Spence, Jonathan, 38, 98, 121

Spratly Islands, claims to, 241

Spring and Autumn Annals, The, 108

Stalin, Josef, 121

standard script (Chinese characters), 83

Starr, John Bryan, 6, 96, 171

State Council, establishment of, 130

student demonstrations
  Tiananmen Square, 159-163, 176
    massacre at, 177-185
  casualties, 178
  dissidents, 181-184
  legacy of, 185
  media coverage of, 179
  world reaction, 179-180

Sun Jianxin, 231

Sun Yatsen, 48, 50-53, 62-67, 95, 264
  death of, 64
  Gemingdang, founding of, 56
  Guomindang, founding of, 53
  San Min Zhu Yi (Three Principles of the People), 62-63

T

Tai Zong, 26

Taiping Rebellion, 39-40

Taiwan, 14
  geography and demographics, 14
  relations with, 220-223
  United States, support from, 221, 268-269

Takla Makan desert, 9

Tang dynasty, 5, 26-27
  artistic developments during, 112-113

Tang, Wenfang, 198

Tao Teh Ching, 24

Taoism. *See* Daoism

television, evolution of, 249-250

Temujin. *See* Genghis Khan

textile industry, 7

Theraveda Buddhism, 76

thought reform initiatives, Mao Zedong, 139-140

Three Gorge Dam, 12
  problems with, 216

Three Principles of the People (San Min Zhu Yi), 62-63

Three Representatives initiative, Jiang Zemin, 172

Three Three Three System, 123-124

Tian Zhuang, 256

Tiananmen Papers, The, 178

Tiananmen Square, 175
  Great Hall of the People, 175
  demonstrations, 159-163, 176
  massacre at, 177-185
    casualties, 178
    dissidents, 181-184
    legacy of, 185
    media coverage of, 179
    U.S. reaction to, 270
    world reaction, 179-180

Tianzang, 197

Tibet
  Buddhism, 16
  geography and demographics, 16
  relations with China, 225-226
Tibetan Buddhism, 16, 77
Tierra, Leslie, 110
Tipitaka, 105
Togrul, 29
Toluia Beki, 31
Tongmeng hui (Revolutionary Alliance), 48
Tongzhi, 41
trade
  Arab traders, 6
  Portuguese traders, 7
  Silk Road, 5
  textile industry, 7
  United States, 273-277
traditional Chinese medicine, 108-110
Trans-Siberian Railroad, 19
transshipments, 273
Travels of Marco Polo, The, 33
Treatises on Febrile and Other Diseases, 109
Treaty of Beijing (Boxer Rebellion), 44
Treaty of Friendship and Alliance (U.S.S.R.),
  135
Treaty of Nanjing (Opium War), 39
Truman, Harry S., 221
Tu Fu, 27, 112
Tung Chee-Hwa, 224
Tzu Shi, 41

U

U.S.S.R. (United Soviet Socialist Republic)
  ideological differences, 146
  support from, 63-64
Understanding China, 6, 171
unemployment, growth of, 290-291
"Unequal Treaties," 39
United States
  Chinese policies, effectiveness, 272

relations with, 264-265
  Boxer Rebellion, 264
  human rights, 269-270, 272-273
  Korean War, 266-267
  most-favored nation status, 270-271
  Nixon, Richard M., 267-268
  nuclear weapon proliferation, 269
  Taiwan, 268-269
  Tiananmen Square massacre, 270
  trade and investment, 273-277
  World War II, 265-266
universities, modern system, 96
Uygur minority, 15

V–W

Vietnam, relations with, 240

Wang An-shi, 28
Wang Baosen, 291
Wang Dan, 181
Wang Dongjin, 290
Wang Honhwen, 147, 154
Wang Jingwei, 65-66
Wang Juntao, 182
Wang Lixiong, 197
Wang Shifu, 113
Wang Wei, 112
water pollution, problems with, 215-216
Wei dynasty, 26
Wei Jianxing, 173, 287
Wei Jingsheng, 177, 182
Wen Jiabao, 284
Wen Zhengming, 114
Western Chamber, The, 113
western region, demographics, 15-17
"White-Haired Girl," 150
wholly foreign-owned enterprises
  (waizi duzi qiye), 276
women
  families, old social order, 91-92
  modern role of, 194-195

prostitution, 196
role of, 197
suicide rates, 195
Woo Ziniu, 256
World Trade Organization, Chinese entry
into, 170
World War II
Chinese role in, 125-128
United States, relations with China,
265-266
*Wrath of God—The Anti-Corruption Bureau in
Action, The*, 253
WTO (World Trade Organization)
admittance into, 293-295
membership in, ramifications of, 298-301
Wu Bangguo, 287
Wu Chinese, 79
Wu dynasty, 26
Wu Guanzheng, 287
Wu Han, 146, 154
Wu Wei, 75
Wu Yi, 287
Wuer Kaixi, 182

X

Xanadu, 32
xi nao (brainwashing), 140
Xi Xia, 29
Xiao (Confucian value), 24
Xie Zhenhua, 215
Xin (Confucian value), 24
Xinjiang Uygur Autonomous Region
geography and demographics, 15
relations with, 227-228
Xiong Shili, 100
Xuan Tong, 49

Y

Yan Fu, 40, 56
Yan'an era, Mao Zedong, campaigns, 123
Yang (light side), 75

Yangzi River (Changjiang), 7, 12
Yangzi River Valley, demographics, 12-13
Yao Wenyuan, 147, 154
Yellow Emperor's Canon of Medicine, The (Nei
Ching), 109
Yellow River, 7
name origin, 11
source, 12
Yellow River Valley, demographics, 11
Yesugei the Brave, 28
Yi (Confucian value), 24
Yin (the dark side), 75
youth, Generation Yellow, 259-260
Yu Baozhong, case of, 212
Yuan dynasty (Mongol), 18, 31-32
artistic developments during, 114
Yuan Shikai, 45, 49, 51-55, 60
death of, 56
presidency of, 54-56

Z

Zao Ziyang, 161
Zen Buddhism, 77
Zeng Guofan, 41
Zeng Qinghong, 288
Zhang Chunqiao, 147, 154
Zhang Hongha, 200
Zhang Junzhao, 256
Zhang Xueliang, 121
Zhang Xun, 55
Zhang Yimou, 256
Zhang Zhidong, 45, 49
Zhang Zhongjing, 109
Zhang Zuolin, 62
Zhao Tingyang, 248
Zhao Ziyang, 158, 160, 166, 204-205
Zhong guo, 4
Zhong Wei, 196
Zhongguo Gongchandang, 98
Zhongnanhai, 288

Zhou dynasty, 4, 22-24
    accomplishments of, 23
    Confucius, 23
    Great Wall
        construction of, 7, 23
    Laozi, 24
    Mencius, 23
Zhou Enlai, 121, 124-125, 130, 140-142,
    148, 150-151, 176, 226
    death of, 150
Zhu De, 67, 130, 140
Zhu Rongji, 170, 211, 298, 300
    early life, 168
    economic reform policies, 170
Zhu Rongji in 1999, 169
Zhuang minority, 15
Zi Feng, 49
zuo feng, 140

A Little Knowledge Goes a Long Way ...

Check Out These
Best-Selling
COMPLETE IDIOT'S GUIDES

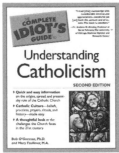

Understanding **Catholicism**

1-59257-085-2
$18.95

Learning **Spanish**

0-02-864451-4
$18.95

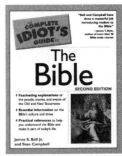

The **Bible**

0-02-864382-8
$18.95

Grammar and **Style**

1-59257-115-8
$16.95

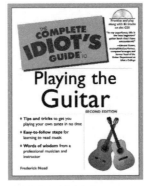

Playing the **Guitar**

0-02-864244-9
$21.95 w/CD

Personal Finance in Your **20s & 30s**

0-02-864374-7
$19.95

The Perfect **Resume**

0-02-864440-9
$14.95

Buying and Selling a Home

1-59257-120-4
$18.95

Windows XP

0-02-864232-5
$19.95

More than *400 titles* in *30 different categories*
Available at booksellers everywhere

ALPH